ASIA'S 'MIRACLE' ECONOMIES

ASIA'S 'MIRACLE' ECONOMIES

Jon Woronoff

M. E. SHARPE, INC.
ARMONK, NEW YORK
LONDON, ENGLAND

© 1986 by Jon Woronoff

Library of Congress Cataloging-in-Publication Data

Woronoff, Jon.
   Asia's "miracle" economies.

   Bibliography: p.
   Includes index.
   1. East Asia—Economic policy. 2. East Asia—Economic
conditions. I. Title.
HC460.5.W68   1986b   338.95   86-20404
ISBN 0-87332-401-3
ISBN 0-87332-402-1 (pbk.)

Printed in the United States of America

Contents

PART THREE: THE PROSPECTS 303

EPILOGUE: LEARNING FROM EAST ASIA

Foreword

There is not much point in trying to analyze a miracle. By definition, it is exceedingly rare and of such an extraordinary nature that it would be hard to replicate. Many of its features cannot readily be evaluated and some defy reason. At most, it can be admired from a distance and held up as a desirable, if unattainable, goal. That is what has been done all too often with regard to the East Asian economies once the full extent of their success was known.

But a careful look at the situation shows that these are quite ordinary countries. They are not ordinary only because they have few natural resources or other wealth but also because, for decades, or more exactly, centuries, they showed no particular predisposition for economic progress. And the methods they applied recently were the standard ones that have been around for years, were used by many with indifferent results, and could be tried again if anyone cares to. The Five obviously did a better job, but not one so exceptional that it could not be copied.

The sad fact of the matter is that the Five only look like prodigies because they succeeded where a hundred others failed. It is only on the background of the regrettable and almost inexplicable failure of so many to achieve much in the way of development that one is forced to regard Japan, Taiwan, Korea, Singapore and Hong Kong with some awe. It is only in this context that one can even think of using such an overblown expression as an economic "miracle."

Such a "miracle" could certainly be worked by many others if they understood how it was pulled off in East Asia. For this, it is necessary to do two things. First, one must cut through the myths and illusions that have been fostered regarding this success in order to see the true dimensions and concrete possibilities. The other is to admit that it did take some doing and will not be that easy to reproduce even if it is clearly within the reach of others.

It is as much in tribute to the successful Five as in the hope of somehow helping the unsuccessful hundred that this book is written. The world cannot afford to have the vast majority of its people living in misery while a small minority enjoys an ease and affluence that is accessible if intelligently sought. It would be a terrible misfortune if the Five were to remain exceptions, a few new faces among the haves, while the have-nots continue to multiply and rot. They should become pathbreakers so that a decent material existence can be attained by all.

JON WORONOFF

PROLOGUE:

LOOKING EAST

It is amazing how hard it can be for people, including the supposed "experts," to perceive even major changes in the world situation until they become unmistakably evident. This blindness is particularly notable in the tenacious failure—or perhaps unwillingness—to realize that a dynamic new center of economic activity was emerging in the East. It required more than a decade after Japan entered a high growth trajectory for it to be taken seriously. Again, not until long after their takeoff were its neighbors Taiwan, Korea, Hong Kong and Singapore acknowledged as rising economies.

It is difficult to understand how they could have been overlooked so insistently. The burst of growth in East Asia after the war was truly phenomenal. These countries, one of them defeated in the hostilities and the others hardly more than backward colonies, were given little chance for success. During the early years, in fact, one could scarcely see any improvement and the dismal forecasts seemed to be right. Then, all of a sudden, growth started coming and remained stronger than anywhere else on the globe.

By now stacks of statistics are available to convince and enlighten the curious observer. All of these countries repeatedly attained more than 10% growth and averaged rates that were not much lower over stretches of two or more decades. Their gross national product doubled, and then doubled again, so that Japan already accounts for about 10% of world GNP and the others a further 3%. Japan presently boasts a per capita income that is among the highest in the world, Singapore has the second best in Asia, and the rest are ranked among the middle-income countries, long since having escaped the category of poor nations.

But these statistics only show part of the achievement. It was not merely a question of taking the original economy they had and boosting production along the same lines. In every country, there was a thorough transformation of the structure as they revamped old sectors and branched into new. The larger ones progressed from light to heavy industry while the smaller constantly added further articles. All made considerable advances into modern services. This both deepened and broadened the economies, making them stronger and more resilient.

Finally, although often neglected or insufficiently stressed, they have all brought very definite benefits to their people. As incomes rose, it was possible to buy more and better food, clothing and housing (the latter sometimes subsidized by the state). The educational systems improved as did the hospitals and social facilities. While the progress was less striking, and sometimes still inadequate, headway was made with social legislation to limit working hours and improve conditions as well as to accumulate funds for social security and welfare.

Yet, it would seem that these achievements were less noticeable than the fact that these activated economies had become so vigorous that they were making waves. It was not long before, for an expanding range of articles, the Five had become ruthlessly competitive. Meanwhile, their technological level rose swiftly, transforming them from copiers into innovators. Their exports kept mounting rapidly in a multitude of foreign markets. While this just meant another source of manufactured goods for some, for others it implied fierce rivalry abroad and also at home. Later on, some of them began investing actively overseas. Ultimately, their presence was felt around the world and East Asia could no longer be ignored.

It was only when they had become a force to be reckoned with that anyone paid much attention. That is strange in a public that clamored for economic progress and launched one "development decade" after the other. Surely the addition of one advanced country and four "newly industrialized countries" or NICs, as they were called, was something worth talking about at an earlier stage. But the Five were barely noticed. It may have been that, rather than doing things in what was generally regarded as the "right" way, they did it in another way. Or it may simply have been that the East Asians were too busy building their economies to participate in the confused and raucous international debates on what the "right" path to development was.

However, once the countries that applied the "right" economic methods and added the "proper" political and social frills had collapsed, it was much easier to see the Third World for what it really was. Of some hundred odd developing countries terribly few were getting anywhere. The average growth rate was only about 5% in the earlier period, falling to 3% or less later on, this representing little real improvement for the population since they often had high birth rates. This made countries which managed to rack up 10% growth and more year after year during the earlier period, and still hefty figures during the slump, look even better.

The rise of the East Asian economies became even more striking due to stagnation in the supposedly advanced nations. Despite a head start that once seemed so large the gap could never be closed, Japan was catching up so rapidly that it pulled ahead of most European countries and actually rivaled the United States in many sectors. This sort of accomplishment could hardly be expected from the other Four, given their smaller size and yet later start. Still, it soon became evident that in sector after sector they were more than a match for the one-time leaders. This process of catching up never really ceased for, when the Five slowed down, the advanced nations slipped even more.

Thus, above an increasingly depressing wasteland of economic mediocrities and failures, these few notable successes stood out prominently. For the first time, people were tempted to "look East" and consider what had been accomplished. In fact, they had little choice. The East Asian Five were playing a significant role in international economic affairs and it was the rare country which did not have to contend with them. This was more than just a question of business as usual. To some, they appeared as a source of inspiration, a model that could be followed by those who wished to develop more swiftly. To others, they looked more like a threat, already serious competitors for domestic firms and increasingly rivals for commercial, financial and technological supremacy.

Alas, this welcome realization of their arrival and an encouraging willingness to let the economic record speak for itself was rather brief. The pendulum quickly swung too far and brought a new kind of blindness. Dazzled by their success, many of the "experts" and some in the general public began praising them as if what they had accomplished were really exceptional. Not content to apologize for having underestimated them, it became fashionable to overcompensate by building the Five up as something truly unique and blowing their noteworthy achievements into an "economic miracle."

In newspapers and magazines around the world, then in weightier works by learned authorities, they were presented as extraordinary phenomena to be admired and copied . . . if only it were possible. The first to deserve this treatment was Japan, once mocked as a producer of shoddy goods, now deemed the only place that could possibly guarantee the highest quality. Japan was

Malaysia's Prime Minister Mahathir "looking East" to Japan

Credit: Honda

dubbed "No. 1" not only for its economy but also the supporting social and political systems. While the NICs did not get the full treatment, since their social and political mores appeared less admirable, they were repeatedly singled out for their economic performance. In an Oriental vein, they became the four "dragons" or the "young tigers."

While the praise was certainly flattering, and made up for some of the earlier disparagement, it hardly helped rectify the misconceptions. The lesser reason for this is that it took so long for the public to realize its earlier mistake and overcome its blindness that what it "saw" no longer actually existed. The pioneering period, when these latecomers had to make almost heroic efforts to get moving, was long since gone. Even the period of robust development as they entered one sector after the other and continued conquering new export markets was some way back. Now they were approaching a comfortable maturity and ultimately a grudging decline in economic growth which could be read in the statistics for Japan and forecast for the others. The recognition, as so often, had come very late in the day.

But the more serious reason why this glorification was more harm than help is that it tended to cover over the rational explanations of their success with more imaginary or illusory ones. There was absolutely nothing superhuman or supernatural about the accomplishments of the Five. Every policy they followed was equally valid elsewhere, every strategy they pioneered could have been adopted by others, and the enviable growth rates were the result of an overall approach and a change in circumstances that could have been used anywhere. The only thing that was miraculous was that they were the only ones to benefit fully from them. Or, perhaps the "miracle" was that so many others had stubbornly applied the wrong policies, strategies and approaches.

Even more regrettable, this new vogue slurs over the negative aspects and makes it look as if there were hardly any hitches. In fact, a closer examination of their development history will show that the Five also made horrible blunders, some of them extremely grave for the economy. The best that can be said is that they made fewer mistakes than others, or did more things right than wrong, and they frequently learned from their mistakes. But it is clear that they did not possess any "magic formula" or "universal recipe" that worked every time and might be sought by others. To find out why they succeeded, it is necessary to sort out the good from the bad rather than assume that everything was in order.

This makes the East Asian economies much more like others which failed because people elsewhere did more things wrong than right, or made too many mistakes, or refused to admit they had made mistakes. There is a difference of degree and not a difference of kind which makes the Five much less "unique" for having succeeded. It is this underlying commonality that is so important since it means that they can be studied to good purpose. It is thereby possible to draw two types of lessons: one from the points where they were basically right; the other, no less significant, from the points where they went wrong.

The time has therefore come to study the "miracle" economies more carefully, and more objectively, to see what can be learned from them. When so many countries have set their sights on economic development, yet merely a handful succeed in any meaningful sense, their experiences must be recounted and analyzed. It is essential to determine which basic policies they introduced, which strategies helped them advance, and which techniques were applied to solve particularly thorny problems. As an increasingly influential economic group, it is also useful to consider how they will affect other countries and the world in general.

It is a pity that it took so long for this insight to be sought, but the awareness is more precious now than ever!

PART ONE:

THE PLACES

What has occurred in East Asia is a fascinating story in itself. Indeed, it has many elements of the ideal success story. Five countries started out at a pitifully low level of economic development, they overcame countless trials and hardships, and finally they managed to rise above most others. This makes it worth telling just to show the world what can be done. The story is certainly rare enough nowadays to make it popular.

But it can serve a much more useful purpose as well. What happened in East Asia is not only interesting, it is equally instructive if stress is placed on how this rise was accomplished. It is generally felt that people can learn from one another and countries can also learn from one another. The biggest problem is to find valid examples. Well, there is every reason to believe that the East Asian Five might be such examples as long as they are not mistaken too often for "tigers" and "dragons."

The first requirement for being an example is to have achieved something of value. This aspect is already obvious. Never has so much development been packed into such a brief span of time. In a matter of decades, these countries began industrializing and quickly transformed the economy from a simple agricultural or entrepot-based one into a distinctively modern type. Employment and income increased rapidly and a degree of affluence materialized that had hardly been expected. The growth rates attained during most of the period were not only high, they were actually unprecedented in previous economic history.

This is certainly a good reason to study the efforts and policies which brought about such results. Still, there would not be much point in taking the Five as examples if they boasted some extraordinary initial advantage. It is not particularly impressive for countries that are inherently rich, that have access to large amounts of capi-

tal, or that own exceptional mineral wealth to do better
than others. There are enough cases of that sort around
and they are hardly useful examples for the vast majority
of countries which are less fortunate.

In this sense, there is no reason why the Five could not
serve as examples for most. They possessed a very
modest natural endowment, much poorer than the
average. They did not have a large domestic market, not
in monetary terms at least, and some of the countries
were extremely small. Japan in prewar days and the
others after the war were complete novices in economic
development and could only count on limited help from
others. The supplies of capital were painstakingly accumulated, largely out of their own earnings.

Only when it comes to the human factor were the East
Asians supposedly luckier. It is widely assumed—in
retrospect—that their people always had some hidden
economic talent. If so, this was certainly not noticeable
during previous centuries or even decades prior to
development. The levels of education and literacy were
no higher, actually often much lower, than in today's
developing countries. There were no planners or
economists, hardly any businessmen or industrialists,
and not even that many technicians or skilled workers.
True, people worked very hard. But it takes more than
hard work to build a modern economy. And it was only a
short while before that the East Asians even got an inkling of what that meant.

There are not many countries which are in a worse
starting position and could therefore not assemble the
basic assets needed to initiate the growth process. In fact,
the majority of nations have a bit more in the way of land
and natural resources, some being far better endowed.
They can also tap capital more easily. Their populations
are usually reasonably educated and can be organized

and trained. By taking the right approach, they could aspire to at least a moderate success and sometimes one that would exceed that of the Five.

The main question is whether they can adopt the right approach. So far most countries have not. But what the East Asians did was not so intrinsically complex or difficult that others could not do the same. On the surface, at least, many of their policies and strategies were very much like those in general use. Promotion of domestic industry, encouragement of exports, introduction of advanced technology, even planning and targeting are things which not only can be undertaken by any country, they have been tried out by many others.

This means that the Five are perfectly valid examples for any who might wish to try a like approach. Admittedly, it is hard to implement such policies in practice. This is where most of the countries failed. But it is no longer correct to think of the ability to succeed as being out of reach or those who succeeded as being somehow "unique."

When Japan first stepped out of rank and began its startling economic ascent, most observers regarded this as a freak occurrence which could hardly be repeated. But it was. It was repeated four times by other countries in the region. Moreover, it was accomplished in places which had an even poorer natural endowment, smaller population and less economic experience. In so doing, they showed that it was more a question of methods than anything else and these methods could be adopted by others. This means that it is far from impossible to follow a similar path to economic development.

Nor could it be argued that instead of one unique case there are now five. It is too widely assumed that the East Asians are an exceedingly homogeneous group and that the parallels are so great that they naturally fall into the same patterns which others might not be able to adopt. True, there are similarities. There are also incredibly big differences between the Japanese, Koreans and Chinese as concerns their outlook and behavior. They did not seek exactly the same goals. And the contrasts are most glaring when it comes to the economic policies they used, whether for planning, finance, investment, labor or otherwise.

The fact that there are five success stories and not one implies that there are five potential models and not one as well as variations on the basic themes. This is extremely significant for would-be successors. It greatly augments the ranks of disciples who can find something in common with one or another of the East Asian masters. Now they can range from very small to fairly large, completely bereft of natural resources to moderately endowed, exceptionally backward to reasonably advanced. And, when it comes to goals, there are even more which seek the same things: industrialization, technological advancement, rising incomes, and economic progress in general.

By ceasing to be unique, the Five become considerably more valid examples for the rest of the world. In addition, they are unusually "exemplary" in the deepest sense, for there is nothing deterministic about economic development. Countries do not have to succed, and there were many occasions when it looked as if the East Asians might not make it. Nor do countries have to fail, no matter how often they failed in the past. The East Asians were widely written off as hopeless when they began, yet they managed to advance. This shows that it is not in a country's stars whether it will achieve its goal but in what does and how it does it.

This applied very clearly to the "mother tiger" and the "four cubs." They developed suitable policies only because they experimented with and improved on what they found. They also realized that it is not so much a question of which techniques are adopted but how well they are implemented. There is no doubt that, in addition to any portion of wisdom, there were many more portions of hard work and dogged determination. If the will were lacking, they would not have gotten very far.

To make the study of their experiences as helpful as possible, the Five are not presented strictly in the order of their rise. Instead, they will be grouped around Japan, which was not only the first to emerge but also provided the underlying theme upon which any variations were made. Going further than it in the direction of state control and institutionalized policy is Taiwan and, considerably more so, Korea. Moving in the other direction are Singapore, which ran a more liberal economy, and Hong Kong, which was as close to unfettered free enterprise as can be found.

The initial presentation is largely descriptive. It delineates the respective roles of the national leaders, the bureaucracy, business community and labor force. Special attention is devoted to the policies adopted to promote development, including special strategies regarding industrialization and exports. Beginning with the early troubles, and their ultimate solution, the evolution in agriculture, industry and services is portrayed. Bringing the story up to date, mention is made not only of the triumphs of the high growth period but also the tribulations of operating in today's more difficult economic environment. And it is taken a step further with a look at the future challenges and prospects for continued success.

All five case histories run parallel in presentation but with considerable variations of emphasis to show crucial differences. This makes it easier to compare them, a primary concern of the book. But it would be most unwise to grade them point by point and then tally up the scores to see which is the "best." There is no such thing since varying starting positions, natural and human endowments, policies and strategies—as well as luck and misfortune—preclude any exact comparisons. Even the statistics are only really suggestive since they are defined and compiled differently in each country and the use of American dollars is merely to facilitate comparison and not evaluate results since what a dollar could buy varied tremendously.

While much can be derived from these five examples, the best way to start learning is by seeing what happened, when and how. If the story were simplified too greatly at this stage, or squeezed into a neat "model" with no loose ends, it would not be very helpful. This would only downplay the problems, difficulties and failures, which are no less instructive than the accomplishments and successes. And it would make it appear as if the miracle-workers knew what they were doing from the outset, although they most definitely did not.

There will be time for drawing conclusions later on. But first a look at the "success stories."

1

Japan's Two "Miracles"

When Commodore Perry's Black Ships arrived in 1853 to "open" Japan, it was not to reveal a highly advanced society reveling in comfort and wealth as some may have dreamed. It did not possess the riches of India or the ancient culture of China. Rather, this was just an ordinary country which had not quite emerged from the feudal era. True, towns and cities were expanding, crafts and petty commerce flourished, and rice production increased. Money was already in circulation and trade existed from one domain to the next. But, no matter how hard scholars try to find some special predisposition for economic development *ex post facto*, Japan was not nearly as far along as most colonies that acceded to independence a century later. If it had remained secluded, there is very little chance that it would have evolved dramatically.

Not only was the country neither rich nor advanced, it did not have much of a basis for autonomous growth. Rule by the Tokugawa clan was a boon in that it put an end to centuries of incessant and bloody strife. People could go about their work, but this work was minutely prescribed to the various classes (nobles, *samurai*, peasants, artisans and merchants) and hard to change. Only over time could those at the bottom of the social ladder, and whose economic contributions were greater, gain some leeway. While agriculture was progressing, it

could not always keep up with population growth, and
the limitations of land and climate restricted its potential. There were few natural resources, aside from some
coal and copper. This meant that there was not much to
trade with other nations, nor could it be hoped that trade
would be undertaken by the natives since the policy of
closed nation cut off most contacts. This was certainly
not an especially favorable foundation on which to build
a modern economy.

The forcible opening of Japan to the outside world
shattered many carefully fostered illusions. The country
was not so powerful that it could simply ignore what was
going on elsewhere and, if it were not cautious, it could
also fall under Western domination. This was
demonstrated by the ships and their cannons which readily demolished coastal fortresses. Nor was it proficient in
new sciences and techniques, as was shown by the West's
greater knowledge of mathematics, astronomy, and
medicine or more practical matters like shipbuilding and
weaponry. These were things that could—and should—
be acquired for the good of the nation. Still, the
Japanese were convinced of their moral superiority, and
it was felt that the best solution was to combine
"Western technology and Japanese spirit" (*wakon yo
sai*).

Faced by a threat from without, and a defial of their
bans, the Tokugawa first promised to repel the barbarians but later seemed to accomodate them. This was
rejected by younger *samurai*, especially in outlying
domains which were traditionally less loyal. In 1868, they
brought about a "restoration" of the emperor which
paved the way for far-reaching reforms. The actual policies were not devised by the Emperor Meiji but his advisors (*genro*) who formed an energetic and foresighted
ruling oligarchy. Once in power, conceding the futility of

trying to ignore or spurn the Westerners, it was decided to accept their presence, learn from them, ultimately outdo them, and meanwhile create a new state which could fend for itself in the radically altered world arena. The principal goals were summed up in the slogan of "rich nation, strong army "(*fukoku kyohei*).

Many of the oligarchs' efforts to modernize Japan were not directed specifically toward the economy, although they affected it immensely. The first steps were naturally to unify the country by breaking down the barriers between the domains and centralizing the administration. This, plus the maintenance of relative peace and stability, provided a broader market and more conducive atmosphere. By depriving the lords and warriors of their privileges, while freeing the peasants and merchants from their subordinate status, it was possible for all to enter new callings and seize new opportunities. Meanwhile, a Western-style legal system was adopted and schools were opened to teach the new learning. The state also took charge of improving the basic infrastructure by building more roads, railways, harbors and so on. To find the right models for these activities, official missions were sent off to Europe and the United States and curious students and businessmen went on their own to see what could be borrowed.

While foreign knowledge was eagerly sought, Japanese governments from Meiji times on were extremely wary of accepting foreign loans in view of the fate that had befallen China and others when they could not repay. To ensure sufficient revenue, the old land taxes in kind were replaced by a levy in cash based on the value of the land. While the amount was roughly the same as before, land owners were now forced to sell their crops for cash which stimulated the commercialization of rice and stifled subsistence farming. It also led to a spread of commercial transactions as other goods were purchased by farmers and, with increasing frequency, land itself was bought and sold. This completely transformed the sector and encouraged other, often more remunerative crops alongside rice, like wheat, barley, tea and also silk culture. By introducing new farming techniques, intensifying irrigation, using more fertilizer and implements, it was possible to boost yields which improved the position of many farmers.[1]

However, the farmers were not the only ones to gain, since the state collected more taxes than before. These were long the major source of revenue, representing 80% in 1880 and still as much as 60% in 1894. The money was used for several purposes which eventually helped the rest of the economy. One was to pay off the *samurai*'s much reduced stipends and compensate the lords for the loss of their property. Another was to build more essential infrastructure and launch special industrial projects. Agriculture financed overall development in a further way, since more funds accumulated with large landowners, some of whom used them for commercial or industrial ventures. In addition to capital, the primary sector supplied much of the supplementary labor as those who lost their land had to seek work elsewhere and there was little room on the tiny farms for younger sons or daughters.

In the secondary sector, the government's influence was less pervasive aside from a number of mining operations and what were regarded as "modern" industries. Some coal and copper mines were owned by the state. Several munitions works were quickly set up. Another priority was shipping, and subsequently shipbuilding, to meet possible strategic needs. The former was heavily subsidized, yet run primarily by private businessmen. But a modern shipyard exceeded the financial and managerial capabilities of existing entrepreneurs and had to be established by the state. To upgrade the textile branch, it had silk reeling and cotton spinning plants built. In addition, the government opened production facilities for cement, glass, chemicals, beer, sugar and several dozen more. Initiated in the first decade or so of Meiji rule, these were usually made according to Western specifications, often erected by Western companies, and supervised by Western personnel until they could be replaced by Japanese.

While only the state could launch such projects, even the state had tremendous difficulties in making them work. The purely technical teething troubles were long and it was not easy to transfer some complex operations to Japanese staff. Often these costly installations had to be subsidized somewhat longer and some just kept on making losses. Caught in a serious financial crisis, of which this was only one aspect, the government decided to sell off its factories. They were usually bought, for extremely low prices, by local businessmen who then made a go of it. With somewhat more industrial experience, far tighter managerial control, and much smaller capital outlays, it was possible to turn a profit in most cases.

After these misadventures, the government was not so eager to float industrial projects on its own. The only major exception was the state-run iron and steel mill in Yawata. The first to be equipped with blast furnaces, it was inaugurated in 1897. Instead, it was preferred to mount programs and take other measures to promote selected industries including shipping, shipbuilding, iron and steel, machinery and chemicals. Where necessary, substantial funds were made available by related banks and, if things did not run well at first, subsidies were also provided. The government shifted its own procurement to such ventures, which gave them a guaranteed source of

work. Legislation was occasionally adopted to keep out
foreign competitors. By then the industrialists were more
competent and more readily overcame any difficulties.
They knew how to run factories, could handle the labor
force, and entered suitable tie-ups with foreign companies if advanced technologies were needed. They were
better at marketing and, just to be certain the market
remained stable, they took to forming cartels with government consent or even initiative.

Thus, the pioneering efforts finally paid off, not for the
government but a small circle of entrepreneurs noted for
their links with influential politicians whose favors were
often instrumental in their rise. The most noteworthy
was Yataro Iwasaki, a former *samurai*, who launched a
giant shipping line (Nippon Yusen Kaisha) through
clever business transactions and also cheap purchases of
ships, state subsidies and contracts, and other help.[2]
From there, he went into trade, engineering and real
estate, founding the famous Mitsubishi combine. The
House of Mitsui, already merchants and bankers under
the Tokugawa, cooperated with the new regime as well
and expanded with government aid.[3] Among those who
bought mines and factories from the state, and then diversified their activities, were Sumitomo, Yasuda, Asano
and Furukawa. The groups thus formed were called
zaibatsu and eventually dominated modern industry and
commerce. In Meiji days, they were beholden to the
oligarchs who sponsored them and perhaps felt some
patriotic zeal. Later on, rather than servants of the state,
the *zaibatsu* manipulated politics. They bankrolled the
parties which owed them favors. Only the military
escaped this control, imposing its will on the *zaibatsu* or
backing new groups of *shinko-zaibatsu* to develop
strategic industries in Japan and the growing overseas empire.

Aside from some "modern" sectors and subsequently the heavy and chemical industries needed for the war machine, successive governments left the economy pretty much to its own devices. Yet, despite a lack of financial backing and, in the earlier period, any protection from imports due to the commercial treaties imposed on Japan, various sectors did emerge. It was certainly not easy. For example, traditional weaving was wiped out by cheap imported cotton goods and some handicrafts became obsolete. But others could be saved by adopting better methods, such as ceramics and lacquerware. New or renovated branches also arose with food processing, fertilizer, cement and simple manufactured articles. The crucial breakthrough came in textiles as silk and later cotton threads and material were fashioned by imported machinery, production techniques improved and, not to be forgotten, workers were pushed incredibly hard. Production grew by leaps and bounds and far outpaced the new-fangled steel, shipbuilding and chemical industries.

These less favored ventures were not usually the work of the *zaibatsu*, although they might partake in any sector which did well. Instead, they were often extensions of shops runs by artisans, some of whom showed more vision and willingness to innovate than their peers. Others were promoted as a sideline by former *samurai*, landlords or merchants who wanted to place their excess cash. The latter were also active in commercial operations involving domestic trade, banking and money-lending. While most units were terribly small, some proved quite vigorous and grew to a reasonable size. Their rise from below, however, was usually blocked somewhere along the line by the *zaibatsu* which increasingly dominated certain industrial sectors as well as banking and trading and used this leverage to buy into or buy up lesser firms.

With production in many sectors growing steadily, Japan soon had a surplus that could be exported. More exactly, these goods had to be exported in order to pay for the costly imports of machinery and essential raw materials. Most of the exports were initially primary produce, especially tea, fish and raw silk. But they were quickly superseded by textiles, which accounted for half of exports by the early 1900s. It was only much later that "modern" products like machinery and metals contributed a modest share. Thanks to cheap yen rates, exports multiplied explosively from ¥61 million in 1880 to ¥1,755 million in 1930. But they were never able to cover the costs of imports and the trade balance stayed in the red throughout.

There was no doubt that the Japanese economy was pressing ahead. But its motion was anything but smooth. Rather, it advanced in fits and starts and went through a painful cycle of booms and busts. The first decade after the Meiji Restoration was a time of fundamental reforms, many of which cost considerable sums such as compensation to the feudal lords and *samurai*, expansion of the bureaucracy and military, and unprofitable industrial undertakings. This led to rampant inflation, which had to be brought down by Finance Minister Matsukata's tight controls in 1881. The economy picked up again and then accelerated during the Sino-Japanese War of 1894–5 and the Russo-Japanese War of 1904–5. While Japan won both, it was rewarded by a huge indemnity from the first whereas it got nothing out of the second and had to pay off crushing national and international debts.

At the dawn of the twentieth century, things were far from bright. The economy fell into a recession and almost seemed on the verge of bankruptcy. It was only revived by World War I, in which Japan did not participate. Its manufacturers and shippers made windfall profits from the Allies while taking over many of their markets in Asia. They also benefited during the ensuing reconstruction period. However, this soon petered out and, while business slumped, the Kanto area was hit by a disastrous earthquake in 1923. The cost of essential relief created a financial crisis for the government and banks and was met by a restrictive policy of the new cabinet in 1929. At the same time, Japan returned to the gold standard and the yen appreciated. Both measures, plus increasing protectionism, hurt business and drove the economy into a domestic recession that was soon absorbed in the worldwide depression of the 1930s.

While the creation of a "rich country" moved much of the population, it cannot be forgotten that the twin goal was a "strong army." Ever since the Meiji Restoration, the army had been revamped to replace *samurai* with modern soldiers, largely conscripted from the peasantry. They put down the Satsuma Rebellion of 1877 and other internal disturbances and then launched into operations overseas. First they conquered Okinawa, then Formosa, gradually imposing control over Korea, which was annexed in 1910. Next, the army took on China, repeatedly encroaching on its territory and then invading Manchuria as of 1931. With the army and navy swelling, more and more funds had to be raised to pay for personnel and masses of weapons, munitions and warships. This drained resources away from some activities but greatly profited others, especially mining, heavy industry and the parallel economies in the colonies. In this way, Japan pulled out of the recession and pressed into a frantic race to prepare for World War II, known there as the Pacific War.

Thus, in the long decades after it was "opened," Japan pursued both goals of economic development and military strength. Its growth rate, which averaged out to 3–4% a year, was rather good compared to its Western rivals and, even more so, other backward countries.[4] But it was not quite an "economic miracle." Part of this merely reflected rapid population growth. It also masked glaring inequalities between big landlords and tenant farmers or landless laborers, company owners or executives and ordinary workers, and especially the powerful *zaibatsu* and weaker companies. Moreover, the economy experienced many ups and down, the former perhaps exhilarating and the latter often disastrous. Worse, whereas living conditions tended to improve in the initial period they were increasingly sacrificed to military strength later on. By the late 1930s, the warlords were ready to risk seventy years of economic progress in a rash gamble for an Asian empire.

This turned out to be a serious miscalculation. In 1945, for the first time in its history, the nation suffered the humiliation of defeat and the presence of an army of occupation. Its political future was uncertain and its economic prospects were even more doubtful. The former colonies were liberated thereby depriving it of seemingly vital raw materials and markets. Meanwhile, six million soldiers and settlers returned to the home islands. Japan was more crowded and resourceless than it had ever been. Some 78 million people then, and now 120 million, would have to live off 377,643 square kilometers of quite mountainous land that could not possibly sustain them at acceptable levels. Yet, the incensed victors seemed intent on having the economy revert to a more primitive state by stripping it of industries and imposing heavy reparations.

Other factors, however, were more positive. The shock of defeat instilled a greater sense of reality in the leaders and people and, for the first time, enhanced the position of the masses against an elite that was to be punished for dragging them into the war. A policy of "democratization" was imposed by the General Headquarters of the Allied Forces (GHQ) and General Douglas MacArthur and his aides tried to bring about an even greater transformation than had occurred under the Meiji oligarchs. Among the principal measures were the adoption of an equalitarian constitution, creation of a political system based on popular representation, educational and agricultural reforms and a renovation of the business sector by disbanding the *zaibatsu*, purging tarnished bureaucrats and financial leaders (along with military and politicians) and promotion of trade unions. This obviously had a tremendous impact on the economy. Freed of stultifying restrictions, individuals could more readily seize new opportunities. With the *zaibatsu* weakened, new enterprises could rise and, even within the older firms, younger managers took over from the owners. Most significant of all, bereft of any military ambitions, the Japanese only had one goal to which their energies could be harnassed—economic progress.[5]

Despite an ardent desire to pull out of the economic morass, it was far from certain that Japan would recover. About a quarter of its factories, infrastructure and dwellings had been destroyed and production fell to a mere 60% of the prewar level. There was massive unemployment, runaway inflation and uncurbed black-marketeering. While there were enough capital, raw materials and labor to resume production in some sectors, this was inhibited by social unrest and the threat of a major upheaval.[6] Since early Japanese governments were relatively ineffectual, it was actually the Occupation authorities who directed the initial steps and had to meet the most urgent needs. The United States provided some US $1.8 billion in aid, especially food and crucial raw materials, a sizable amount in those days. It also relented on the demands for reparations, which were ultimately quite modest, and even retracted measures which it was feared might hurt the economy such as the dissolution of *zaibatsu*-related companies.

It was only painstakingly that overall production attained the prewar level in 1949 (although it was considerably lower in per capita terms). The situation was still touch and go when the Korean War broke out, giving the economy the stimulus it needed in the form of massive "special procurements." More important, emergence of a Communist threat in parts of Asia convinced Washington to strengthen Japan as a bulwark of the "free world." This not only reversed the earlier course of economic containment but brought ready access to capital, technologies and trade. From then on, the Japanese did quite well on their own going through a succession of booms so unprecedented that they were often named after mythical ages, Jimmu boom, Iwato boom, Izanagi boom. These were reasonably long periods of rapid growth that occasionally hit 13%, followed by slumps that bottomed out at still impressive rates of 5% or so. To the Japanese, this came as a continuing surprise, although they eventually got accustomed to high growth and regarded anything else as abnormal. Foreign observers, who had never expected a Japanese resurgence, were even more startled by this emerging economic superpower.[7]

This aroused an urge to find the architects of such a formidable success. The usual conclusion was that it could be traced to a combination of politicians, bureaucrats and big businessmen who were working closely together within what was dubbed "Japan, Inc." While all three obviously had a significant impact, and merited much praise, they were hardly alone and did not deserve all the credit. It was also essential to determine the relative effectiveness of each partner, something most analysts got wrong.[8]

Most conspicuous were the conservative politicians who formed the Liberal Democratic Party and clung tenaciously to power year after year, ultimately providing some four decades of political continuity. Since changes in prime minister were more a result of shifting factional alignments than elections, it made for even greater stability. This created a propitious atmosphere in which to implement economic measures and introduce long-terms policies. And it was even better because the LDP proclaimed economic progress as its primary goal and promised to bring ever greater prosperity. This won it widespread popular support while the opposition parties, which could not produce a viable or credible counterproposal, continued to languish. But it was not so much the backing of the people as of specific segments, including the farm vote and big business which filled its campaign chest, that kept the LDP in office and oriented it toward liberalism attenuated by a willingness to help vested interests.

For all its prominence, it would be presumptuous to claim that it was the party, or more generally the political leadership, which brought about the nation's economic rise. Most politicians had no economic training or business experience, nor even a global view or consistent policy, and they were mainly interested in specific and concrete deals. This could mean getting infrastructure built in their home constituency or convincing companies to locate plants there in return for suitable aid. They rarely got further than pork barrel politics or using connections. Only some few demonstrated statesmanship or a grasp of the overall needs, occasionally buttressed by personal experience in the economic bureaucracy or business

world. Among the most decisive were Prime Ministers
Shigeru Yoshida, Hayato Ikeda, Kakuei Tanaka and
Takeo Fukuda.

But it took considerably more than this to actually run
an economy and most postwar governments never really
got the knack of it. They applied the standard tools
of economic management such as fiscal spending or
"pump-priming" to stimulate growth and interest rates
or "window guidance" from the Bank of Japan to slow
it down if overheated. Alas, they rarely took the right
moves at the right time and often made things worse.[9]
With such a track record, it would be hard to believe that
the more grandiose gestures could be credited with
galvanizing the whole economy as is frequently intimated. Prosperity did not come just because of Ikeda's
"income doubling plan" nor could the economic
slowdown have been arrested by Tanaka's scheme of
"remodeling the archipelago."[10]

A far bigger role in economic management was played
by the bureaucracy since it included people with technical knowhow and entrusted with specific tasks related to
the economy. It was they who came up with the ideas
and worked out the policies which were then fed upward
to the political leaders who adopted them, often with
little understanding or ability to review or amend them.
The bureaucrats were also responsible for the implementation of innumerable rules and regulations governing
economic matters as well as of the more comprehensive
plans and programs. While their status was respectable,
the bureaucrats never resumed the dominant position
they held during the wartime controlled economy, when
they could allocate resources and issue directives to mere
businessmen.

The limitations were most evident when it came to planning, a seeming innovation for a capitalist country but

not so far removed from wartime experiences. Despite periodic efforts at centralization, most plans were just a juxtaposition of the views of different ministries and agencies with some political window dressing thrown in. The contents were very loose and descriptive, explaining what sort of policies and practices were desired.[11] Aside from occasional projects, however, there was little concrete and most proposals were not even backed up with financial allocations. For the private sector, the targets were purely indicative. This made any forecasts a mixture of econometric projection and wishful thinking. It is therefore not surprising that most of the plans had to be revised, or merely discarded, well before completion. Whereas the targets were often exceeded earlier on, they remained hopelessly out of reach in later years. Meanwhile, the planning apparatus was constantly downgraded.

Comprehensive planning was simply not the Japanese way of doing things. They did not have a taste for such grand and global exercises, much preferring the practical and particular. Nor was the government itself strong enough to implement a true plan, had it been adopted. This weakness arose primarily from the sectionalism and rivalries that existed between the relevant ministries and agencies. Thus, what usually happened in practice was that specific bodies and, within them, specific divisions and bureaucrats, would tackle specific projects and do whatever they could to make them work. In this narrower, concrete and highly personalized setting, they were often able to accomplish extraordinary feats. The outcome was an intricate web of relations and arrangements that did not differ so much from Meiji days.

The most illustrious of these bodies is the Ministry of International Trade and Industry which grew out of the earlier Ministry of Commerce and Industry (and the wartime Munitions Ministry). This combination of trade and industry was symbolic since trade, for which read primarily "exports," became the basis of much subsequent growth. And in industry, for which it was directly responsible, it spearheaded Japan's resurgence in two ways: by increasing industry's share of total production and by upgrading specific industrial branches. Although it did not have the largest personnel or budget, MITI was entrusted with more of the postwar economic policy than any other body, including the Economic Planning Agency which it usually dominated. Its action was most authoritative in the initial period when business circles were still disorganized and scarcities prevailed. But it managed to find some task of value to one clientele or another throughout its career.[12]

MITI's most notable activity is what has come to be called "industrial policy." On a higher and broader level, it published white papers and "visions" tracing the past experiences and forecasting the future paths of industry as a whole or specific sectors. While useful in conveying a general impression, and arousing public interest, most of these exercises were rather academic and quite hazy. Where it was really effective was in promoting individual branches and even individual products. In so doing, it made extensive use of all possible means of protecting and promoting "infant industries." It repeatedly showed more ingenuity than others and came up with some tricks that were unknown abroad. Also, when its powers under formal legislation ran out it engaged in informal but no less persuasive advice-giving and arm twisting known as "administrative guidance."

In order to protect domestic products from foreign competition, it cut off imports by introducing tariffs and quotas or, later on, formalities and regulations that served as non-tariff barriers. It also kept foreigners from manufacturing locally by restricting investment. Local companies were encouraged by granting them fiscal incentives including tax exemptions and rapid depreciation of equipment. Government banks were instructed to provide cheap loans and other financial support included outright subsidies. Meanwhile, much of the necessary infrastructure was built at public expense. The state then directed its own purchasing toward national suppliers and private companies, which also wanted MITI support, were encouraged to do the same. This could have resulted in fat and lazy enterprises, and occasionally did. But they were jolted out of their complacency by outside demands for liberalization which were feared and likened to a "second coming of the Black Ships." Here, MITI held off as long as possible but also prepared its dependents by rationalization, modernization and mergers.

Electronics in the early days

Credit: FPC/Kyodo

Within the broader industrial policy, the real action was with sectors that were "targeted" at one time or another. There were many such and they changed periodically. The first effort was to restore coal and steel production by concentrating resources there. In the early 1950s, fertilizer, textiles and shipping were added. By the 1960s, it was more a question of creating internationally viable operations in synthetic fibers and petrochemicals, machinery and electronics. About then shipbuilding and automobiles were given a strong push. Subsequently, and especially after the oil crisis, MITI shifted from heavy and chemical industries to the so-called knowledge or technology-intensive sectors, including nuclear energy, aerospace and computers. As soon as any new item arose, it might be picked up, and thus biotechnology, robotics, and new materials were seen as industries for the future. From this list it is evident that there was more concern with potential than comparative advantage, and MITI adopted a "dynamic" rather than a "static" approach. While it was argued somewhat abstractly that the targets were chosen on purely economic grounds, it is more likely that helpful prerequisites were access to influential MITI bureaucrats or politicians and a sector that looked "modern" at the time.[13]

The Ministry of International Trade and Industry was not the only body doing such work. Other ministries and agencies also protected and promoted sectors of special interest. The Health Ministry carefully nurtured a domestic pharmaceutical industry. The Ministry of Agriculture, Foresty and Fisheries looked after the suppliers of farm machinery or fishing boats and gear. The Ministry of Construction helped the cement producers and makers of building equipment. In a sense, the Ministry of Finance also fostered "infant industries" like banking, securities and insurance. Certain semigovernmental corporations also did their bit. Nippon Telegraph and Telephone procured its material from favored makers of telecommunications equipment and computers and Japan National Railways bought its rolling stock domestically. Meanwhile, the Science and Technology Agency provided basic research on a broad range of subjects, including rockets and satellites, and smaller research institutes turned out prototypes for local manufacturers free of charge.

While the Ministry of International Trade and Industry clearly usurped the leading position, it was partially counterbalanced by other bodies. The Economic Planning Agency, although it did not have any practical activities or pet projects—and perhaps just for that reason—was able to develop a broader view and think of other sectors which were being neglected. It also had to consider the drawbacks to some of these efforts such as pollution, urban congestion and the impact on consumers. While its words of advice were not often heeded, the Ministry of Finance could not be ignored. It drew up the national budget which included those of all ministries and agencies which it had to approve. It could thus keep the others in line somewhat (on total if not specific allocations) and also prevent the national budget from snowballing. On the whole, it was a brake on economic development in the eyes of MITI, which would gladly have pushed harder. But this at least ensured a degree of prudence and enhanced the economy's stability.

In spite of all this, it would be foolish to assume— as is increasingly done—that the principal impulse for Japan's economic development came from the bureaucracy or government. There is no question that they were extremely useful for any specific help they could give. But it did not take very long for the positions to be reversed and for businessmen to take the lead. This derived from their capacity to organize and expand companies, to recruit and train workers, and to conquer domestic and overseas markets. They did not need much encouragement to improve production methods, raise the technological levels, or boost scale. Nor did they really have to be told which products had potential. The ability to get along on their own was shown most strikingly by the proclivity to develop sectors which had not been targeted or which enjoyed little government backing. And it was demonstrated most pointedly by firms which were not initially members of Japan, Inc. and often rose despite it such as Sony, Honda, YKK, Kyocera and others plus masses of smaller ventures.[14]

Far more important than this, and less realized by outsiders, the businessmen were gradually altering the power relationship. They began financing the politicians who had to repay their debts by seeking favors for business circles in general (*zaikai*) or even specific sectors. With the years, they also became considerably less dependent on the bureaucrats. They were soon able to obtain their own funds from related banks, or by issuing stock, and they could get technologies from overseas partners or create their own through R&D. Each time capital, investment or trade restrictions were liberalized, they enjoyed less protection and had less reason to tow the line. Eventually, whatever support might be forthcoming from MITI or other bodies was quite secondary. With this, businessmen ceased paying as much attention to "administrative guidance" as they once did.

Meanwhile, they provided more of the input for national policy in areas that concerned them. Through leading business organizations like the Federation of Economic Organizations (Keidanren) or the Federation of Employers Associations (Nikkeiren), they influenced government policy and programs and even cowed it into an administrative reform. As for the ministries and agencies, it was the businessmen in the field who knew far more about actual needs than any bureaucrats, and they were always consulted on upcoming operations. In fact, it was this system of feedback from industry that kept the bureaucrats moving in the right direction, although the businessmen sometimes overstated their case and got more than they deserved. When it came to targeting, it was the businessmen more than the bureaucrats who decided which sectors should be selected. More intimately, over the years certain companies established close relations with certain bureaucrats who aided them and, in return, were rewarded with cushy jobs after retirement (*amakudari*).

In referring to the role of business circles, it should not be forgotten that there were definite categories of companies with more or less clout. The most influential were those which grew out of the old *zaibatsu*. Some were never really dismembered and others quickly came together again under the wing of the related bank. It did not take long for Mitsubishi, Mitsui, Sumitomo, Fuyo, Dai-Ichi Kangyo, Sanwa and other groups or *keiretsu* to emerge. While looser than before, they certainly had advantages over smaller groups or individual companies. Many major manufacturers also created their own groups of suppliers, such as Hitachi, Toshiba, Toyota and Nissan.[15] The upstarts which succeeded, like those previously mentioned, eventually gained acceptance. But there was little concern for the needs or wishes of the vast majority of small and medium enterprises (99% of the total with 70% of the labor force) which were engaged in more backward or labor-intensive industries, services or distribution and frequently acted as suppliers or subcontractors to bigger firms.

While business circles were able to reverse the situation

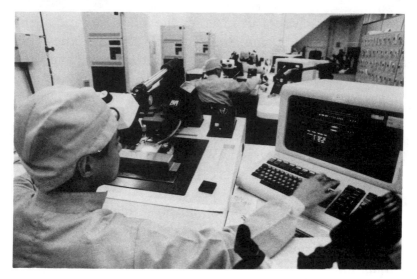

Electronics in the high tech age

Credit: IBM-Japan

within Japan, Inc., labor was never able to assert itself adequately and remained a very junior partner. There had obviously been a striking change for the better. Before the war, workers were regimented and pressed into service, on occasion by labor bosses. They were miserably treated and poorly paid with little thought as to their health or safety. When they tried to organize, this was adamantly opposed by the employers who were backed by the government. This was altered by labor legislation imposed by MacArthur's advisors and since generally accepted. Workers were entitled to seek work freely. They could band together in unions to demand improvements. In fact, the trade union movement spread rapidly and still includes about a third of the labor force. It is supported by opposition parties, especially the Socialists and Communists. Gradually, working hours were reduced, holidays and vacations extended, safety and other regulations tightened up. With time, not only wages but also retirement benefits and social security increased.

Rather than resist worker demands, managers found it advisable to bring part of the working class under their domination in other ways. Due to a passion for loyalty, companies offered lifetime employment which appealed strongly to workers just after the war when losing a job could be disastrous. This system was sharply reinforced with regular promotions, seniority wages, special bonuses and assorted fringe benefits. Ultimately, the advantages of belonging were so great that employees hesitated to leave.[16] Yet, while lifetime employment was portrayed as the typical Japanese system, it never covered more than a quarter of the labor force and excluded most women, part-time workers, subcontractors and smaller companies in general. There, employees faced considerable job insecurity and endured lower wages, longer hours, and worse working conditions.

After the war, Japan's basic problem was not how to run an economy. It already had eighty years of experience. The real lack was capital since much of its physical plant had been damaged or destroyed and government and personal finances were run down or dissipated by inflation. Yet, despite the urgent needs, the government was not willing to seek more than modest sums abroad in the form of loans. To do otherwise would create unwanted dependence. Nor was foreign investment really desired since that implied letting potential competitors into the market. If anything, restrictions on investment were stricter than before and some multinationals which had previously done business in Japan were not allowed back in.[17] This meant that the easiest way of partaking in the economy was by licensing products or technologies, which is what the government wanted. During the Oc-

cupation, there was considerable American aid in cash
and kind which helped Japan through the period of extreme shortage until it could get back on its feet. After
that, it was pretty much on its own and determined to
rebuild the economy primarily with domestic funds.

The main source of these funds was the population as
a whole, no longer just the farmers, and taxes were levied
at gradually mounting rates. The pressure, however, was
moderated by the fact that once the economy got into
swing revenues increased largely due to higher incomes.
Indeed, in early years, tax rates were occasionally
lowered and companies were granted all sorts of exemptions and rebates. More of the money was derived from
the savings of a traditionally frugal people. The urge to
save was, of course, accentuated by a lack of public
welfare to fall back on and widespread desires to own a
home and educate the children. Thus, saving also grew
apace, particularly at bonus time. The only drawback
was that interest rates were kept relatively low at the
behest of the financial authorities. This was more
bearable given rather mild inflation, but it still did not
offer much of a return. Nevertheless, with few alternatives, the Japanese ended up by putting as much as 20–
25% of their disposable income into savings. Together
with public saving, this added up to 30–37% of GNP.[18]

This was supplemented by the government, whose action was constricted by a modest budget and the few
directly productive activities it undertook. The public sector consisted of little more than housing, highway and
regional development agencies. It also had indirect control over the tobacco and salt monopoly, national
railways, national airline, and telephone and telegraph
operations run by public and semi-public corporations
like JNR, JAL, NTT and KDD.[19] Its essential contribution was therefore to create a broad and solid infrastruc-

ture of highways, bridges, dams, ports and so on. Part of this came from the national and local budgets and an appreciable share fron the Treasury Investment and Loan Program. The TILP, whose funds were drawn from postal savings and pension plans, made generous allocations to state corporations, banks and agencies as well as specific infrastructural projects. While the limits on government spending could be regretted, it was certainly advantageous that it taxed private companies less and left them more money to use. It also helped tremendously by keeping defense expenditures down to a mere 1% of GNP.

This made it feasible to pump tremendous sums into productive investment, with gross domestic capital formation reaching a formidable 30–37% of GNP. Some of the money was channeled through a dozen state banks, the most prominent being the Japan Development Bank and the Export-Import Bank. But more eventually came from the commercial banks, national and regional, and cooperative institutions. The city banks, related to the *keiretsu*, took the lead in feeding funds at very modest rates to major manufacturers and traders. With interest rates low, largely because savers were paid less, they were enabled to expand quickly on what looked like perilously high leverage but remained safe due to "overloaning" by the Bank of Japan. Later on, however, many companies increased the amount of reinvestment and raised funds by selling shares on a lively stock market. By the 1980s, their debt-equity ratios were less extreme and dependence on banks slackened. It was finally possible for bankers to think of lending to smaller companies or even consumers, except that they were now pressed into absorbing government bonds.

Agriculture, although plainly dwindling, still represented about a third of gross national product and occupied about half of the work force shortly after the war. It naturally had to be revived—and quite urgently— given the food shortages, but not in its previous state. Earlier practices had resulted in a concentration of owner- ship among large, often absentee landlords, while 40% of the land was farmed by tenants. To avoid a return of social tensions which were regarded as a cause of militarism, the Occupation authorities drew up plans for a reform which had to be imposed on the Japanese government. As of 1946, much of the land was trans- ferred from the landlords to the tenants and holdings were limited to three hectares. This gave a new impulse to agriculture, since the owner-cultivators worked hard to boost output. Still, with the average household only farming some 1.2 hectares, there were distinct limits to what could be done and many left for the cities or sea- sonal work in factories, entrusting the farm to mother, grandmother and grandfather. By the 1980s, agriculture only accounted for 4% of GNP and a tenth of the labor force, most of that just part-time.

This time farming was very different from what had ex- isted before. In certain ways, it was more efficient than ever due to an exceptional use of fertilizers and pes- ticides, improved varieties, irrigation, farm machinery and advanced methods. Rice yields were among the highest in the world, so high indeed that there was occa- sionally too much. This created severe problems for the government, which paid heavily subsidized prices for rice and then sold it more cheaply to the consumers. To diver- sify production, the Ministry of Agriculture launched programs to promote other grains, fruits, vegetables, meat and dairy products. However, since Japanese farmers were not inherently competitive, this often re- quired restrictions on imports and more subsidies, pushing these prices far above international levels as well. The outcome was a relatively prosperous farm population, and one that was not really worth its keep but had to be protected for political reasons.

Fortunately, the essential thrust of postwar development came from manufacturing. The sectors which made the biggest contributions to growth were, not surprisingly, those that had been singled out by the government for particular attention. Part of their headway came from special support since they had ready access to funds and, for a long time, almost guaranteed markets for the local industry although individual companies competed fiercely against one another. That is probably why those which survived were sufficiently tough to take on foreign rivals. What they did to strengthen was their own formula, which varied, but invariably contained elements like steady improvement of production techniques, usually replacing people with machines, unceasing efforts to upgrade technologies and boost scale, and constant rationalization to cut costs and keep wages from rising unduly.

Ever since Meiji days Japanese industrialists had been obsessed with a concept of heavy-and-chemical industries as the driving force of a modern economy. They had come closest to their goal during the war and now in peacetime they simply adopted another tack. Despite American preferences that light industry be encouraged initially, and fears that a resource-poor country could not succeed, one of the very first steps was to revive the steel industry. In some ways, it was lucky that a new start was necessary since the new mills were far larger, used the vastly more efficient LD converters, and could be located on the seaside which facilitated delivery of raw materials and shipment of exports. This worked, as the steel produced was of very high quality and sufficiently cheap to export. One after another, blast furnaces went up and capacity rose to almost 150 million tons. Similar attempts were made for other metals like aluminum and copper. Fine chemicals, and then petrochemicals, were the other prong of this drive and oil-based *konbinato* were soon rising in different parts of the archipelago.

With these basic inputs produced locally, it was far easier to develop downstream activities. Shipbuilding, a major consumer of steel, was given priority because it was comparatively simple and helped promote the merchant marine. Using relatively cheap labor, and good Japanese steel, it was possible to produce a broad range of ships including mammoth oil tankers since the shipyards were also built to scale. Japan ultimately had the foremost shipbuilding industry, about as big as everyone else's put together. Truck manufacture, also less complex, got off to a fast start. Motorcycles, which required less capital, followed. Here, due to innovative companies like Honda, Yamaha and Suzuki, Japan almost gained a world monopoly. Automobiles came somewhat later and the initial results were quite disappointing. Only when the assembly plants had been upgraded, and especially the vendor networks organized and improved, could progress be made. By the 1960s, Toyota, Nissan and others turned out good cars, but small ones that were not so popular abroad. The oil crisis changed all that and not long after Japan's automobile industry was vying for first place with America's.

Meanwhile, the machinery industry was expanding since local manufacturers were constantly renovating plant and equipment and had an almost insatiable appetite for more productive units. With this, machine tool makers moved ahead and some firms branched into robotics. Optics did well with cameras by Canon and Minolta, and then photocopiers, along with Ricoh. Electrical equipment underwent an even greater metamorphosis, evolving into electronics. Due to extremely efficient assembly techniques, Japan became a top producer of radios, televisions and video tape recorders. It also made telecommunications gear of all sorts. Casio captured the calculator market while Seiko got the biggest chunk of digital watches. However, the burning ambition was to dominate the most vital sector, computers. Starting in a middle range, leading companies like Fujitsu, Hitachi and NEC worked up to main frame and down to microcomputers. For crucial elements like semiconductors, they quickly gained an advance over the Americans.

By the 1980s, Japanese companies were looking for new openings. There were no longer many around, but some few began to catch on. To ensure its power needs, nuclear energy was backed by Japan, Inc. so resolutely that even when other countries had second thoughts it pushed ahead. Having created robust pharmaceutical and chemical industries, it was not surprising that biotechnology was picked up. While not all of the so-called "new materials" might pay off, one already was as Kyocera developed high-grade ceramics. Japanese companies had long eyed aeronautics and some were producing military planes under license. But, aside from a small turbojet, no indigenous commercial aircraft had been designed. Finally, in the early 1980s, it was decided to cooperate with American makers rather than go it alone. For satellites and rockets, however, Japanese pride won out and the goal was again 100% national products.

With so much attention devoted to the "sunrise" industries, little could be done about the reputedly "sunset" ones. They were left to shift for themselves and it was occasionally hinted that, if they could not get by, they might just as well disapperar. Yet, while the older, labor-intensive sectors shrank as a whole, they hardly vanished. During the 1950s and 1960s, they actually did fairly well since labor costs were low and they enjoyed a comparative advantage. Many continued thriving even after that because they were increasingly automated and produced at incredible scales. The most striking examples were simple objects like pens, music box movements and zippers, the latter monopolized by YKK. As for textiles, it simply passed from one phase to another as silk was partially replaced by cotton, and that by nylon and synthetic fibers and all eventually coexisted. Even garments flourished by moving into high fashion. And toys adapted to the electronics age. Meanwhile, as handicrafts regained popularity, makers of pottery, bamboo dolls or kimonos could get by. Under such conditions, one can only wonder how much better these sectors would have done if not starved of funds, personnel and status.

During the high growth period, only two basic types of industry were visible, the more backward but still passably successful light and the more advanced and smashingly successful heavy and high tech industries. Subsequently, however, a third category became conspicuous. This was an assortment of branches regarded as depressed or declining. By this was not meant the older cottage industries, for which there was little concern. Rather, it included many of the former success stories which had come upon bad times and had to be cared for. Among them were fertilizer, plywood, pulp and paper, aluminum and others hurt by skyrocketing energy or raw material costs. Many more were suffering from inadequate demand, all the more painful since they had considerable excess capacity, like shipping, shipbuilding, petrochemicals and even steel. In earlier days, they had been targeted and strenuous efforts were made to build them up. Now they were protected by special measures until they could be scaled down to a point where they might conceivably survive.

Despite its dynamic nature, the secondary sector only grew moderately as a share of total gross national product. It was already quite large by 1955, some 24% of GNP, and only expanded to 43% in 1970, after which it shrank to 38% in 1980. More revealing are the changes that took place within the sector. Mining, largely coal and copper, almost disappeared. Within manufacturing, the light industries faded and textiles, in particular, declined from 13% to 5% from 1955 to 1980. Chemicals also slipped from 16% to 11%. Metals (both crude and fabricated) remained at about 15%. Machinery, on the other hand, rose from 15% to 23% and transport equipment from 7% to 11%. Changes in export composition were yet more noteworthy. Textiles dropped from over 40% to under 5%. Chemicals and metals increased moderately. The biggest change came from machinery and transport equipment which together climbed from a mere 12% to over 60% of total exports. With that, Japan had little need to import manufactured goods and most of its emphasis was on raw materials (20%) and fuel (40%).

Nevertheless, in absolute terms, secondary production increased substantially, more than forty times over from 1955 to 1980. But exports expanded even more rapidly, 65-fold, making it a vital impetus. Most of this growth arose from aggressive sales by manufacturers once they had satisfied the domestic market or wished to boost scale. It was facilitated by greatly improved quality and low prices. These prices were low only partly due to rationalization. Tax rebates in early years and a cheap yen throughout were just as helpful. While Japanese exports quickly penetrated world markets, and seemed excessively abundant, this was due less to the export ratio which was a modest 13% than the sheer size of the Japanese economy which represented 10% of world GNP and 8% of world trade by the 1980s. Although, to judge by the export ratio, industry did not seem overly dependent the same could not be said of specific branches where exports accounted for more than half of total sales, such as automobiles, motorcycles, machine tools, cameras, watches, and certain electronics. This made resurgent protectionism a serious threat.[20]

While the tertiary sector never received as high a priority, it continued expanding from 30% of GNP in 1960 to 58% in 1980. At that time, it employed over half of the total labor force. This was gradually bringing Japan into a postindustrial era it was not yet comfortable with. That is because services had traditionally been a backwater, far less esteemed than manufacturing, and some parts were still insufferably inefficient. Other segments, however, had made notable progress.

Most service establishments were quite small, a welter of restaurants, bars, amusement centers and household helpers. When they modernized, it was more often by offering Western food, beverages or sports than through efficient service. More disturbing was that the scale of distribution operations, retail and wholesale, also remained small. With twice as many outlets for a given number of customers as the United States or parts of Europe, distribution was dreadfully complex and costly. This occurred despite the rise of department stores, chain stores and convenience stores since the older establishments continued to exist and the newer ones were not all that cheap or effective. Only for the introduction of modern services like leasing, consulting or software were the signs more positive. Communications were also improving in what the authorities wished to make an "information age."

The latest in integrated steel mills

Credit: NKK

Financial activities, on the other hand, did somewhat better. Japan developed a dense network of banks, insurance companies and securities houses. They all prospered due to booming business as well as government protection. As noted, the Bank of Japan set interest rates so as to keep corporate borrowing cheap, but also to guarantee an adequate spread for the bankers. Insurance rates were kept high by the Ministry of Finance so that even small or incompetent companies could get by. To avoid excessive competition between different intermediaries, it drew boundaries between banking, trust, stock and bond sales, pension business, and so on. Foreign competitors were kept out completely at first and only let in when most of the market was occupied. Not until the 1980s was true liberalization undertaken which intensified competition but also enhanced efficiency and promised to bring down costs for the consumers.[21]

Where Japan apparently excelled was foreign trade. There, in contrast to domestic distribution, highly efficient and large scale operations arose amidst lesser trading houses. These were the general trading companies (*sogo shosha*) which also reformed despite the Occupation edicts. This time they were even bigger and more diversified, handling literally thousands of articles. They dealt in imports of raw materials and other bulk products, some domestic processing and distribution, exports of machinery and certain consumer goods, and financing of suppliers and clients. They also invested widely abroad, especially in raw material extraction or to handle sales. They succeeded due to their far-flung networks of national and international offices and the huge turnovers which allowed them to charge very slim commissions. They also gained immeasurably from being members of the leading *keiretsu*, which provided a base clientele and facilitated financing. If anything, their success may have been too great. The top nine *sogo shosha* (Mitsubishi, Mitsui, C. Itoh, Marubeni, Sumitomo, Nissho-Iwai, Toyo Menka, Kanematsu-Gosho, and Nichimen) controlled nearly 50% of total exports and 60% of total imports.[22]

Thus, the Japanese economy grew vigorously during the 1950s, 1960s and early 1970s, averaging some 10% a year. This "miraculous" growth had various causes. One was quite simply luck, as for the booms sparked by the Korean and Vietnam Wars. More determinant, and more praiseworthy, was the ability to get two "virtuous circles" moving. One arose when increased production induced investment in plant and equipment which resulted in yet more production. The other emerged as exports stimulated production which flowed into more exports. Each turn of these wheels was driven by falling prices deriving from greater efficiency and scale. When one mechanism was not operating, the other usually was. What was disconcerting was that rising domestic consumption only rarely propelled the economy and that it was increasingly export campaigns that pulled it out of a recession.

But the "miracle" began flagging after the oil crisis of 1973. The economy slowed down to about 5–6% for the rest of the decade and a mere 3–4% in the early 1980s. While this was still better than other advanced countries, it was hardly impressive for Japan. Obviously, with oil so essential for production, transportation, and equally as a raw material, spiraling prices knocked the cost structure out of kilter and made Japan uncompetitive for some goods and raised the prices of others enough to discourage sales. But it would be misleading to put all the blame on the oil shock, as many Japanese did. Production was bound to slow down anyway because local manufacturers had already boosted output so high, introduced so many new products, and conquered so many markets that there was not much room for growth. The first "virtuous circle" stalled. The second was more brutally interrupted by neo protectionism which impeded sales of most leading exports. Meanwhile, even the domestic market became sluggish due to stagnating purchasing power and near saturation for some articles. The situation was further aggravated by budget deficits and a ballooning national debt.[23]

For the Japanese population, the postwar prosperity was an unquestionable boon. Per capita income kept rising smartly during the 1960s and early 1970s and more hesitantly thereafter. By the 1980s, the Japanese were earning more than the British or French and seemed likely to pass the American level by the end of the decade. Admittedly, the yen could not buy as much as an equivalent amount of pounds, francs or dollars given the prevailing high prices. But the Japanese could at least purchase more food and clothing, move into their own home, and fill it with masses of consumer goods, rice cookers, gas ranges, refrigerators, televisions, VTRs and the like. Where they did considerably less well was in the dwelling itself which was often cramped and uncomfortable, not quite a "rabbit hutch" but not much better. And they had inadequate leisure since the poor "workaholics" still put in many more hours than their counterparts in the West.

More serious deficiencies affected society as a whole. By devoting so much of the national wealth to productive investment, there was not enough left over for social overhead. Amenities like plumbing, sewerage, piped water and even paved roads were inadequate and parks and gardens clearly insufficient. Lack of physical planning led to urban congestion and rural depopulation and pollution seriously blighted the country. While health care, social security and welfare were more widespread, costs kept rising implacably and just when it was most needed efforts were made to weaken the safety net. Such problems were more acute for those in the lower tier of the dual structure. For, although the extreme gaps of prewar times closed somewhat, it was still evident that blue-collar and service workers, employees of small firms, high school graduates and women in general were disadvantaged by a supposedly meritocratic system that helped those who did not need it more than those who did.[24]

For all its shortcomings, there is no doubt that Japan was an "economic miracle" of uncommon proportions. This tiny, inherently poor and terribly overcrowded nation became one of the most productive in the world. In many sectors, it not only caught up with its Western rivals, it passed them by. However, obsessed with productive capability as it had earlier been with military might, it forgot most other things. Among them were living conditions, human relations, natural beauty and spiritual fulfillment. This may have been too high a price to pay and certainly a less productive but more fruitful economy would have made it a happier society. If it could finally adopt a more balanced approach in the coming years it would be on the way to a real "miracle."

NOTES

1. Two good studies of this period are William Lockwood, *The Economic Development of Japan*, and Takafusa Nakamura, *Economic Growth in Prewar Japan*.
2. See William D. Wray, *Mitsubishi and the N. Y. K.*, and Kunio Yoshihara, *Sogo Shosha*.
3. See John G. Roberts, *Mitsui: Three Centuries of Japanese Business*.
4. Nakamura, *op. cit.*, pp. 2–4.
5. The best overall studies of this period are Takafusa Nakamura, *The Postwar Japanese Economy,* and Tatsuro Uchino, *Japan's Postwar Economy*.
6. See Joe Moore, *Japanese Workers and the Struggle for Power*.
7. This included, among others, Herman Kahn, *The Emerging Japanese Superstate,* and P. B. Stone, *Japan Surges Ahead, The Story of an Economic Miracle*.
8. See Jon Woronoff, *Inside Japan, Inc.*
9. See Uchino, *op. cit.*
10. Kakuei Tanaka, *Building a New Japan*.
11. If you don't believe this, just look at the various plan documents. See also Miyohei Shinohara et al, *The Japanese and Korean Experiences in Managing Development*, pp. 6–14.
12. See Chalmers Johnson, *MITI And The Japanese Miracle*.
13. The tendency of MITI to target almost everything was noted by various observers. See Miyohei Shinohara, *Industrial Growth, Trade, and Dynamic Patterns in the Japanese Economy*, p. 22.
14. See Woronoff, *op. cit.*, pp. 86–110.
15. See Dodwell Marketing Consultants, *Industrial Groupings in Japan*, Tokyo, 1984.
16. See, among others, Tadashi Hanami, *Labor Relations in Japan*

Today, Taishiro Shirai (ed.), *Contemporary Industrial Relations in Japan,* Jon Woronoff, *Japan's Wasted Workers,* and M. Y. Yoshino, *Japan's Managerial System.*

17. Even by 1983, foreign investment only reached $4.8 billion, which was a rather paltry sum for an economy as large as Japan's.
18. It should be noted that the savings rates peaked at the higher levels about 1970 and have been declining since.
19. The tobacco and salt monopoly and Nippon Telegraph & Telephone were "privatized" in 1984–5.
20. See Jon Woronoff, *World Trade War.*
21. See Stephen Bronte, *Japanese Finance: Markets and Institutions.*
22. See Kunio Yoshihara, *Sogo Shosha,* and Alexander K. Young, *The Sogo Shosha.*
23. See Jon Woronoff, *The Japan Syndrome.*
24. See Tadashi Fukutake, *Japanese Society Today* and *The Japanese Social Structure.*

2

Taiwan, Industrial Island

Despite its engaging name (derived from the Portuguese for beautiful), the island of Formosa had not been quite a tropical paradise for its inhabitants. Relatively underpopulated, it attracted hordes of land-hungry settlers from the Chinese mainland who cleared the forests and drove back the aborigines. Under the Dutch, it briefly became a trading center. Once freed by Cheng Ch'engkung (Koxinga), and incorporated into Fukien Province as of 1683, the Chinese population multiplied even more rapidly. For a while it looked as if tea production might generate much needed earnings. But this failed due to poor care of the plants and adulteration of quality. And the dreams of good fortune faded.

Only after Formosa was ceded to Japan, in 1895, was its potential finally realized and something done to harness its considerable agricultural assets. Among the newer cash crops, none was more valuable than sugar cane with land under cultivation expanding swiftly and advanced farming methods boosting yields. Rice was also grown more systematically and production rose sharply with more irrigation, fertilizer, and the introduction of superior varieties. In order to get these crops to the market, and to administer the colony effectively, the Government-General busily improved the until then rather deficient infrastructure, constructing essential roads, railways, and harbors.

This was the first period of real development the island had seen after centuries of neglect under Chinese rulers. Its inhabitants benefited from improvements in nutrition, health and education. They also learned from the extension service how to farm more productively. But they were not permitted to rise high in society since most top, and even many relatively subordinate positions in the administration, commerce and industry were held by Japanese immigrants. The Chinese were farmers, but they hardly participated in the initial industrialization which was confined largely to sugar refining and other operations run by major Japanese combines, although some opened small rice mills. How much the islanders actually gained from their overlords was most uncertain since much of it was paid for by massive amounts of sugar and rice that were exported to Japan, pretty much at prices fixed by the Japanese.[1]

While not directly involved in the Pacific War, the budding economy was seriously blighted. Young men were conscripted as soldiers and, toward the end, ports and factories were bombed. Meanwhile, the Japanese squeezed the island for food and gave ever less in return. Much of the infrastructure was dilapidated and the food processing installations run down. Then, as the Japanese withdrew, the key administrators and technicians who made the system function left and could hardly be replaced. More detrimental, the whole economy had been designed as an appendage of Japan, exporting food, importing manufactured goods. There was no alternative market for the sugar and rice so that growth proved spurious. For such reasons, Taiwan's production in 1945–6 amounted to less than half the peak of the colonial period.

Reversion to China did not help much, given the dire economic state of the war-torn country that was soon engulfed in civil strife. Not much could be done by the beleaguered Nationalist Party (Kuomintang) as it fought to hold on to the mainland. When it moved to Taiwan in 1949, the situation seemed to take a turn for the worse. In its wake came over a million refugees, mainly politicians, military and bureaucrats who had to be provided for. As the site of the Republic of China, a National Government was established alongside the Provincial Government, saddling the populace with a double administration. Faced with Communist provocations and attacks, the Kuomintang's first priority was to strengthen the armed forces in order to hold on and perhaps one day reconquer the mainland. It was not until the United States began supplying economic and military aid and, in 1954, signed a mutual security treaty that the military peril receded. However, the bombardments continued a while and the need to be prepared for all eventualities never ceased.

The danger without was not the only threat to Taiwan's survival. The need to bolster the military establishment and serve as the remaining bastion of Free China placed a tremendous burden on it. The cost of receiving so many refugees would have been onerous at any time, but it was aggravated by shortages of food, housing and jobs. Military expenditures absorbed most of the central government's budget and, to cover its massive deficits, more money was printed. The inevitable result was inflation which raged out of control in the early 1950s. Some of the measures taken to combat it only added to the problems. Price controls were imposed on many products and, due to shortages, there had to be rationing. To suppress imports, multiple exchange rates and licensing were introduced. To stimulate at least some domestic production, industries were protected and subsidized. While the inflation gradually subsided, the economy was deprived of its vitality and pushed in the wrong directions.

As late as the mid-1950s, there were justifiable doubts as to whether Taiwan's economy could ever be restored. Periodically, it appeared on the verge of collapse. Even when the crises were overcome, it had to be remembered that this was basically a small nation of only 36,000 square kilometers which was inhabited by 5 million people after the war and an almost stupefying 20 million people today. With the agricultural sector severely weakened, hardly any industrial sector, and not enough exports to cover the costs of vital imports, it had very little going for it. As for labor, which was all it could boast, most youthful and energetic elements were in uniform while women and older people looked after the productive apparatus where they were still too numerous and often unemployed. It is not surprising that the forecasts ranged from depressing to disastrous.

It was only thanks to American military and economic assistance that the country could pull out of the tailspin. Military aid took some of the pressure off the government which could finally turn to economic issues. Economic aid was channeled into agriculture and infrastructure. The funds, which were substantial, made a big difference. But the stress on economic matters and the possibilities of influencing and expediting policy gained by American AID experts and others were even more significant in getting the Republic of China to reorder its priorities and seek economic development more rationally and vigorously.

They were the ones who proposed the concept of planning, both to give the efforts coming from the government and the private sector a sharper focus and to have a clearer idea of where the aid money was going. They also convinced the government to relax or cease some of the restrictions and regulations that hampered normal commercial undertakings. This resulted in a series of measures, introduced as of 1959 and ultimately formalized in the Nineteen-Point Program of Economic and Financial Reform. They included the dismantling of various trade and foreign exchange controls, adoption of a single exchange rate, and promotion of foreign investment. Freed from these bonds, local businessmen could act more efficiently and purposefully.

Although the government only played a rather feeble and sporadic role in economic development during the 1950s, it was definitely enhancing its position and spreading its activities which took a notable upturn in the 1960s and thereafter. The most prominent sign of this was the reinforcement of the planning machinery which grew out of the old Economic Stabilization Board (ESB), became stronger and more centralized under the Council of International Economic Cooperation and Development (CIECD), and was finally institutionlized in the Economic Planning Council (EPC) and today's Council for Economic Planning and Development (CEPD).

They drew up a series of usually four-year plans, the earliest of which goes back to 1953. The first two, under the ESB, were largely lists of desired projects that might be funded by aid donors with only scant reference to the rest of the economy. The CIECD, which formulated the fourth and fifth plans (1965–72), coordinated the policies of the relevant ministries and oversaw the implementation of selected projects. The EPC and CEPD engaged in broader planning, national, regional and sectoral and made forecasts of future developments which became very rough "targets." Although they did not select or supervise projects, this being left to the ministries and agencies concerned, they did try to overcome inconsistencies or conflicts.

While repeated transformations of institutions and shifts in policy may seem to indicate a lack of continuity or stability, it should not be forgotten that much of the economic personnel remained throughout. Some earlier planners or bureaucrats rose through the ranks to become ministers of finance or economic affairs, such as K. T. Li and Chao Yao-tun and others went even higher, to posts as premier, vice-president or president, like Chen Cheng, C. K. Yen, Sun Yun-suan and Yu Kuo-hwa. At the summit, it was clear that Generalissimo Chiang Kai-shek took close interest in what was being accomplished and his son, Chiang Chung-kuo, participated more actively since 1972 as premier and then president.

Moreover, the changes made it possible to experiment with different forms and degrees of planning and adopt a system that was broad and comprehensive but left enough latitude to government ministries and agencies to pursue their own ends. Since the CEPD came directly under the premier and the plans were adopted by the Executive Yuan, they enjoyed considerable prestige. But they were not regarded as sacrosanct and could be modified as needs arose and even superseded in practice by one-year plans or specific programs. Planning was only indicative for the private sector, which could go its own way but tended to weigh the possible advantages of conforming with official goals and policies. This made the exercise somewhat more effective and purposeful than in Japan if hardly constraining.

Some things the planning bodies were not able to do were often taken care of by other ministries and agencies whose action must also be considered. The most significant was the Ministry of Economic Affairs, with very broad competences for manufacturing, mining, commerce and public enterprises. It tended to single out specific sectors which were to be promoted and protected and eventually undertook a long series of such operations. Most recently, it decided to back a number of "strategic " industries including electronics, telecommunications, machinery and automotive. Such activities were handled largely by its Industrial Development Bureau while the Board of Foreign Trade, whose primary task was to promote exports, also had the crucial function of impeding competing imports.

For most other ministries, economic development came as an additional task to their current operations, but one that could hardly be neglected. The Ministry of Finance and Bank of China were instrumental in accumulating and distributing funds, not only of the government but also the commercial banks. The Ministry of Communications supervised, and fostered, railways, navigation, aviation and telecommunications companies, both public and private. The Council for Agricultural Planning and Development was responsible for advancement of the primary sector. The National Science Council and a new Science and Technology Advisory Group promoted more practical technology transfers as well as R&D.

Although the government usually stuck to broad and general supervision, it has intervened more directly on certain occasions. Most conspicuous was the launching, in 1973, of the "ten major construction projects" for a total cost of some US $8 billion. They consisted not only of infrastructural ones like the north-south freeway, Taichung harbor and Chiang Kai-shek International Airport. There were also key industrial ventures such as the integrated steel mill, shipyard, and petrochemical complex. Twelve further projects of a similar nature, including more nuclear power plants, were initiated in 1979 and expected to cost roughly US $5.7 billion. It goes without saying that the initiative for these programs came from the highest level while the timing was partially influenced by the need to get the economy out of the doldrums after the first and second oil shocks.

Whether intended or not, such projects gave a strong impulse to the burgeoning public sector. Initially, the government had restricted itself to basic transportation, like the railways and China Airlines, post and telephone, and utilities, the most important enterprise being Taiwan Power. The Ministry of Economic Affairs also inherited some operations from colonial times which engaged in mining, sugar refining and production of phosphates or fertilizer. However, as new plants went up, the state directly or indirectly began running huge corporations like China Steel, China Shipbuilding and Chinese Petroleum. Whereas some enterprises did well, more were just passable and a few got into financial difficulties and had to be scrapped, merged or rationalized. This put an end to a possible invasion of the private sector by bureaucrat-industrialists.

Given the nature of the regime, there is no doubt that there were definite temptations for the government to play an even more dominant part in the economy or, at the very least, for the "public sector to spearhead Taiwan's economic development."[2] But it never went too far. This may have stemmed from contrary advice from aid donors and especially the United States or fear that this would discourage sorely needed foreign investment. Evidently, the Kuomintang's own ideology militated against excessive state involvement and made it stress the vital role of free enterprise. In addition, its leaders were extremely occupied with more fundamental issues of domestic and foreign policy, defense and the threat from Communist China. When planning slipped back into a decentralized mode and public enterprises got into trouble, whatever illusions there may have been about directing the economy from above were dissipated and the public sector ceded most of the ground to the private sector.

While welcome, it was not as if the potential entrepreneurs had been waiting for government consent or support to make their own efforts. Numerous firms, the majority of them unincorporated, were launched because people thought they saw possibilities in some commercial opening and had to do something to pull themselves out of the morass of chaos and poverty. The initial steps were taken during the 1950s when little could be expected of the government and when, if anything, it burdened the business community with undesired restrictions and regulations. As planning became more effective and tempting incentives were given those who cooperated, some businessmen accepted a degree of official guidance. But most of them preferred avoiding any unnecessary red tape or interference.

There was never any shortage of entrepreneurs in the Republic of China. Indeed, there often seemed to be too many. This makes one wonder where they all came from. Some were merchants and industrialists who fled the mainland. They were able to inject useful skills and knowhow, even if not too much capital. A further contribution was made over the years by Overseas Chinese who lived in developing countries of Southeast Asia that appreciated their talents less and often thwarted their efforts. On occasion, they suffered from discrimination and open attacks. Partly out of patriotism, and partly to play it safe, they diversified their operations and set up factories on the island. Gradually a very dense web of commercial dealings arose with contacts in the far-flung Chinese diaspora.

The bulk of the entrepreneurs, however, were native

Taiwanese. This was not only due to the fact that they represented the vast majority of the population but also that they tended to be excluded from the military and political apparatus in earlier years, as this was reserved for Mainlanders, and could only prove their ability or attain greater wealth and status through material success. Some had learned how to do business during the Japanese occupation. Others found out by watching the first Chinese entrepreneurs. Younger generations occasionally acquired the essential knowhow at school or abroad. But the largest share picked it up by working in existing companies and then left to found their own.[3]

A far from negligible source of entrepreneurship has arisen from foreign firms. American multinationals soon set on Taiwan as an excellent site to enage in offshore production in order to procure cheap components or articles for use or sale back home. Often they were forced to cut costs this way because of Japanese competition. Later on the Japanese themselves had to subcontract work to Taiwan in order to remain competitive. In fact, Taiwan was the most popular base for the Japanese who understood the people and customs more, or at least thought they did. And the locals knew how to take full advantage of these links.

Firms in Taiwan, like others run by Chinese in Hong Kong and Singapore, were initially very small. Many of them were simple family operations. The personnel consisted of the proprietor, his wife and children, sometimes other relatives and employees from the same city or province. The premises were cramped and crowded in the extreme. It might be some small space in a make-shift factory or merely their own living quarters. The machinery was rudimentary and most of the work was painstaking and time-consuming manual labor. To any outsider, this inevitably looked like a "sweat shop." Perhaps it was. But there was not much alternative at the time.[4]

Over the years, however, there is no doubt that the space increased and the equipment improved, at least for those who made a go of it. While the mass of firms were still relatively small, there were a fair number of larger ones employing several thousand workers in reasonably decent, if hardly luxurious premises. Where more care was lavished was on the machinery. In textiles, for example, the industry vaunted an extraordinary number of jet looms for a developing country. The electronics factories were also more methodically and efficiently run. Among the leading local firms were Nan Ya and Formosa Plastics, Far Eastern Textiles and, for electronics, Tatung and Sampo. Other larger units were subsidiaries of or joint ventures with foreign companies.

Many of the smaller firms, originally independent entities making common articles, gradually slipped into the position of subcontractors. They supplied the countless components needed to assemble finished electronic, metal or plastic products or parts for automobiles. While the system worked after a fashion, it was not terribly convenient or quality-conscious and it was thus decided to restructure it with satellite factories serving "parent" factories. Meanwhile, even many of the larger companies were just subcontractors for foreign multinationals. They made parts for leading manufacturers or furnished products that were sold by major distributors in America and Europe. They worked on an OEM (original equipment manufacturer) basis under which the finished articles bore the trademark of the foreign buyer rather than their own, although a less conspicuous "made in Taiwan" label could be found somewhere.

No matter how crucial the entrepreneurs were in taking the lead, there is no question that the workers were just as essential in the development process. Most of those in the factories were younger children of farmers, forced to enter industry by a lack of land but also eager to grow with these expanding sectors. In government and corporate offices, many were Mainlanders and their children with more white-collar tastes and pretensions. On the whole, people worked hard, although there were often justifiable complaints of waste and sloth in the bureaucracy and state enterprises. There was also a gratifying degree of stability and job mobility was only moderate. This commitment may have arisen from time-honored traditions, or the government's appeals to work earnestly for the good of the nation, or the fact that so many were employed in family firms. When employees did move, it was often from a desire to become their own boss, in keeping with the ancient Chinese saying that "it is better to be the bill of a chicken than the anus of an ox." In such cases, they usually ended up working even harder than before.

While there were bound to be hidden reserves of initiative among potential entrepreneurs and untapped energy among the working people, it is a bit of a mystery as to where the capital could have come from to reconstruct and then expand the economy. During the first decade, it was certainly not the state, for it was spending revenue faster than it was raised and printing money to make up the difference. This was the practice which had led to runaway inflation on the mainland and, until the early 1950s, it was undermining Taiwan's economy as well. There is no reason to believe the government desired such a policy, it simply could not meet the overwhelming needs with what it had. Once the crisis was over, however, the past experiences encouraged it to be even more financially responsible and conservative than most.

During the 1960s and 1970s, with a brief relapse in the

early 1980s, the government managed to balance its budget and usually ran a surplus. This was an exceptional feat considering that the country still had to mount an army of half-a-million and devoted as much as 12% of GNP and 65% of government expenditures to defense right into the 1960s and only somewhat less subsequently. The Bank of China continued a comparatively restrictive policy which kept inflation down to moderate levels aside from two unavoidable flare-ups after the oil crises of the 1970s. Even when some of the responsibility for fixing interest rates was delegated to the Bankers Association of Taiwan, the Central Bank could influence interest policy and curb monetary expansion as needed. This stricter approach, although a welcome relief from earlier practices, did limit the possibilities of counter-cyclical policy and easier money to stimulate the economy when it slowed down.

Containing administrative and military expenditures was only one side of the picture. Over the years, the government was able to boost its receipts by more effectively collecting the sums due. Since wages and profits were steadily growing, the increase in state revenue was substantial even without raising taxation to prohibitive levels. Corporate income tax, for example, only reached 25%. The money was then pumped back into economic development and various infrastructural projects as well as state enterprises. As costs of other items were held down, these headings eventually accounted for about 30% of the total outlay.

But the biggest portion of the money needed to promote the economy evidently came from the people. Part of this was a compulsory transfer from agriculture to industry. As the primary sector was initially predominant, some of the surplus had to be extracted from the farmers. This was done in various ways, the most direct being a land tax. Since rice had to be sold to the state, by fixing the purchase price considerably lower than the market price additional amounts could be derived. Finally, fertilizers and other inputs bought from the state or cooperatives were sold well above cost, providing another gain. These practices were most pronounced and prevalent during the 1950s and were gradually phased out in the 1970s, by which time the industrial sector had come into its own.

A very large share of the essential investment, and no one could really calculate how much, came from the businessmen themselves. At first, the banks could not supply very much funds and conditions for loans were extremely strict. Thus, budding entrepreneurs had to use their own money or what could be borrowed from family, friends or local moneylenders to launch their ventures on the skimpiest basis possible. Then, slowly and fitfully, as earnings came in, some of the profits could be directed toward reinvestment and expansion. Since this was their own money, or that of close associates, it was carefully used and frequently multiplied. Only much later, and only for the more successful ventures, was bank credit available.

The government tried to make up for these lacks by strengthening the banking system. It owned or controlled a number of specialized banks, medium business banks and even commercial banks. There was also an Export-Import Bank. Other institutions were cooperative banks and credit societies and the postal savings system. While their assets grew and more and bigger loans could be made, under guidance from the Bank of China most were equally conservative in their approach and demanded stiff security for loans. Only the foreign banks, which were increasingly eager to have a presence, were willing to lend money based on future prospects. They, however, were not always able to evaluate possible risks and eventually realized why solid collateral was a necessity.

Of course, the banks could not offer much funds as long as the population hesitated to entrust its money to them. This was the case during the first postwar decade when inflation regularly exceeded interest rates and saving was less purposeful than buying concrete assets or foreign currency. This penchant was finally broken by raising interest rates to higher levels while bringing inflation down. Then the normally thrifty Chinese rediscovered the virtues of saving and Taiwan's saving rate rose beyond 30% of GNP. With more abundant funds, the banks could lend more and, with less inflation, they could do so at more affordable rates for borrowers.

What is most amazing is the extent to which the Republic of China managed to do without external financing. This could be traced to the sad lessons learned many decades before when its predecessors became over-indebted to foreign powers. The only exception was the massive American aid, over US $4.1 billion from 1949 to 1967.[5] This was essential to save the country from bankruptcy and get the economy moving again, but it could not really be credited with the subsequent economic resurgence. Most of the money went into military expenditures or infrastructure as opposed to directly productive commercial or industrial investment, which came from local sources. Aside from that, borrowing was quite limited and the debt-service ratio remained under a remarkably low level of 5%. Thus, the bulk of the impressive gross capital formation which revolved around 30% of GNP was generated domestically.

Where foreign contributions made a notable difference was in direct investment. Leery of borrowing, the government was nonetheless willing to accept an even more intimate role in the economy by foreign companies which could provide capital and knowhow and also, by having a palpable stake, reinforce the island's position in the world economy. To attract investment, tax exemptions and deferrals, repatriation of capital and profits, and especially 100% ownership were offered. Investors were helped by an Industrial Development and Investment Center under the Ministry of Economic Affairs. This resulted in a massive influx of funds amounting to US $3,850 million from 1962–83, almost a third coming from Overseas Chinese and other large shares from the United States and Japan.

No matter how beneficial, most of the investment only came after Taiwan had proven that it was politically and economically viable. Any hint that it was not, such as derecognition by Washington or subtle pressure from Peking, worried and sometimes inhibited investors. Thus, the investment basically supplemented local efforts and was undertaken because of perceived commercial gains or due to the good and cheap labor force rather than special incentives. This meant investors were seeking a concrete return, one they frequently obtained to judge by the amount of reinvestment. Where they contributed most to economic progress was by launching or refining key sectors like electronics, chemicals, machinery and automotive, where the bulk of the investment was made.[6]

To get the most out of investment, Taiwan undertook a number of interesting experiments. One was to establish "export processing zones" as of 1966 in Kaohsiung (KEPZ), Nantze (NEPZ) and Taichung (TEPZ). The advantage to investors was to find specially-designed and largely self-contained industrial estates with factories and utilities installed, local labor readily available, and easy access to ports and airports. Exemption from import duties was a further counterpart for the government's main aim, namely export of all production. With was many as 80,000 workers and US $2 billion and more of exports annually, these zones were a great boon. The only thing they did not do adequately was to upgrade skills, since most of the output was of simple, labor-intensive products. So, in 1980, a novel version was unveiled at Hsinchu Science-based Industrial Park which attracted high tech industries due to the availability of trained technicians and engineers and proximity of technical schools and institutes like the Electronics Research & Service Organization (ERSO).

With its most trying problems under control, the government was finally able to concentrate more on economic development and overcome some of the constraints and bottlenecks that were beyond the scope of individual actors. This applied particularly to agriculture where Japan's earlier success left a very mixed legacy. The physical infrastructure had to be restored and amplified and the extension service and credit institutions of the colonial period refurbished, a relatively straightforward if arduous task. Far more important was to change the whole basis of the sector which was no longer competitive internationally for rice or sugar and had to produce more food to feed a vastly augmented population. This meant a shift to crops like sweet potatoes, corn, fruit and vegetables as well as more fishing.[7]

The other pressing task, almost a prerequisite to everything else, was to improve the situation of land ownership. Over the years, too much land had accumulated in too few hands, often those of Japanese settlers or Chinese collaborators. This reduced many farmers to the status of tenants who had to pay rents which averaged 50% and ran as high as 70%. Land reform had been promised by the Kuomintang and, since

Keeping rice production productive

Credit: GOI

it had to win popular support, the move could not be avoided even if it encountered some resistance. Eventually, it went through in stages. In 1949, rents were reduced to a uniform 37.5%. Then much of the land that had been confiscatcd from the Japanese was sold to tenants. Finally, through the Land-to-the-Tiller Act of 1953, holdings over three hectares were acquired from large landowners and sold to tenants and others at moderate prices and payable over extended periods. The landlords received commodity bonds and stock in government enterprises in return, generally regarded as inadequate but not unacceptable compensation.[8]

It is extremely difficult to attach an exact value to the land reform since many of the effects were more moral than material. Admittedly, smaller farms were less rational and productive. Yet, once cultivating their own field, farmers would be more strongly motivated to use it well and upgrade it.[9] This was essential for the success of the other government programs to promote agriculture through more irrigation, greater use of fertilizer and pesticides, introduction of improved varieties and new crops, and application of modern farming techniques. This was part of a policy of "developing agriculture by virtue of industry and fostering industry by virtue of agriculture." For, as must be evident, much of the growth in output came not from harder work but more industrial inputs like chemical fertilizers and greater use of agricultural implements like tillers and tractors which were increasingly manufactured domestically.

Despite relatively modest government funding, and actually an outward transfer of resources to industry, it was possible to revitalize the primary sector. As production grew, a result of larger yields rather than more land, it could meet the local demands for food and still export considerable amounts. Output more than doubled from 1952 to 1982, which was impressive, and exports increased much more rapidly despite the anticipated decline of sugar and rice shipments. The sharpest rise was for processed and canned foods. While farming was still thriving, its share of net domestic product continued shrinking, from 36% in 1952 to about 9% in 1982.

It had always been assumed that industrialization would be a much tougher assignment and there were doubts as to how much could be accomplished with a poor population and shaky foundation. Little industry had existed during the colonial period and much of that, oriented toward processing of sugar and rice, was useless. Still, during the 1950s, humble entrepreneurs established small shops and factories to make a number of simple products like shoes, bicycles, rubber and leather articles, and electrical apparatus. Agriculture encouraged fertilizer and farm implements and construction stimulated building materials. Cotton textiles were woven and turned into ordinary garments. And this gradually developed into larger operations which included synthetics as well. By the 1960s, however, the possibilities of easy import substitution had already been pretty well exhausted.[10]

In these endeavors, the government provided little initiative or financing, most of this coming from the private sector. Its help consisted mainly of protecting the precarious, and often inefficient and costly producers from foreign competition. This was done by imposing tariffs on competing products, and luxuries in general, so that local products could be more readily sold. If tariffs were not enough, it added quotas and sometimes just prohibited specific imports. But it was relatively easy to import any necessary equipment and raw materials, this partly through loans and partly due to an overvalued NT dollar. Alas, once most obvious substitutes were being produced domestically, there was not much room for expansion and the economy stagnated.

This led the government, advised by American experts, to suggest a switch to export production or at least an end to measures that discouraged or discriminated against exports. The primary goal was not even to boost exports so much as to stop the constant bulging of imports which resulted in incessant trade deficits. Whatever its rationale, such a change in policy alarmed most businessmen, bureaucrats and economists. They could not imagine Taiwan's rudimentary manufactured articles as ever being competitive on world markets. And they had never seen a successful example of a developing country selling enough such goods to balance trade. Still, they had to admit that, without more exports, importing would have to stop soon and it was grudgingly agreed to try the new strategy.[11]

Export promotion became the official policy as of the early 1960s as indicated by the new slogan of "developing agriculture by virtue of industry and fostering industry by virtue of foreign trade." To ease the transition, it was decided to grant special incentives to exporters including low-interest loans, rebates on customs duties, and remission of various taxes. The exchange rate was also lowered.[12] While it was the government which initiated the move, imaginative entrepreneurs soon saw the advantages and turned out suitable articles for sale abroad. In fact, the shift into export activities was so dynamic that there were often excessive production and competition and cartels had to be formed to avoid disrupting foreign markets.

While it might be assumed that a new phase implied new products, this was not the case. The top exports throughout were just an extension of earlier import substitutes. This is obvious for textiles and garments, which maintained the number one position. It was even more so for footwear, number three, of which Taiwan was soon the world's principal supplier. It was also a major producer of toys, bicycles, sewing machines and digital watches. Only electrical apparatus showed a striking transformation as electronics were added and gave it a momentum that would eventually make the sector the second biggest export earner. Thus, exporting turned supposedly hopeless "sunset industries" into renewedly hopeful "sunrise industries" despite all the fears of businessmen and quibbling of economic theoreticians.

Thanks to this effort, Taiwan's exports expanded at a stupendous rate of some 27% a year during the 1960s and 1970s, only slowing down with the recession of the early 1980s. Most of these exports were manufactured goods which made exporting the primary engine of industrial growth and further upgrading of industry the key to continued export prowess.[13] By 1983, exports had risen to a fantastic US $25 billion, far exceeding the US $20 billion worth of imports. In fact, much to everyone's surprise, the balance of trade turned in Taiwan's favor as early as 1971 and stayed that way during most of the ensuing period, allowing the country to accumulate substantial reserves that could cushion any unexpected setbacks. The only serious concerns were a continuing overdependence on exports to the United States and a gaping deficit with Japan.

Although the economy was progressing smoothly, there were limits to this policy as well. Or so the government thought. Too much reliance was being placed on a narrow range of articles and most of these were a bit old-fashioned. To move ahead, it was necessary to launch a number of daring projects which the existing entrepreneurs with their limited capital and technological ability could scarcely handle. These projects, however, were highly desirable because they broadened and strengthened the industrial base. They stood a particularly good chance of succeeding since they often supplied essential materials for downstream manufacturers and did so by choking off imports. That is why this has been called the "second" import substitution stage which, unlike the first, was mounted basically by the public sector during the 1970s.

The three crucial operations for steel, shipbuilding and petrochemicals were part of the "ten major projects." Each one was, indeed, monumental with regard to cost and scale. Already in its first phase, with a capacity of 3 million metric tons, China Steel could meet most local needs and it kept expanding with the economy and then beyond it to take up exporting, with an ultimate goal of an 8 million ton capacity. China Shipbuilding possessed the world's second largest drydock and could turn out nearly any kind of ship. Chinese Petroleum, along with the second refinery, had crackers and other facilities for dozens of derivatives. Other installations of a somewhat lesser scale, but also run by state corporations, were an aluminum refinery and a copper smelter.

While the original plans made perfectly good sense, and should have worked without a hitch, serious difficulties cropped up in most of these industries. Some of the trouble was due to lax management by bureaucrats, although China Steel under Chao Yao-tung was very tightly and efficiently run. More fateful was the vast increase in oil prices which affected just about every project by hiking energy or raw material costs. This was most harmful for aluminum and copper, which could not be produced competitively, and it hurt some of the petrochemicals which became more expensive than imports. China Shipbuilding was caught by the general slump in new ship orders. Only China Steel made profits and expanded. When Chao became Minister of Economic Affairs in 1981, he put an end to this phase by closing down some ventures and reducing others. At the same time, he actually initiated one of Taiwan's most ambitious attempts at targeting, this time in the automotive sector.

Automobiles and trucks were already being produced by a number of companies through tie-ups with foreign makers. Most prominent were Ford-Lio Ho, largely owned by Ford, Yue-Loong, which cooperated with Nissan, and San Yang, connected with Honda. None of them, alas, possessed sufficient scale. While it might have been safer to expand (or merge) the existing operations, Chao thought it was more effective to launch major new ones. For heavy trucks, it was agreed to have local makers cooperate with Japan's Hino. For automobiles, the solution was a joint venture between China Steel, several other local firms, and Toyota. This would result in a huge plant producing some 300,000 units a year, half of them intended for export, when completed in 1990. The main plant was expected to cost US $550 million and, with improvements in the network of parts vendors, the overall investment would exceed US $1,000 million. But this was not to be. After Toyota refused to guarantee enough exports, and ministers changed, the project collapsed and was replaced by a more modest and pragmatic, if also dispersed, approach.[14]

Thus, the three decades or so since 1950 witnessed a far-reaching industrial revolution. Industry as a whole was magnified some fifty times over. The growth rate reached 20% a year in the peak period from 1963–72 and remained above 10% before and after. This obviously brought about a major shift in the relative shares of sec-

From subcontractor to top supplier of sewing machines

Credit: Janome

tors as the primary dwindled and the tertiary held its own while the secondary managed to attain over 40% of gross national product and just under 40% of the labor force. An interesting sidelight on the inner workings of the economy is that the public sector, which accounted for over 50% of all industrial production (especially mining and utilities) before the takeoff slipped to a minor position by the 1980s when the private sector boasted over 80% of the total thanks to its role in manufacturing.

Even if the progress was not quite as striking, there was a gradual renovation of the service sector. One reason for this slower advance was that most activities were reserved solely to domestic enterprises that were sometimes stymied by regulations and red tape. The latter was the case for commercial banking. Although more foreign banks were allowed in, their operations were restricted, and local banks remained somewhat parochial because they were not really exposed to competition. The same applied to insurance and shipping, both of which showed moderate growth. Tourism and hotels did reasonably well, especially as long as Taiwan offered the only glimpse of the "real China." But it was subsequently hurt by political events and the fact that some of the tourist trade attracted the wrong people for the wrong reasons, no matter how lucrative.

With exporting such a crucial factor, it was felt that local traders should organize to handle this more efficiently. The need was especially great since Japanese *sogo shosha* seemed to be getting a big chunk of the business. The primary weakness was the excessive fragmentation of local efforts split among some 10,000 trading companies, 36,000 exporters and 27,000 manufacturers. The Board of Foreign Trade therefore attempted to rationalize the sector by offering incentives to "large trading companies" and hoping the smallest ones would eventually drop out. Yet, while some larger units emerged, they did not do particularly well. It was extremely difficult to convince local manufacturers to entrust them with sales or procurement of essential inputs and the competition from smaller firms remained tenacious. Worse, as soon as trading companies expanded too much, there was a tendency for some of the staff to break away and open their own offices. Surprisingly enough, this did not keep exports from attaining as much as 50% of GNP, vastly superior to Japan's trade performance.

Despite the priority on boosting production and exports, there was an abiding interest in social welfare. This arose from the third of Dr. Sun Yat-sen's Three Principles of the People or *Min Sheng* which could be construed as "people's livelihood" as well as the wish to make the Republic of China a showcase for the Kuomintang. There was thus considerable investment in basic infrastructure like roads, railways and urban transport and amenities like electricity, water supply and sewerage. Hospitals and clinics were opened throughout the island. The biggest push arose for education and the system was soon one of the best in Asia. Alas, some of the most highly educated never returned from advanced study abroad and it was only recently that the brain drain could be reversed.

Meanwhile, the inhabitants splurged on what they regarded as symbols of the good life, such as electric fans and rice cookers, radios and televisions, and more automobiles than the roads could carry. New housing went up and the quality improved somewhat. Despite the hang for modernism, the Chinese family held together rather well and broader social circles flourished. This was partially due to deep-rooted traditions but also the fact that so much of the economy consisted of small family concerns. It was just as well since unemployment insurance, retirement benefits and old age pensions were still insufficient and had to be supplemented by savings and family solidarity.

Such betterment was only possible because of the dramatic upswing of the economy. The growth rate was phenomenal by international standards: 8.3% during the 1950s, 9.1% during the 1960s and 10% during the 1970s. It was even more "miraculous" given the heavy defense burden. During this period, gross national product augmented about ten-fold. Per capita income naturally lagged somewhat but still showed a five-fold increase to reach US $3,000 by 1983. This wealth, by the way, was quite equally shared to judge by certain surveys.[15] This generated a cozy degree of affluence which pleased the people and enabled the regime to gleefully point to the situation on the mainland where the average person only earned US $335.

It is not easy to predict the future of Taiwan, nor has it ever been. Until the 1950s, it was generally assumed that the economy would collapse or—at best—just muddle through. In the 1960s, when it turned to exports, this was regarded as a futile attempt to keep things moving. Then, by the 1970s, when the prospects had never been more encouraging, it was struck by the oil crisis and, yet more ominously, the American decision to recognize Peking.[16] This led to a derecognition of Taipei by numerous countries which, it was feared, would undermine the economy as well. But other methods were found for dealing with old trading partners and there was little economic damage. The Republic of China continued walking a political tightrope while performing its economic juggling act, not an easy position for anyone. But it has managed not to fall and should be able to keep its balance for a long time to come.

NOTES

1. See Samuel P. S. Ho, *Economic Development in Taiwan,* pp. 25–40 and 91–102.
2. See Ho, *op. cit.,* p. 117.
3. See Robert H. Silin, *Leadership and Values,* for case studies of entrepreneurs and how they operate.
4. See Ho, *Small Scale Enterprises in Korea and Taiwan.*
5. See Neil H. Jacoby, *U. S. Aid To Taiwan.*
6. See Denis Fred Simon, *Taiwan, Technology Transfer and Transnationalism.*
7. See Ho, *Economic Development in Taiwan,* pp. 41–69 and 147–85.
8. See Cheng Chen, *Land Reform in Taiwan.*
9. See Martin M. C. Yang, *Socio-Economic Results of Land Reform in Taiwan.*
10. See C. Y. Lin, *Industrialization in Taiwan.*
11. See Shirley W. Y. Kuo, *The Taiwan Economy in Transition,* pp. 207–310.
12. See Kuo-Shu Liang and Ching-ing Hou Liang, "Trade Strategy and Exchange Rate Policies in Taiwan," in Wontack Hong and Lawrence B. Krause (eds.), *Trade and Growth of the Advanced Developing Countries in the Pacific Basin,* pp. 150–86.
13. See Kuo, *op. cit.,* pp. 135–74.
14. What was to be the greatest of all targeting operations was also in many ways the riskiest and most controversial. Its collapse was not necessarily an economic setback.
15. See Joel Bergsman, *Growth and Equity in Semi-Industrialized Countries,* and John C. H. Fei et al, *Growth with Equity: The Taiwan Case.*
16. For the multiple effects of the oil crisis, see Kuo, *op. cit.,* 181–222.

3
Korea, Man-Made Miracle

While hardly enviable, the starting points of Japan and Taiwan were considerably more auspicious than Korea's. Although its feudal society attained a high cultural level, it never advanced as far economically. This was partly due to the constraints of strong Confucian traditions that placed the peasants and merchants on the lower rungs of a hierarchy dominated by aristocrats (*yangban*) and scholars with scant concern for practical matters. But progress was also blocked, and the economy periodically disrupted, by incessant fighting between rival kingdoms sharing the peninsula and devastating invasions from Manchuria and Japan. It was not until the seventeenth century that a centralized and relatively independent state could arise and modest advances were made in agriculture and commerce. Alas, to maintain stability the country was turned into a "hermit kingdom" which rejected intercourse with the outside world.

When the Western powers demanded that Korea be opened, the resistance was stubborn and lasted much longer. But it proved futile as foreign countries imposed their influence and vied for domination. China, which maintained its traditional claims, was itself being partitioned and quickly lost any tenuous control. The real struggle arose between Japan and Czarist Russia, with the British, French and Americans trying to salvage what they could for themselves or vainly calling for an "open door." However, as Japan vanquished its rivals in the Sino-Japanese and Russo-Japanese Wars, it became the principal contender and established its domination. Korea was turned into a protectorate in 1905 and, five years later, was annexed and absorbed into the Japanese empire.

As in Taiwan, this brought a new era of economic development. While the administration (and police) were reinforced, the indigenous population was directed toward productive activities. Agriculture was renovated to grow more rice as well as cotton and silk. Petty commerce proliferated while Japanese *zaibatsu* organized larger operations. Of primary interest were gold and mineral ores, some of which were processed locally once electricity could be generated. There was even a bit of heavy and chemical industry later on, part of it for military production, while small local firms produced textiles, foodstuffs, and other articles. To expedite change, roads, railways and ports were built and children were given a basic education, albeit one designed to implant Japanese culture. Korea was turning into a booming and valuable colony. But it was doing so for the good of Japan which squeezed it for rice and put its industry at the service of the home economy and then more specifically the war effort.

During the Pacific War, there was an inevitable propensity to neglect the economy and let it run down as mines and factories were pushed frantically to produce. The same applied to much of the infrastructure which gradually decayed. By the time the Japanese withdrew, in 1945, part of the productive machinery and infrastructure was in very bad shape and could hardly be used. While these facilities were physically confiscated by the new government, some could not be restored and went to waste. In other cases, they could not be run effectively because most of the key posts in commerce and industry had been reserved for Japanese employees or immigrants and Koreans lacked the requisite skills. There were not even enough educated officials to administer the new state. Worse, much of the agriculture, mining and manufacturing relied on raw materials or equipment from Japan, which was also the sole market, and these links were completely severed.[1]

The already unfortunate situation was aggravated by the division of the peninsula into American and Soviet zones. This brutally rent the existing economy asunder. Much of the rice was grown in the south while most of the mining, heavy industry and power generation were located in the north. As the border solidified, what became the Republic of Korea (or South Korea) was cut off from badly needed raw materials and electricity as well as a market for its agricultural produce. With only light industries on its side, it also had a rather lopsided structure which was strained by the need to absorb the larger share of the population. The breach was compounded by the human suffering of countless divided families in a divided nation dominated by differing and antagonistic regimes.

Slowly and painfully, the Republic of Korea did revive and reshape an economy which could cope with some of its many problems. But the political situation within remained chaotic and pressure from the Communist regime in the North continued. Then, in June 1950, the Democratic People's Republic of Korea attacked without warning. The capital of Seoul was quickly overrun and its army moved southward, pushing as far as Pusan. If not for American troops under General MacArthur, backed by United Nations forces, the South would have fallen and been absorbed. Instead, the North Korean

troops were gradually driven back as bitter fighting ranged over most of the peninsula and reached as far north as
the Chinese frontier. The war dragged on as troops from
Communist China joined the fray. In the end, the front
stabilized near the 38th parallel. But the war only ended
with an armistice and not peace as the two sides faced
each other over the demilitarized zone and prepared for
the next round.

South Korea, which now had to construct a viable
economy alone, possessed a very modest natural endowment. It had a rather small area of 99,000 square
kilometers with a large population of 20 million after the
war and about 40 million today. This made it one of the
most densely populated countries in the world. The land
consisted of many mountains and few plains and those
with only moderately fertile soil, irregular supplies of
water, and an indifferent climate. There were hardly any
mineral resources aside from some coal, iron and
tungsten. Even its geographical location did not help
much. It is not a vital link between East and West but
rather the point where the "free world" ends at a barrier
more impenetrable than ever existed in feudal times.
Whatever assets it had gained during Japanese rule had
now been pretty well dissipated and in most modern sectors it was almost starting from scratch.

There was a limit to how much could be accomplished
by the early governments under Syngman Rhee. It was all
he could do to hold the country together, torn as it was
by conflicts between more liberal or conservative politicians often moved by class interests and wracked by Com-
munist-inspired propaganda and subversion. Even after
the Korean War consolidated his position, Rhee concentrated heavily on political issues in an effort to weaken
his opponents and establish a system in keeping with his
views. Although it was now somewhat illusory, his

primary goal remained reunification and he even talked of a "march north" to enforce this. Meanwhile, he failed to take essential, and perfectly feasible, actions to improve the economic situation in the truncated south. This was unwise since economic stagnation only exacerbated the political divisions and his attempts to stay in power met with growing resistance. Ultimately, Rhee was forced to step down by student-led demonstrations. While the new government of Chang Myon recognized the need for economic progress, it was too weak to take the lead and was sorely undermined by the continuing political agitation.

On May 16, 1961, General Park Chung Hee seized power in a bloodless coup. There was no doubt that this time a resolute leader was in charge and disposed of the necessary might to impose his will. But no one really knew what Park intended to do or expected very much of his rule. They were somewhat surprised when, rather than military or political goals, he made economic advancement the top priority.[2] This is assuredly what was most wanted by the population, although they doubted a military man could do much about it. Still, as long as the president followed this path, showing that the country could pull itself up by the bootstraps, he won active support or at least passive acquiescence from the people. He could thus be reelected several times, albeit in increasingly dubious circumstances. And his rule was only ended by an assassin's bullet in October 1979. But the army's influence was not over. After a brief interim in which democracy might have been restored, General Chun Doo Hwan came to power with a pledge of resuming the economic program and bringing about a "second takeoff."

While Park doubtlessly overstayed his welcome, there is no question that he was more directly responsible for his country's resurgence than any one man in most other places. Before the military takeover, there had been only feeble and sporadic attempts at restoring the economy. Many of them were foisted on Syngman Rhee by his American advisors since it was only U. S. aid that kept the country going and this could not be continued forever. Yet, while some useful measures were adopted, not much came of these efforts. This made the sudden activation even more striking. Hardly had the new regime consolidated its position than an Economic Planning Board was established, plans were drawn up and implemented, and the state played a leading role in promoting growth. While it had to do so given the initial weakness of the private sector, there was an even greater urgency since American assistance would soon be terminated.

The center of much of this activity remained the Blue House, the president's residence. Park assumed broad control over everything relating to economic development which could not help but reflect his views. But these views still had to be focused and formulated. That was entrusted in a special staff of advisors who counselled the president and generated many more of the specific policies as time went by. Some of the initiatives, however, came straight from the president and were pushed through whether or not they received much support. They included the first highways and an integrated steel mill. Park took a keen personal interest in many projects, visiting the work sites himself to see how things were progressing and urging his subordinates on to greater exertions. The same practices were resumed by President Chun, but with some differences. As a newcomer, he paid more heed to his advisors and left more of the decisionmaking to the appropriate bodies. He also admitted the need to relax the system and introduce economic, social and political reforms.

No matter how centralized or authoritarian a state, effective formulation and implementation of economic policy require the cooperation of the whole governmental bureaucracy.[3] To ensure this, various mechanisms were adopted. None was more significant than the creation of the Economic Planning Board whose minister was also the deputy prime minister and more directly accountable to the president. The EPB enjoyed very broad powers since it was entrusted with development planning, budgeting (usually the prerogative of the Ministry of Finance), statistics, price policy, fair trade administration and, until recently, foreign cooperation and investment promotion. To handle ongoing economic management, it regularly convened meetings of ministers or vice-ministers from the spheres most directly involved in economic matters, including the Ministries of Trade and Industry, Finance, Transportation, Communications, Agriculture and Fisheries, Energy and Resources, and Science and Technology. For longer-term and more fundamental issues, its primary task was planning. This gave the EPB a much higher status and wider scope than the other ministries and made it a super-ministry of sorts. In the hands of men like Chang Key-young or Nam Duck-woo, it has consistently proven to be a more powerful and effective organization than its counterparts in Japan or elsewhere in the capitalist world.

The five-year plans issued regularly by the Economic Planning Board, starting in 1962, were increasingly competent and professional. They included general policies and goals as well as more specific sectoral programs. Forecasts were made for the major parameters and, on the whole, they were reasonably accurate. To make the medium-term plans more precise and concrete, they were converted into annual plans, first in the form of an overall resource budget and later an economic management plan. This created a "rolling plan" which was more amenable to revisions and rectifications imposed by changing circumstances. But what gave them a solid reality, and kept them from degenerating into mere visions, was that they were always backed up by allocations in the budget and support from the relevant ministries. The chances of implementation were greatly enhanced by the fact that bureaucratic careers could be advanced or retarded by ability or inability to perform. This clearly made Korea a "hard" state in which orders tended to be carried out.

In a liberal economy, the government is expected to provide the essential infrastructure and certain basic services. In developing countries, it has since become common to add more commercial or financial tasks. Korea, not surprisingly, undertook all this and more.[4] To accomplish these functions, the government established over twenty special corporations, many of which were not unusual for a capitalist nation.[5] There were housing and highway agencies, a telecommunications authority, tourism and trade promotion bodies, and several banks. Power generation, for both conventional and nuclear plants, came under the Korea Electric Power Corporation (KEPCO). But it went somewhat further by engaging in coal and tungsten mining, fertilizer production and oil refining. And it went much further by launching shipbuilding, automobile assembly and steelmaking ventures.

Such encroachments on the private sector could be explained by a lack of capital or managerial ability among existing businessmen, especially in earlier years. This forced the government to go ahead on its own if it were

Exploiting Korea's edge in electronics

Credit: KOTRA

not to sacrifice what looked like worthwhile projects. Alas, although some of these operations were well run, it was hard to avoid a bureaucratization that stifled initiative and masked profitability. Some cases became so acute that the corporations had to be wound down or sold off while others were subsidized. Thus, in later years, planners definitely preferred leaving productive ventures to private entrepreneurs and there was mounting interest in privatization of existing state enterprises. With this, the trend which had led to a rather large public sector was reversed.

Getting the bureaucracy moving, despite any inertia or caution, was much simpler than bringing the private sector into line. This was not just a small group of paid employees who were doing their job and following orders but millions of individuals in countless callings who were eager to earn a proper living or risking their own money on projects they had faith in. They did not necessarily appreciate government pressure, much less interference, although there were many ways of influencing their action. One of the gentlest was simply to inform them in which direction the government felt the economy should be heading. That was a primary purpose of planning which, for all its rigor in the public sector, was purely indicative for private entrepreneurs. The plans and programs listed sectors which were expected to rise, some of which were singled out as "strategic," and by deduction also a feeling for which ones could be expected to decline. Compliant or ambitious businessmen would obviously prefer the former to the latter.

However, sectors were not merely targeted, special incentives were granted to those who entered them. This could take the form of tax exemptions, customs rebates, access to foreign exchange, and other forms of promotion as well as protection of the industry until it became competitive. In addition, it was always easier to obtain credit for projects in targeted sectors, usually at exceptionally low interest rates. This was provided not only by state banks such as the Korea Development Bank or Korea Exchange Bank but also the commercial banks which remained largely under government control. If there was still hesitation, the bureaucracy involved would try to convince leading companies to comply, emphasizing the advantages of any new policy, offering assistance and also stressing the disadvantages of not participating. In cases where the national interest was at stake, such "administrative guidance" might even come from the Blue House. There was also relentless pressure to attain production or export targets, which may explain why they were so often reached or exceeded. This resulted in a "Korea, Inc." that was similar to the Japanese phenomenon except that it was even better coordinated and the business community was clearly the junior partner.

The predominant role of the government is more comprehensible when one considers that there was not much of a private sector to begin with. Since the Japanese had dominated commerce and industry and used their own people in most administrative and technical posts, few Koreans developed a familiarity with modern ventures. While there were some local entrepreneurs and others fled south, the total number was not very large. In the course of time, and with the challenge of two periods of reconstruction, businessmen did arise in building, foodstuffs and light industry. But those who fared best during the 1950s engaged in less reputable pursuits. It was possible to buy former Japanese enterprises cheaply from the government, or obtain a protected position for production of import substitutes, or corner the market for goods in short supply. The black market flourished and racketeering prospered. Naturally, success here depended less on business acumen than government (or police) connections, with favors returned in cash.

This led to a general impression of business as shady and disreputable and businessmen who grew rich were automatically assumed to be corrupt. In fact, just after the military coup, the most visible ones were arrested and their fortunes confiscated. There was even talk of executing some. Instead, it was decided to rehabilitate and use them until a new generation of less tainted entrepreneurs could be fostered. No one knew just how to go about creating businessmen and, for its own corporations, the government usually installed former generals. Yet once the opportunities for legitimate undertakings existed, there was no shortage of people who tried to seize them. While some only launched rather modest ventures, and others eventually failed, there were enough to engender a growing and virile business community.[6]

In the fullness of time, this might have resulted in a sufficiently large pool of talent to transform the whole economy. But the government was in too much of a hurry to wait. In addition, some of the projects were just too complex or costly to be tackled by private businessmen alone. Thus, it tried to fill the gap by supporting carefully selected entrepreneurs who had risen on their own and showed particular promise. They were enabled, and sometimes almost obliged, to start up more and more operations, especially in the "strategic" sectors. There they received generous assistance. This policy of backing winners led to the emergence of some extremely large groups, not only by Korean but even by international standards. Known as *chaebol,* they were not very different from Japan's *zaibatsu* in that they were loose conglomerates with supreme authority vested in the group's founder. Ultimately, there were some thirty or more *chaebol* of various sizes and compositions, the most prominent being Chung Ju-yung's Hyundai, Lee Byung-chul's Samsung and Kim Woo-choong's Daewoo.

This resulted in a rather premature polarization of the corporate structure into a select circle of very large groups and a multitude of smaller firms. The bulk of the latter were in services and distribution. In manufacturing, they were active in sectors where scale did not matter as much, such as toys, sporting goods, footwear or garments. Others were producing the countless parts and components needed to make finished products like electronics, automobiles or ships. While some manged to maintain their independence, more and more were drawn into the supplier networks of leading *chaebol*-related assemblers as mere subcontractors. When this was not

possible, the assemblers would set up their own subsidiaries to produce the necessary parts.

While the smaller units remained paternalistic in their
management, not very different from updated family
firms, the larger ones began experimenting. It was obvious that they had to introduce more efficient methods
or the economies of scale would be wasted. This was not
so easy with quite heterogeneous companies in many
groups, especially since the owners did not really want
them to become too autonomous and liked to shift funds
and personnel from one to another as the need arose.
Some presidents, with a more authoritarian bent, tried to
introduce Japanese techniques with recruitment straight
from school and lifetime employment. Others preferred
the more impersonal and "scientific" methods of
American management. But most were a mixture of old-
style Korean and modern Japanese and American types.[7]

It was not much simpler to form a capable, modern
labor force since, when Korea gained its independence,
the population was still predominantly rural and
agricultural. Even those who lived in towns or cities had
little previous contact with industrial activities since these
had been reserved for the Japanese. The educational level
at that time was not very high and there was considerable
illiteracy. What was saddest, however, was that the new
classes of educated youth being turned out by the hastily
expanded schools were not of much more use. They were
not taught the right things due to curricula that were overly academic and insufficiently technical. Until the system
could be reformed, most graduates would not have the
necessary skills or attitudes. This, as much as an actual
shortage of jobs, explained why unemployment ran as
high as 15–20% into the 1960s.[8]

Nevertheless, the burgeoning industrial sector absorbed

more and more employees and, if they lacked the appropriate skills, they were trained on-the-job. Most farm children ended up in factories while those from the cities, especially graduates of better schools, got white-collar jobs. In some ways, the most significant category was the bevies of girls who worked a few years before marriage and proved ideal for delicate assembly operations. On the whole, the Koreans worked longer and harder than their counterparts in the region. They were admittedly less docile and disciplined than the Japanese, but more dedicated to the company than the Chinese. Yet, the biggest virtue—in the eyes of most businessmen—was that their wages were still much lower. This gave Korea a precious advantage on highly competitive world markets . . . as long as the labor force was well used.

Back in the 1950s, given the chaotic situation and a growing mood of despondency, the Korean people were in no position to raise the capital needed to restore the economy. Not only was there little saving, and this of a very palpable kind, there was a degree of dissaving. Wages were spent as fast as they were earned and assets were sold off to buy food or clothing. The worst culprit was the government which consistently ran a budget deficit and printed money to pay its debts, fueling a raging inflation. It was widely felt that the only thing which saved the economy from collapse was American aid, military and civilian. The latter, consisting largely of foodstuffs, ultimately totaled US$4 billion, a very appreciable amount. There was some question as to whether the country could survive when this was cut off. Syngman Rhee seemed to think not, and used every possible stratagem to get more aid. Park Chung Hee, realizing that could no longer work, and for reasons of national self-respect, wanted Korea to make the necessary efforts on its own.

The new regime therefore brought the budget into balance.[9] Painful as it was, expenditures were reduced and revenue was boosted through higher tax rates and stricter collection. This permitted a considerable expansion of the budget over the years and also a notable increase in state spending on the economy. Economic development accounted for 20–25% of the total and social development (including education) a similar amount. This was an impressive showing given the need to maintain a strong military establishment which absorbed 30% and more of the budget and 5–6% of GNP. By balancing the budget, and controlling monetary expansion, it was possible to bring inflation down to tolerable levels during the 1960s although it flared up again during the frantic growth of the 1970s.[10]

Now that the government had mended its ways, it appealed to the population to save more. These exhortations were of little avail as long as the advantages were slim. However, as inflation subsided and then, in 1965, interest rates were raised substantially to guarantee a positive return, saving ballooned quite dramatically. Private saving rose from about 7% of GNP before the interest reform to as much as 19% by the late 1970s. (Together with public saving, the rate attained 25%.) But the level slipped a notch each time inflation reduced the benefits. Most of the money flowed into the commercial banks. But, even higher rates—and correspondingly higher risks—prevailed on the unorganized or "kerb" market which gathered amazingly hefty sums from the petty savings of some and the unrecorded earnings of others.

Like Taiwan, and unlike Japan, Korea turned outwards for financial support and investment.[11] But its priorities were different. Although accepting foreign investment from the onset of the Park era, it was initially very cautious and restricted projects to certain areas while reserving others for domestic entrepreneurs. Moreover, at first, investors were limited to minority shares and joint ventures were strongly encouraged. To direct investors toward export-oriented activities, two Free Trade Zones were opened in Masan and Uri. In this way, the government got some of the things it wanted, such as employment of more labor and induction of technologies in key sectors such as electronics, petrochemicals and machinery. Its more dynamic companies, which often set up the joint ventures, found useful partners. However, the total value of foreign investment which reached US$1,700 million by 1983 was less than hoped for and proportionately less than obtained by some other countries in the region.[12]

Foreign loans, on the other hand, were generally welcome once Korea ceased getting aid. It continued receiving concessional rates from friendly countries and the International Development Agency for some while and then graduated to the World Bank, becoming one of the most successful examples of its aid and advice. By the 1970s, government bodies and private companies (albeit with state guarantees) could even borrow from foreign commercial banks. The outcome was a tremendous amount of external debt which ran into a cumulative US $40 billion by 1983. This permitted levels of investment and capital formation that were much higher than could have been financed by domestic saving alone, which was to the good. But it also entailed high debt servicing which fortunately never rose above the danger point of 20% of GNP. Still, as the economy grew, the share of foreign saving became progressively smaller.

After the Pacific War, Korea was still a predominantly agricultural country with farming accounting for over half of employment and gross national product. It was therefore essential for the sector to remain viable and preferably grow to generate a surplus for other areas.[13] But little could be done without correcting the social inequities that had arisen before and during the period of colonization. Most of the land was owned by a relatively restricted group of big landlords (Japanese and Korean) and the majority of the tenants had to pay huge rents in crops and labor. While admitting the problem, the early independent government did not wish to tackle this because it relied on landlord support. Nevertheless, under persistent pressure from American advisors, a land reform was carried out in two stages. In 1947, the land confiscated from the Japanese was distributed. Then, in 1949–50, all holdings in excess of three hectares owned by Koreans was sold at low prices to the tenants.

This created a vast number of owner-farmers who were eager to take advantage of the opportunities offered by advanced methods, improved varieties, more fertilizer and better farming implements. They also received state aid for essential infrastructure, especially irrigation, extension work and credit. With this, rice yields could be raised sharply while new crops and livestock were introduced. But there was a limit to how much could be accomplished with such small farms. Farm income rose more slowly than industrial wages and there were much less amenities or cultural facilities in the rural districts. Not until the late 1960s, when the government found its political base in the countryside had weakened, was the process reversed. Efforts were made to improve farm earnings whether through higher rice prices or diversification to more remunerative crops. While this was effective in attaining parity, the drain on the budget led to later reductions in subsidies and hopes that the gap could be closed by more off-farm income or less farmers sharing whatever income there was.

Noteworthy improvement also resulted from a novel experiment that had a far greater impact than was ever expected. It started in 1971 with a grant of free cement to thousands of rural villages, initially to see what they would do with it. Some interesting self-help projects actually ensued and it was decided to continue the program. This was subsequently institutionalized as the Saemaul Undong or New Community Movement in which each village, then province, under its elected leaders would work out plans of how to use further government aid. Much of the necessary capital and materials thus came from the state, while the farmers and villagers contributed their free time, to build increasingly impressive projects including irrigation ditches, roads and bridges, communal facilities and better housing. The movement later spread to urban areas, where factory workers and civil servants were enrolled and asked to participate in self-development and community improvement. Although it never caught on as well in the cities, the Saemaul Undong retained a very strong influence in the countryside.[14]

Industrialization got off to a rather poor start in the 1950s. With a narrow domestic market, more imports than desirable, and a very unstable political and economic environment, it was hard for businessmen to operate. Those who did best often benefited from artificial scarcities or special favors. During the 1960s, however, as the country got down to work and greater stability encouraged more rational and productive investments, a fair number of light industries emerged. Many were related to daily needs, such as food processing, footwear and garments. There was also increased production of cement and plywood for housing and infrastructure. Chemical fertilizers were manufactured locally for farming. And the textile industry not unsurprisingly became a major sector.[15] Many of these activities were quite rudimentary, run by small and undercapitalized firms. Others grew more than could be imagined, with huge shirt factories managed by Daewoo, footwear facilities by Kukje, and foodstuffs from Samsung and Lotte. Ssangyong eventually built the world's largest cement plant.[16]

Despite this growth, the government feared that the possibilities were being steadily exhausted and adopted legislation to promote heavy and chemical industries toward the end of the decade. Among the first were oil refineries to meet the swelling demand for fuel. Oil was also used in adjacent complexes to produce a broad range of petrochemicals. Encouraging as the development appeared, the industry was later hurt by rising costs

Textile production goes mechanical

Credit: KOTRA

of crude and naphtha. The key project, however, was to be an integrated steel mill. Repeatedly turned down by Western bankers and aid donors as too big and complicated for Korea, it was finally erected in cooperation with the Japanese. By 1973, the first phase of the government-owned Pohang Iron & Steel Company (POSCO) was completed and three more were undertaken. Then it was decided to build a second mlll. With its termination in the late 1980s, Korea will be one of the world's top ten makers.

With indigenous suppliers of steel on the way, the planners targeted several sectors that were major consumers. The first was shipbuilding. The industry was originally quite backward, consisting mainly of small firms which produced rather simple boats, most of them wooden. Upgrading seemed less promising than helping ambitious companies to construct huge modern shipyards with special incentives, ready access to funds, and aid in sales. As of 1975, major projects were completed by Hyundai, Samsung and Daewoo, while the initially government-owned Korea Shipbuilding & Engineering expanded somewhat. This boosted capacity to 4,000,000 G/T, including facilities that could handle the largest and most sophisticated vessels. What proved harder than increasing capacity was filling it, given the sluggish market since the oil crisis and fierce competition worldwide. Yet, although coming from behind, Korea quickly overtook America and Europe to become the world's number two producer after Japan.

Another avid consumer of steel was the automotive industry. Automobile and truck production resulted mainly from private initiative after the government's initial effort failed. That company was eventually absorbed by a joint venture between Daewoo and General Motors. It was later challenged by an aggressive operation of Hyundai, which managed to take over much of the market. In addition, there were some smaller makers producing motorcycles and trucks. With little government support, these companies continued boosting capacity and modernizing facilities or constructing completely new factories. What the government did do was to keep out imports, thereby reserving the domestic market. But, only partly due to the oil crisis, this market never expanded as rapidly as hoped. And exporting was more difficult than expected. This left the industry in a tight position that was unlikely to improve much before the end of the 1980s.

The move into heavy machinery, machine tools, power generators, telecommunications equipment and several allied sectors was even more precipitate after they were designated "strategic" industries in the late 1970s. The government had already carried out several targeting exercises and, expecting generous support and protection, eager (often *chaebol*-related) companies rushed in too quickly. Since they had little experience in these sectors, they went into joint ventures or licensing agreements with foreign firms. Most of the funding was obtained from state or commercial banks. But the technologies turned out to be much more complex than anticipated. Worse, the domestic market was unable to absorb products at a high enough level to justify economies of scale. This time it was clear that some businessmen had bitten off more than they could chew and the government had to rescue one of the largest ventures which was turned into Korea Heavy Industries & Construction (KHIC).

The field in which progress was smoothest and most rational was electronics. Electronics actually covers a multitude of aspects and Korea's path was highly sensible. It started with labor-intensive operations. First, it made parts and components, eventually making

whole products aside from some special items. Finally, it
learned how to produce them. Since assembly was also
labor-intensive, it kept up with the stream of new articles
going from radios to televisions, to VTRs and even computers. The earlier efforts were restricted to household
appliances and consumer products which had broader
markets, and required less complicated technologies,
before tackling electrical machinery and industrial equipment. Parts were usually delivered to large domestic
assemblers or multinationals while exports of finished
products initially took the form of OEM, being sold
under the brand name of others. Only when they had fully matured did some Korean companies try marketing
their own goods under their own names. The leaders
were Lucky-Gold Star, Samsung and Taihan, joined
more recently by Daewoo and Hyundai.

Within the process of industrialization, it was not so
easy to determine where import substitution ended and
export promotion began. It was clear that the 1960s
brought a definite shift in priorities from simple import
substitution to strong promotion of exports, less for
reasons of industrial policy than to cover the continuous
and worrisome trade deficits. Tax, customs and other incentives as well as special financing were offered to boost
exports and, even more decisive, the exchange rate was
lowered.[17] Yet, during the 1970s, with strong emphasis
on basic industries, automobiles and machinery, a new
period of more sophisticated import substitution began.
By the 1980s, the situation was somewhat more balanced,
although there was no doubt that exports still enjoyed a
residual preference.

Looking at specific products, it was even harder to find
any cut-off point between import substitution and export
promotion. Producers of what were usually regarded as
pure import substitutes were eventually exporting

massive amounts of cement and plywood. For textiles, garments and footwear, some local producers nearly forgot the domestic market in their triumphant penetration of foreign markets. The first integrated steel mill was obviously built to meet local requirements and just exported when there was a surplus. The second will make steel much more export-oriented. However, the move could also be in the opposite direction. Most ships were exported but, when orders were slack, the government urged national shipping lines to "buy Korean." Electronics had always been oriented toward exports. Yet, when some articles encountered trade restrictions, the makers were delighted to find that demand had grown at home.

Of the Five, exports were probably most decisive in reshaping the Korean economy because this was a country with no prior tradition of trade and where the ratio of exports to GNP was a pitiful 4% in the early 1960s. Thanks to incentives, more favorable exchange rates and repeated exhortations (as well as some arm-twisting) from the government, the ratio rose to an impressive 40% by the early 1980s. This was only possible because exports kept increasing much more rapidly than overall production, attaining an average rate of 35% a year from 1962–82. The biggest portion of this naturally came from manufactured exports whose share of the total soared from under 20% to over 90% during the same period. The foremost market throughout was the United States, followed by Japan and Southeast Asia, with a major advance into the Middle East in the late 1970s. Despite this extraordinary growth, imports were also expanding from a higher base and the balance of trade remained somewhat negative due to unsated needs of raw materials (especially oil) and capital goods.

Thus, within little more than three decades, Korea

managed to put together an amazingly broad and diversified manufacturing sector. It consisted of ordinary light
industry products and more complex electronics, basic
materials and assembly branches. Heavy and chemical industry (which includes electronics) actually outpaced
light industry and accounted for over half of total output
by 1979. Industry as a whole quickly superseded
agriculture as the secondary sector's share rose from a
mere 9% after the Korean War to 15% in 1961, and
about 29% in the 1980s. It was the growth of manufacturing, at some 17% a year during the 1960s and 1970s,
which gave the crucial impetus to the economy. And it
was the increase of manufactured exports, at well over
twice that rate, which led manufacturing growth.

While still the largest sector, representing more than
half of GNP, the tertiary branches obtained rather mixed
and more often lackluster results. There was a marked improvement in transportation and communications and
more electricity was generated. Distribution, on the other
hand, remained terribly disorganized and most services
were far from efficient. Although the banking system
grew, excessive government regulation and protection
discouraged initiative and even rationalization. This was
bound to change under the new rules as equity in the leading commercial banks was sold to the public, primarily
the *chaebol*. Moreover, as industrial growth slackened,
entrepreneurs would be attracted to opportunities in
certain areas which had been previously overlooked, including travel and hotels, entertainment and leisure in
general.

Only two activities showed outstanding performance.
One was trading. A breakthough here was critical given
the stress on export promotion. Without effective national traders, the export targets could never be attained
or, perhaps more disturbing, could only be met by rely-

ing heavily on foreign buyers and Japanese *sogo shosha*. When the welter of small exporters failed to mobilize fast enough, the government mounted a crash program for creating General Trading Companies or *chonghap sangsa* in 1975. By setting up extensive overseas networks, and handling a broad range of goods, the GTCs could function more efficiently. In an amazingly short time, some companies—most often *chaebol*-related—did develop the necessary skills and the top nine quickly took over more than half of total exports.

The other success owed relatively little to government support. Acquiring knowhow and gaining experience from the many infrastructural and housing projects in the country, some local construction firms shaped up very quickly. When Korea was hit by the recession, and contracts were hard to find, a few of them were daring enough to seek work abroad, especially in the Middle East. It was initially assumed that they could not possibly compete against bigger and more technologically advanced contractors from America, Europe and Japan. Indeed, on highly complex projects they could not. But, for a middle range, where the use of skilled manpower was more decisive, they did very nicely. In fact, they did so well that by the 1980s the Korean contractors were firmly established and signed contracts worth billions of dollars a year. Although the boom could obviously not continue forever, any decline was cushioned by diversification into Asia and Africa.

While these aggressive development strategies had been extraordinarily effective in launching the economy, transforming the various sectors and attaining rapid growth, they were not without drawbacks.[18] Among them were irksome levels of inflation, excessive support of certain industries and a corresponding neglect of others, and an incipient polarization between companies,

The world's biggest shipyard in an unexpected place

Credit: KOTRA

social groups and individuals that threatened to reverse the earlier trend toward equality.[19] These problems were subsequently aggravated by the oil crisis which had a drastic effect on an increasingly oil-based economy with few local sources of energy. Already by the end of the Park era, the need for change had been conceded. But more basic reforms were proposed and then implemented under Chun Doo Hwan who promised a "second take-off" but also talked of "liberalization" and a "welfare state."

There was no change in the consensus that continued growth was necessary for Korea, which had since become a semi-industrialized country but still had a long way to go. Growth was a must to provide more jobs and increase the assets of a country which was far from affluent. This time, however, it was desired to avoid inflation because of the social unease it created as well as the distortions that arose in the price structure and priorities. The government was therefore determined to prevent an overheating of the economy and used monetary tools especially to this end. To the surprise of many, it was possible to bring inflation down to uncommonly low levels and yet maintain impressive growth.

Other reforms went much further in revamping the previous system. It was felt that while planning and intervention were warranted for a small and primitive economy, Korea's economy had become too large and complex to be subjected to central control. The more command elements, including targeting, had to be discarded and businessmen were urged to follow the market signals more than the plan. To ensure this was done, strategic sectors would no longer benefit from special tax treatment or access to funds and bankers were advised to judge loan requests on their intrinsic merits. Meanwhile, in sectors where excess capacity had arisen, companies were asked to cut back, merge or specialize. Where the government should help out in the future was with more general aspects that affected all sectors more or less equally, such as promotion of productivity and research and development.

These reforms could obviously not be carried out without a degree of liberalization. Internationally, it was decided to allow investors into more sectors and to permit 100% ownership. Foreign banks were more readily authorized to set up branches in Seoul and were promised equal treatment. More painful to local manufacturers, steps were taken to lower trade barriers and liberalize imports. Some domestic changes were even more significant, such as increased autonomy for commercial banks. This would theoretically also give smaller firms a greater chance to obtain credit. Just in case, certain measures were adopted to aid smaller firms and, to protect them from the *chaebol*, the antimonopoly law was reinforced. An indirect result of all this was to enhance the role of the business community which became a full-fledged partner in a renovated Korea, Inc.

At last, there was more emphasis on social matters. Education, which already enjoyed high priority, was now seen not only as a means of increasing skills needed for development but also giving youngsters an equal opportunity to get ahead. Although efforts were made to maintain farm income, workers were more subject to market forces. The only signs of concern were the introduction of employee-management councils and establishment of a Labor Ministry. Now that much of the economic infrastructure had been completed, it was possible to provide more social overhead and amenities. Housing was also upgraded. While these projects were useful as such, they were just as important in stimulating the economy when it slackened and became a "second engine" for growth. Finally, medical insurance, social security, and welfare schemes were initiated or expanded. Even if there was no intention of going as far as the West in any of these particulars, this was still a big step for Korea.

As noted, these reforms were not designed to slow down the movement but to make any future growth more balanced and sustained. Korea could thus build on what had become quite an enviable record. From 1954 to 1961, the economy expanded by 4.4% a year, much of it due to postwar reconstruction and increased population. But the growth rate shot up to 9.3% during the Park era which included an amazingly swift recovery from the first oil crisis. After his assassination, there was a year of negative growth and widespread fear of an impending debacle. Instead, the economy rebounded and seemed capable of attaining the government's target of 7-8% for the 1980s. While somewhat lower than before, these rates were even more "miraculous" at a time when most other countries were seriously slipping. As for the individual Koreans, the rise in per capita income from a meager US $90 a year in 1961 (the level of India) to a more substantial US $1,560 two decades later (seven times the level of India and twice that of North Korea) was a well-earned reward.

NOTES

1. For the pre-independence period, see Edward S. Mason et al, *The Economic and Social Modernization of Korea,* and Sang-Chul Suh, *Growth and Structural Changes in the Korean Economy, 1910–1940.*
2. Studies on the Park regime include David C. Cole and Princeton K. Lyman, *Korean Development, The Interplay of Politics and Economics,* and Michael Keon, *Korean Phoenix.*
3. See Bun Woong Kim and Wha Joon Rho (eds.), *Korean Public Bureaucracy.*
4. For the role of government, see Leroy P. Jones and Il SaKong, *Government, Business, and Entrepreneurship in Economic Development,* pp. 38–165.
5. See Il SaKong, "Macroeconomic Aspects of the Public Enterprise Sector," in Chong Kee Park (ed.), *Macroeconomic and Industrial Development in Korea,* pp. 55–98.
6. For more about the role of entreprenuers, including case histories, see Jones and Il, *op. cit.,* pp. 166–373.
7. See Jon Woronoff, *Korea's Economy: Man-Made Miracle,* pp. 231–9.
8. See Noel F. McGinn et al, *Education and Development in Korea.*
9. See David C. Cole and Yung Chul Park, *Financial Development in Korea.*
10. See Sang Woo Nam, "The Dynamics of Inflation," in Chong Kee Park (ed.), *op. cit.,* pp. 55-98.
11. See Anne E. Krueger, *The Development Role of the Foreign Sector and Aid.*
12. See Sung-Hwan Jo, "Direct Foreign Private Investment," in Park (ed.), *op. cit.,* pp. 129–84.
13. See Sung Hwan Ban et al, *Rural Development.*
14. See In-Joung Whang, *Management of Rural Change in Korea: The Saemaul Undong.*

15.   See Yung Bong Kim, "The Growth and Structural Change of Textile Industry," in Park (ed.), *op. cit.,* pp. 185-276.
16.   For more on the specific sectors and phases of industrialization, see Woronoff, *op. cit.,* pp. 31-88.
17.   The most comprehensive national studies of export promotion policies are on Korea. See, among others, Wontack Hong, *Trade, Distortions and Employment Growth in Korea.*
18.   See Parvez Hasan, *Korea: Policy Issues for Long-Term Development.*
19.   See Mason et al, *op. cit.,* pp. 408-44, and Hakchung Choo, "Economic Growth and Income Distribution," and Sang Mok Suh, "The Patterns of Poverty," in Park (ed.), *Human Resources and Social Development in Korea,* pp. 277-369.

4

Singapore, Capitalist Haven

When Sir Stamford Raffles set up a trading post in Singapore, back in 1819, there was little more to recommend the island than location and a deep water port. It was sparsely inhabited, had no visible wealth, and even the port was ignored by many sailing ships because it was not on the major commercial routes that were then determined by the trade winds. Still, it managed to attract traders almost from its inception. This is partly because Singapore was inserted in the colonial empire being staked out by the British in Malaya and Borneo in heated competition with the Dutch in Indonesia. But its real pull was that, unlike the Dutch, the British ran it as a free port which welcomed ships of all flags.

Not until the 1860s, when steamships replaced sailing vessels and the Suez Canal was opened, was the port's true potential shown. It became a popular coaling station on the new routes between East and West and was rapidly integrated in the commercial channels. The island was a handy place to collect rubber and tin, and perhaps process them, for shipment to Europe. It also received foodstuffs and manufactured goods from Europe and America and broke them into smaller lots, so they could be distributed by local merchants throughout the region. This entrepot function contributed immensely to its rise. By the early twentieth century, it was a bustling center where people could seek their fortune or simply a new start in life.

Japanese conquest and occupation, from 1942–45, put an end to what seemed like a golden age. The old trade links were cut and few new ones replaced them. There was little work for the inhabitants who were increasingly desperate. There was only a brief respite when the British restored their rule after the war. For, in a greatly changed world, colonialism was being rejected. In Malaya, they faced a Communist insurrection, which could be contained, and calls for independence, which could not. Singaporean leaders also demanded self-government. But they were worried about the island's fate on its own, an entrepot without a hinterland. In 1963, they opted for merger in the Federation of Malaysia. This only provoked President Sukarno of Indonesia, who launched a "confrontation" that deprived it of a major market. Then, only two years later, the Federation fell apart and Singapore was cast out.

Thus, on August 9, 1965, the Republic of Singapore had to start anew. For the first time, it was perfectly clear just how poor the place inherently was. The 618 square kilometers consisted largely of marsh and jungle. There was little arable land and little agriculture. There were no natural resources. And there were far too many people. Due to immigration and high birth rates, the population grew at a vertiginous pace. From the few thousand who lived there when Raffles arrived, it had risen to almost a million after the war and about 2.5 million today. The port was still there, more precious than ever, but it could hardly generate enough business to keep things going.

People appeared to be the only potential asset. But certainly not in their existing state. The population was divided among several races, Chinese (77%), Malays (15%), Indians (6%) and others (2%). For all the talk of multiracialism, there were ethnic tensions and even open violence. This was only exacerbated by bitter political conflicts as Singapore approached independence. There were repeated strikes and riots, instigated by Communist activists or sympathizers, and this merely subsided somewhat when the People's Action Party, socialist and aggressive, won the 1959 elections. While PAP's leader Lee Kuan Yew became the self-governing state's first prime minister, the party itself was torn between moderates and radicals and the pro-Communist elements were driven out in 1961. This was not the end, since they took many of the local branches with them and formed an opposition Barisan Socialis as well as underground movements. It took years for Lee to reconstruct a united party that could rule the nation effectively.[1]

Given the struggle for power and the socialist ethos of the party, to say nothing of the dominating personalities of those who led it, it was not surprising that the government should play a strong and sometimes decisive role in economic development.[2] This role, however, was not at all what had been expected. The emergence of the People's Action Party seriously alarmed business circles, whether the larger British and foreign companies or more modest Chinese ones. So great was the fear that some actually withdrew and there was a noticeable flight of capital. While the ascendancy of moderate leaders was hopeful, even more encouraging was their increasingly realistic and pragmatic approach. Without repudiating socialism, it was clearly admitted that Singapore's situation was different and the most urgent task was not to manage or share the existing wealth but to create much more.[3] This left room for an active private sector.

In such a small country, with such dynamic leaders, it is hard to define the scope of the government and there is a tendency to see its hand everywhere. There is no doubt that Lee Kuan Yew and his team, especially the long-time finance minister and deputy prime minister Dr. Goh Keng Swee, gave economic progress extremely high priority.[4] There were nagging problems that had to be solved, like massive unemployment and miserable living conditions, if the ruling party were to continue enjoying popular support. But there were even more basic issues, none of which was more crucial than how to shape the new economy. As socialists, they clearly had to consider social advancement and welfare and draw a balance with more purely economic pursuits. These matters were almost as political as economic and could obviously only be settled at the highest level.

It was also at this level that fundamental development strategy was forged. There was no longer any future for Singapore as an entrepot and it was necessary to move into other activities. But, which? Agriculture was out. Manufacturing was an alternative, but not if sales were limited to the local population. One way of escaping this was through the merger with Malaysia. For two years, efforts were made at import substitution for this larger market. As of 1965, it was impossible to continue the policy. More resolutely than elsewhere, Singapore's leaders turned to export orientation. The first products encouraged were labor-intensive to sop up some of the unemployment. By the early 1970s, more capital-intensive projects were launched.[5] Then, in the 1980s, there was stress on high tech and "brain services."

Many of the specifics were spelled out in development plans for varying periods which were issued intermittently as of 1961. While planning seemed to indicate a greater degree of government intervention, the plans were actually quite general and, for the private sector, purely indicative. Although they highlighted sectors in which growth was sought and where investment should be made, most of these efforts were reserved for ordinary businessmen. Pressure was rarely used to obtain compliance. Instead, incentives were offered to companies which entered "pioneer industries," the list of which was periodically revised to reflect current priorities. Firms which qualified for pioneer status received tax exemptions for five to ten years, accelerated depreciation of capital expenditures or R&D, and possible financial assistance. This was actually a form of targeting, but certainly more attenuated than in other parts of the region.

The government seldom went beyond this framework to promote or protect companies. "Infant industry" measures were adopted during the early 1960s, and then ceased as the priority switched to exports. Companies which did export were granted tax and other incentives that could be added to pioneer industry benefits. Yet, on the whole, the government tried to avoid any action which might benefit one sector at the expense of others or could distort the allocation of resources. With a free port, it could hardly engage in undue protection or promotion. And, trusting in the market mechanism, it preferred following a liberal tack as much as possible. Where it was most willing to intervene was thus in the more neutral yet essential tasks of providing basic infrastructure, running an honest and efficient administration, and creating a suitable climate for business.

Relevant government machinery was then activated to accomplish these ends. The more general supervision came from several ministries, especially the Ministry of Finance at first. The Ministries of Trade and Industry, Communications, National Development, and Labour were also instrumental. But a particularly significant role was assumed by some of the more than three dozen statutory agencies related to these ministries and which were kept sufficiently small and autonomous to be more flexible. Among the most active were the Economic Development Board, Jurong Town Corporation, Public Utilities Board and Singapore Tourist Promotion Board (Trade and Industry), Housing and Development Board and Urban Redevelopment Board (National Development), Port of Singapore Authority and Telecomunications Authority of Singapore (Communications), Monetary Authority of Singapore and Post Office Savings Bank (Finance), and National Productivity Board and Central Provident Fund Board (Labour).

The most influential economic body, especially in the initial period, was the Economic Development Board established in 1961. Originally under the Ministry of Finance, and then the Ministry of Trade and Industry, it was responsible for development planning of a general and sectoral nature. Its primary task, however, was to promote investment. It could handle enquiries from potential investors and help them make all necessary arrangements, including acquisition of land and facilities, recruitment of manpower and access to financing. It could also go out and look for desirable investors and introduce them to Singapore, a more purposeful task. To accomplish its aims, the EDB could grant pioneer status, and the corresponding incentives, to qualified investors. It could even buy equity in suitable companies, a prerogative that was transferred to the Development Bank of Singpore in 1968.

Important as these functions may be, they reveal more a limitation than an extension of government influence over the productive sectors. Most industrial and commercial undertakings were left to private companies which might—or might not—be helped by the EDB and DBS. Even when the Development Bank of Singapore participated in such companies, as it has repeatedly done, it only took a modest share of most ventures and more to help out than to dominate. Moreover, it always left the managerial power to the owners. There were some few exceptions to this rule since, for historical or tactical reasons, the government invested more heavily in certain enterprises including two shipyards, a shipping line (Neptune Orient) and a general trading company (Intraco).

What the government did most, and also best, was to supply the appropriate infrastructure and business climate. Through various statutory agencies, it built, maintained amd managed modern ports and airports. The road and highway network, already excellent, was being supplemented by a mass rapid transit system. Telecommunications and utilities met the growing needs. Going somewhat beyond the call of duty, it constructed nearly twenty industrial estates in which fully equipped manufacturing facilities were available at reasonable cost. Some of them were specialized for aviation, petrochemicals or high tech while the largest, Jurong, was more general. Run by the Jurong Town Corporation, established in 1968, these estates accounted for as much as 70% of total manufacturing output.

Even if not usually regarded as "economic" aspects, there were a number of activities whose effect was far from negligible. Physical planning was one. In an area as densely populated as Singapore, it would have been wasteful and chaotic to let the city grow haphazardly. The Ministry of National Development therefore maintained a master plan, which was periodically updated, to make the best use of existing land. It also provided for public and middle-income housing as well as urban renewal. The old slums in the inner city were quickly replaced by office buildings and outlying districts were provided with comfortable dwellings. By grouping housing units, and reorganizing the transport network, it was much easier to get about. Planning also helped the city to preserve an attractive appearance.

While education is important anywhere, it was much more decisive in Singapore where the only asset was people and the government placed particular stress on not only imparting knowledge but inculcating proper attitudes and behavior. This task was not so easy given a multiracial population with several vernacular languages and an assortment of Chinese dialects. The solution was to encourage bilingualism, with English emerging as the common language and then the principal one. This alone drew foreign investors. But they might not have come as gladly if the curricula had not been revised to correct the earlier academic bias. Increasing stress was put on science, mathematics, commercial and technical subjects in secondary school. Students could then enter vocational or technical schools or proceed to the university, more of whose courses were commercial or technical, the polytechnics or the technological institute. This was supplemented, in various ways, in school or in society, with moral training designed to foster good citizens and good workers.

A final effort of the state, and one whose economic significance is too readily overlooked, was to promote family planning. While all Five did this, none were more energetic than Singapore. It was vital given a 3.5% natural increase rate at independence, high even for a developing country and especially worrisome for such a crowded place. With the full backing of the national leadership, the campaign was extended and intensified under a Family Planning and Population Board as of 1965. Families were urged not to have more than two children and the rate was brought down to a low 1.2% by 1980 with a future goal of zero population growth. This meant, in its simplest expression, that more funds could be devoted to productive investment. It also implied that the priority could shift from industries which created more jobs to those which made better use of existing manpower. For the population at large, it brought a more modern lifestyle in which child rearing took up less time and more care could be devoted to fewer offspring.

Thus, with very few exceptions, the government did leave productive undertakings to the private sector. When local entrepreneurs failed to respond, as sometimes happened, it gave them a nudge or turned to outside entrepreneurs to blaze the way. That explains the existence of the "pioneer industry" scheme which was introduced as early as 1959. By making the incentives available to all companies, domestic and foreign, it was apparently being neutral and not influencing events. But this opening for multinational corporations was already rather symbolic for an avowedly socialist regime.

The main difficulty was not that Singapore lacked entrepreneurs but that they were in the wrong sector. There were more than enough traders, what with the British and other foreign merchant houses and smaller Chinese or Indian wholesalers, retailers and importers. Not many of them, however, were willing to enter manufacturing which was more needed and promising. Even if the long-term prospects of trading were bleak, they did not feel the pinch yet and relatively few responded to the blandishments and harangues of the political leadership. They joined the motley ranks of small manufacturers and processors whose number was occasionally reinforced with Overseas Chinese. During the earlier period of import substitution, local manufacturers actually performed rather well. However, when export orientation received the priority and more sophisticated articles had to be produced, it was much harder to adjust.

At this point, the government made particularly pressing appeals to foreign entrepreneurs to take up local production and exporting. They were offered a battery of incentives and guarantees of their investment. While tempting, this was only partially the reason for accepting, since such arrangements had become almost standard throughout the region. Far bigger attractions were the central location, the comprehensive infrastructure, an efficient administration and a capable work force. They also liked Singapore's atmosphere. In one sense, this just meant a pleasant place for expatriates to live. More important for the investors, of course, was that the authorities left business to businessmen and rarely intervened in their affairs. By now there are thousands of multinational corporations and foreign residents and companies account for about a fifth of total gross domestic product and a much larger proportion of manufacturing and modern services.

Naturally, it was not easy to make the city-state a haven for MNCs. There was resistance from radical political groups and misgivings in certain segments of the ruling party. There was also anxiety among older expatriate and indigenous firms that they would be overshadowed and perhaps crushed. Some of the forebodings, by the way, became realities and the opening did not bring only benefits. But there was ultimately much less friction than feared because most of the multinationals went into "pioneer" sectors, namely areas in which there was little or no local presence. Moreover, many of them produced for export or engaged in offshore banking and services. National firms, on the other hand, were frequently involved in light industry as parts suppliers or makers of articles for domestic consumption or in distribution and more traditional services. This was a dual economy of sorts, but one in which there was more separation than direct competition.

Since Singapore is the only one of the Five which made such strenuous efforts to bring in multinationals, it is worthwhile considering the motives. Most urgent, at the outset, was probably that the country simply could not generate entrepreneurs fast enough. The need for more capital was perhaps the second reason. But the financial factor was not really the most conclusive in the long run. More important was to obtain the sophisticated technologies needed to enter new fields. Obviously, they could have been licensed as elsewhere. But multinationals tended to pass on older technologies while reserving the best for their own operations, and they knew better than any licensee how to use them in practice. Fourthly, the multinationals possessed extensive marketing networks and could export regularly and substantially. Having realized the advantages, the big question eventually became, what if the multinationals left? But there was no indication they would as long as the atmosphere remained congenial.[6]

In a way, the labor situation was similar since there were far too many potential employees for the work initially available, and most of them were not very suitable. With 5% unemployment in 1957, and 9% in 1966, it looked as if it would be impossible to create enough jobs for the existing labor force and masses of newcomers. Yet, Singapore's workers were far better paid, had more fringe benefits and bonuses, and also higher expectations than anywhere else in the region. With politicized trade unions, they continued agitating for more and work stoppages were frequent. This was certainly not the sort of labor force with which to lure new companies, all the more so since they lacked the necessary technical skills. If the economy were to advance, an indispensable prerequisite was the creation of a more orderly and efficient work force, another unusual assignment for a socialist regime.

With habitual energy and resolution, the political leadership took on the trade unions and gradually brought them into the National Trade Union Congress (NTUC), allied with the PAP. In 1968, new basic legislation was adopted and duly enforced. The Empoyment Act countered the efforts to inflate wage costs by stipulating working hours and fringe benefits, restricting overtime and retirement benefits, and tying bonuses to performance and productivity. The Industrial Relations Act clarified that recruitment, promotion, transfer and dismissal were mangement functions. In addition, machinery was instituted for conciliation and arbitration of labor disputes. Then, in 1972, a tripartite National Wages Council (NWC) was established to recommend reasonable wage guidelines. To justify wage hikes, and absorb them safely, more emphasis was placed on productivity and the National Productivity Board was reactivated in the early 1980s. At the same time, Singaporean workers were advised to "learn from Japan" and become model workers.

With a bit more imagination and spunk, the Singaporeans never became model workers and there was much lamentation about inefficiency and especially job-hopping. But they were certainly much better than they had been and good enough to attract quite demanding investors. With economic expansion, jobs multiplied and by the 1970s there was only some frictional unemployment and, a bit later, a need for tens of thousands of "guest workers" to fill lesser positions. After subsiding somewhat, wages began to rise again and the NWC actually suggested that they be raised in order to overcome the tight employment situation and upgrade job opportunities. Naturally, at the same time, companies were

Singapore's financial center towering above the old city

Credit: STPB

urged to automate, robotize and computerize and, if they could not keep up, perhaps find another base for their operations.

By opening the economy so widely to foreign interests, Singapore repeatedly seemed to be going out on a limb. A look at its external finances, however, gave a more sober view. From the very outset, the government made a strict distinction between foreign debt and foreign investment. Loans, from the World Bank, Asian Development Bank or the capital market, were quite limited and never added up to more than a modest share of government borrowing. Foreign investments, on the other hand, kept flowing at exceptionally high levels, reaching a cumulative US $4,710 million by 1983. This represented a big chunk of total investment and was a form of dependence. But, unlike bank loans, it was not necessary to pay interest immediately and ultimately return the principal. Investments stayed put, and any transfer took the form of profits and dividends which were usually paid somewhat later, more evenly and only if the project had been a success. Meanwhile, it contributed to production and exports, generating income for the employees and taxes for the state.

Still, if the foreign contribution were too great in proportion to the national contribution, there could be an undesirable overreliance on others. The PAP leadership had no wish for this. Moreover, when the economy was being opened to investors, nobody really knew how many would come and it was first necessary to create a proper infrastructure and administration to entice them. Hence, the government began tapping local sources of revenue, gradually raising its take in income and other taxes as well as sales of land, utilities and services. To show its soundness, it regularly ran a budget surplus and pumped over 40% of its own expenditures into "development," a quarter of this economic services and the remainder largely social and community services. Meanwhile, a considerably larger amount was added by the leading statutory boards.

Obviously, given its needs and a taste for thrift, the government promoted saving. It was originally voluntary and modest sums were collected by the commercial banks, the postal savings bank and local *chit* funds. They grew with time, but certainly not fast enough to relaunch the economy. Thus, the Central Provident Fund which had been created in 1955 was reinvigorated and turned into a form of forced saving. Every Singapore resident had to pay part of his wages, with an equivalent share coming from the employer, into a fund which accumulated until the person reached the age of 55. He would then get the money back in a lump sum (with interest) or, if he so desired, the money could be used earlier to buy a flat in a public housing project. With CPF beneficiaries steadily increasing and the contributions raised to a whopping 50% of total wages by 1984, the sums that accrued were enormous. The CPF, postal savings bank, and even commercial banks and insurance companies bought government securities and thereby financed development expenditure.

That explains how domestic borrowings could swell so prodigiously as to make foreign borrowing pretty much superfluous. It also explains how the national saving rate could rise from a negative level in 1960 to a remarkable 40% of GNP in 1980, outperforming even the Japanese. However, since gross national saving was still supplemented by foreign saving (including loans, investments and retained profits), gross capital formation was even higher, some 46% of GNP. While the foreign input was considerable even in the 1980s, it was nevertheless a dwindling share of the total, slipping to about a tenth. This meant that more and more, voluntarily or otherwise, the Singaporeans were themselves financing the economy and reducing external dependence.

In Singapore, plans for economic development usually concentrated on manufacturing. This was because the city-state had no agricultural or mineral resources to speak of. To some economists, this lack of a primary sector appeared as an advantage. True, it did simplify the question of where to put one's priorities and avoided cumbersome development costs or subsidies. But, certainly when a country was as poor as Singapore after the war, an agricultural base would have been a precious source of work, and food, and along with minerals might have provided some of the capital to finance industrialization. This lack turned out to be particularly unfortunate after independence when neighboring countries ceased sending their commodities for processing. Whole branches which processed rubber, tin, coconut and vegetable oil, timber and other tropical produce gradually shrank and sometimes disappeared.

Luckily, as an entrepot, Singapore could use some of the trade currents to its own advantage. Especially during the import substitution phase, local merchant houses began manufacturing simple products on their own or through others and a number of rudimentary industries arose. Nearly all of them were markedly labor-intensive and required quite ordinary technologies. They included foods and beverages, textiles, garments and footwear, leather and wood products, furniture, paper, printing and so on. There was also a lively demand for building materials and one rather ambitious venture was launched, automobile assembly. However, when Singapore lost its hinterland and its neighbors also introduced labor-intensive import substitution policies, the markets for many of these articles shriveled and the automobile plant had to be closed down. Two decades later, most of these industries were still around and a few produced more than before although, as a whole, they were a diminishing share of production.

This was partly because some new sectors had done so well. Almost all of these were more capital-intensive, a few highly so, and most were predominantly export-oriented. What is interesting is that many of them issued directly from the pioneer industry program, although no one knows if they would not have come anyway. One of the earliest showed the government's drive and foresight as it converted the old British military base into a center for shipbuilding and repair. Two of the first ventures, Keppel and Sembawang Shipyards were established to use these facilities. Japan's Ishikawajima-Harima Heavy Industries was encouraged to open the Jurong Shipyard, the biggest in the region, of which the government was part owner. This gave a strong impulse to heavy industry and, even in a sagging market, the companies could adapt by building oil rigs. More recently, aircraft servicing and components shored up the transportation equipment sector.

Petroleum refining was another major effort, this time left basically to international oil companies which benefited from pioneer status. It did not take long for petroleum to become the principal industry, accounting for about a third of manufacturing output if considerably less of value added and a minimal share of employment. Its future, oddly enough, was perennially in doubt. It did extremely well during the Vietnam War but seemed bound to collapse when Vietnam halted purchases and some neighbors began refining their own crude. But there was always enough more needed by other countries and passing vessels to keep the refiners busy. Again tempting fate, in the 1980s, a huge petrochemical complex was established, largely by Japanese companies and with participation of the government.[7]

The sector whose development was most satisfactory, as regards not only output but employment, was machinery and appliances including electrical and electronics. Hardly existant at independence, it rose to 28% of industrial output and 37% of industrial employment. This was also a result of heavy investment by multinationals, mainly for sourcing purposes. They manufactured relatively few finished products but huge amounts of parts and components. This carried over into such sophisticated areas as computers, with production of semiconductors, disk drives, keyboards and printers. Metal products, aside from machinery, continued plodding along at a reasonable level. Precision equipment and optical goods, however, were hurt by the failure of Rollei which was one of the few notable mishaps.

With this, manufacturing contributed significantly to a transformation of the economy. Its share of gross domestic product climbed from 12% in 1960, to 20% in 1970, and 29% in 1980. Its share of the work force expanded even more during that period, from 8% to 28%. While the growth rate was about double that of the overall economy in the earlier period, it began slowing down and other sectors have since made an even greater contribution. Some of them were stimulated by the government, directly, as for construction, or indirectly, as for banking. Others were primarily a result of private initiatives, in particular tourism. A few, however, seemed to be just an added bonus which Singapore got for having the most attractive living and business environment in the region which made it an ideal site for company headquarters.

Proportionately, construction has shown exceptional vigor, increasing from 2% of GDP in 1960 to as much as 8% in the 1980s. This derived from several series of projects launched by the government for one reason or another. The primary, seen as essential to run a modern economy, was to improve infrastructure with roads and highways, ports and airports, industrial estates and schools, and a host of other useful things. Secondary for the economy, but primary for social welfare, was a simultaneous program of public housing and urban renewal. The Housing and Development Board built nearly 800,000 flats and shops from 1960–83 which housed over 1.7 million people or 70% of the population. No matter how valuable, this was a calculated risk for the government since it was investing huge sums for indirectly productive purposes. If the economy did not catch up, it would be hard put to bear the costs.

Transport and communications also grew commendably. Part of this was due to an upgrading of post, telephone and telegraph services. More came from the continuing expansion and improvement of the harbor run by the Port Authority. Emerging as the world's second busiest port, it catered to many of the regional needs due to its greater efficiency. With the opening of the Changi Airport, Singapore could also handle the rapidly increasing traffic, an appreciable share of which was carried by Singapore Airlines. But the most dynamic service was tourism with arrivals reaching the 3-million mark by the 1980s. Luxury and modest hotels, parks and beaches, plus the traces of traditional cultures and cheap shopping, turned the island from a mere transit point into an inevitable stopover and form of "instant Asia."

Financial and business services rounded out the sector, providing the essential banking, insurance, brokerage and consultancy needed to do business in and around the Lion City. While not originally planned, the decision to permit Asian dollar operations had gratifying spinoffs. Initially just a supplement to the Eurodollar market, it soon became an autonomous and vigorous market of its own. Since no taxes were paid by individuals, and a reduced rate by banks, turnover grew by leaps and bounds to US $112 billion by 1983. At that point, the number of Asian Currency Units (ACUs) was 131. Meanwhile, the number of commercial banks rose to 108, merchant banks 41, finance companies 35, and insurers 75, making the city-state a major regional financial center and a kind of Asian Switzerland.

The only basic sector which showed a relative decline during this period was trading, not at all surprising since the entrepot business was often in the doldrums. During the 1960s, as its neighbors expanded their own commercial and industrial facilities, re-exports periodically slumped and it was not really until the 1970s that new opportunities were found to enhance them moderately. Domestic exports, on the other hand, increased very rapidly and more than made up the difference. With this, the share of domestic exports shot up from a ludicrous 6% in 1960, to 50% in 1972, and 63% in 1983. This trend would probably continue, although for the traders both categories were welcome and entrepot business was a precious supplement most other countries did not have. It explained how Singapore could boast an export (including re-export) ratio of over 130%. Yet, even then, the trade balance remained negative and could only be covered by invisible earnings and capital inflows.[8]

Considering its unenviable political and economic situation upon independence, it might be regarded as a "miracle" that Singapore survived—let alone thrived—as a separate entity. By all standards, its performance was astounding, including the usual yardstick of GDP growth which was 8.4% for the 1960s and 9.4% for the 1970s. It still did quite well into the early 1980s.[9] Even two oil crises and a worldwide recession could not stop it, although it was slowed down.[10] The average Singaporean was nicely compensated, given a per capita GDP of US $5,196 in 1983, the second highest in Asia. With imported food and consumer goods bought from the cheapest source, comfortable and subsidized housing for most, a pleasant environment, and relative security, he was even better off than that figure would imply.[11] Yet, ever ambitious, the Economic Development Plan for the Eighties set a growth target of 8–10% a year to reach Japan's 1980 GDP by 1990.

NOTES

1. See John Drysdale, *Singapore: Struggle for Success.*
2. See T. J. S. George, *Lee Kuan Yew's Singapore.*
3. For the views of one who helped shape it, see C. V. Devan Nair, *Socialism That Works, The Singapore Way.*
4. For Goh's own views on economic development, see Goh Keng Swee, *The Economics of Modernization.*
5. More on the troubles of the earlier period can be found in You Poh Seng (ed.), *The Singapore Economy.*
6. See Kunio Yoshihara, *Foreign Investment and Domestic Response.*
7. Jon Woronoff, *Japan's Commercial Empire,* pp. 150–1.
8. See Lim Chong-Yah, *Economic Development in Singapore,* pp. 36–40.
9. For a recent summing up, see You Poh Seng (ed.), *Economic Development in Singapore in the Last Quarter Century.*
10. For some of the problems, past, present and future, see Lim Chong-Yah, *Economic Restructuring in Singapore.*
11. While the Singaporeans often griped about paying so much into the Central Provident Fund, this gave them more savings to fall back on than any other East Asians.

5

Hong Kong, Capitalist Paradise

Hong Kong had not even been sought by the British Crown. It was acquired almost accidentally, in 1841, during the campaigns undertaken to open China to trade and, for a long time, it appeared less valuable than Macau or a concession somewhere on the mainland. On the face of it, the island and the small patch of territory on the opposite shore that was later obtained, were of little intrinsic worth. The land was not very hospitable, there were no natural resources or other assets, and climatic conditions were wretched. This led Viscount Palmerston to write it off as "a barren island with hardly a house upon it."

The only thing it did offer was a reasonable harbor, once it was improved, and a convenient site for transshipment of goods from other parts of China or up the Pearl River to Canton. Yet, what ultimately made the place so attractive was not its location but the fact that it was a free port where traders of many nations could operate without the constraints they faced elsewhere. Thus it was that the entrepot business continued growing over the decades bringing an unanticipated prosperity to the international community and a soon vastly larger horde of Chinese.

The thriving colony suffered a tremendous setback when it was conquered by the Japanese and integrated in their empire in 1941. By the time the Pacific War was over, much of its infrastructure had decayed and most of the earlier settlers had fled. It was not certain how the British could restore it or, indeed, whether they would hold on to it for long since the civil war in China was rolling south and only stopped at its border. This triggered frantic flights of refugees who doubled the postwar population and then doubled it again.

With a population of 600,000 in 1945, 2.6 million in 1955, and nearly 6 million now, it was hard to imagine how the city-state's meager 1,052 square kilometers of land could possibly accomodate them. With no raw materials, and henceforth condemned to import all basic inputs, food and even water, it was far from certain they would ever get by. In fact, for decades after the war people could be found living on rooftops or hillsides. There were hosts of unemployed and many who were just partly employed or worked as itinerant hawkers and petty domestics as well as swarms of beggars. It was felt that only massive charity could enable the inhabitants to survive.

Although much help came, it was never enough, and it did not accomplish the most important aim. If Hong Kong were to become viable again, it could not live off an international dole as opposed to its own efforts. But, who could mobilize the teeming masses and channel their energy in more productive directions? In any other place, it would be assumed that this was the role of the government and, in a colony, it was almost natural to look upward. Alas, to the dismay of many, the approach adopted by the Governor and his aides was anything but one of strong leadership in economic affairs. To some, they seemed to stand aloof as mere onlookers.[1]

Hong Kong's rulers from the earliest days had abided by a policy of strict non-intervention in economic matters and left the organization and conduct of business to those most directly involved, namely businessmen. They placed credence in a philosophy of *laissez-faire* and free enterprise that was becoming increasingly outdated in other parts of the world.[2] While somewhat more involved than the theory, it was still the most liberal economy in the capitalist bloc.[3] And criticism poured down on them then, as it does today, for apparently doing nothing in times of need.

Yet, to their way of thinking, this "doing nothing" was not really an act of disconcern but an expression of faith in the ability of economic laws (and human nature) to solve most of the problems that might arise. Rather than push the economy in one direction or another and decide how fast it should grow, this was left to businessmen who encountered greater or lesser opportunities in one sector or another. Rather than promote reputedly promising industries, it was left to comparative advantage to determine whether investors should enter them and to supply and demand to make them expand or contract. There were no incentives to export rather than import aside from market needs and the chances of making a profit. Even the currency was allowed to fluctuate in keeping with business rather than government spending plans or fears of inflation or stagnation.[4]

This meant that there was not only no need for planning, targeting or industrial policy, there was no desire to have them since it was beyond the capacity of anyone to determine abstractly which actions were right. More particularly, it was not the role of the government to take such decisions because then it would be interfering in the most intimate affairs of the private businessmen. Worse, if it intervened and were wrong, it would be held to blame and expected to make some sort of compensation. And, even if it were right for a given sector, it was likely to inconvenience others and would certainly cost the taxpayers money.

But the Hong Kong government did accomplish a number of tasks which it regarded, and would probably have been conceded by a reborn Adam Smith, as falling within its realm. It had to provide a series of common services that could not be taken care of by commercial enterprises for one reason or another. And it had to supervise the companies entrusted with others. Thus, over the years, the Colony was endowed with the necessary courts and police force, public transport, post and telecommunications, and utilities. These services were not only good, on the whole they were also cheap.

The government also had to create the broader infrastructure for a modern economy. The port, an essential asset, was expanded and equipped. More roads and highways were built, an airport established, and a mass transit railway provided. It ran a reasonable, if not always superior, educational system on its own and subsidized private schools. Education was gradually upgraded and oriented toward vocational and technical training, with specialized institutes, universities and polytechnics. Public health was looked after and modest public assistance offered. And it went uncharacteristically far with two less customary tasks. It increased the territory's modest size through land reclamation and undertook public housing projects that eventually lodged almost half of the population.

On certain occasions, when the need was pressing enough, the government might deviate from its stern course of non-intervention. It was convinced to lease land or factories at lower rates to selected industries which were deemed in the interest of the overall economy. It blocked some rents during the rash of speculation. It imposed more controls on banking, the stock exchange and futures markets. It sought foreign investment and supported a trade promotion body. When the Hong Kong dollar came under pressure, more due to political uncertainties than because of its underlying tone, it was finally pegged to other currencies and artificially adjusted.

But this was not the usual approach. Normally, the government stood pat. This was not easy since there are strident and almost incessant demands in any society that something be done for one sector or another. This could imply helping out companies whose business had slumped, exporters who supposedly could not operate with adverse exchange rates, tenants who found rents prohibitive and low-income groups with claims on social justice. This was frequently accompanied by weighty arguments from academics and irate criticism in the press to the effect that, by doing nothing, it was letting the economy drift hopelessly from one crisis to the next.[5] Then came the invidious comparisons with Japan, Korea or Singapore, which were doing so much more for their people. And, of course, there were always means of pressuring any government. In such circumstances, it would seem that intervention was the simpler alternative and this may explain why it was so much more prevalent.

Yet, for all its alleged indifference, there was a definite developmental thrust. Business was the Colony's life-blood and it was impossible for the government not to be very concerned with the source of its sustenance. This was shown by the way in which it accomplished its rather limited tasks, which were hardly left to chance. For example, the infrastructure was not decided on in an impromptu manner or created after the needs had become painfully obvious. There was a long-term "outline" plan which foresaw most of the necessary projects well in advance. This also made it easier for public works to be held back in the upswings and moved forward in the downturns so as to stabilize the economy.[6]

Moreover, there was a remarkable continuity in the key economic personnel which allowed those in charge to acquire exceptional familiarity with the situation, actually more than existed in some highly interventionist states that constantly shuffled ministers. There were departments of trade, industry and construction. But the crucial position was clearly that of Financial Secretary, whose global understanding of the problems compared favorably with the specific views and interests of those in the private sector. Most Financial Secretaries served rather long terms and often held other posts before or after.

Among the most notable were Arthur Grenfell Clarke in the 1950s and Sir John Cowperthwaite in the 1960s, who shaped the government's philosophy and presided over the Colony's recovery. More recently, Sir Philip Haddon-Cave, since moved up to the post of Chief Secretary, developed a policy of "positive non-interventionism" which showed that there was infinitely more method to what was done than appeared at first sight.[7] While most of the officials were traditionally civil servants, or bureaucrats if you will, the latest Financial Secretary was a businessman who had run one of Hong Kong's biggest companies, Sir John Bremridge.

Despite the abundant lip service paid to the "common people" in most right-thinking circles, it is amazing how little confidence is generally placed in their faculty to solve problems effectively. It was regarded as almost a betrayal that the government should not take the lead in reviving the economy and thereafter in directing it. Yet, by so doing, it left the initiative to those further down . . . and they responded. There was not the slightest

doubt that Hong Kong owed its prosperity to the people
and also that they did an incredibly good job of boosting
it on their own. (They probably owed an equal debt of
gratitude to the government for giving them the chance,
although that is another matter.)

Still, one can readily understand the qualms that were
expressed when the process first began just after the war.
There were hardly any indigenous entrepreneurs
available since most of the managerial posts had been
held by expatriates, many of whom had since disappeared. So had many of the former Chinese
businessmen. Moreover, whatever entrepreneurial talent
there was had been geared principally to commercial
operations, related either to the entrepot business or
distribution. This included the big banks like the
Hongkong & Shanghai Bank, the British trading houses
and *hongs* like Jardines and Swire, and multitudes of
Chinese merchants. There were precious few industrialists of any sort and that is what was most needed.

Fortunately, among the hordes of refugees the territory began receiving were rather small numbers of
entrepreneurs. Some were manufacturers coming from
nearby Canton, others from further afield and especially Shanghai. The latter were specialized in textiles and
the foresighted arranged to have their machinery shipped to Hong Kong before it was too late. These outsiders
formed a very creative core and launched some of the
seminal ventures. When things settled, innovative businessmen were attracted from Europe, America or the
Chinese diaspora. Later on, leading American, European and Japanese multinationals set up offshore facilities.

The economy could never have blossomed if many
more entrepreneurs had not joined in, this time locals.
By the 1980s, between 10,000 and 15,000 companies were
being founded each year with a cumulative total of over

100,000. But these were only the registered corporations. With single proprietorships and partnerships as well as hawkers and the self-employed there were over twice as many "entrepreneurs" around. For a labor force of about 2.5 million, this worked out to one boss for every dozen workers. Under such conditions, many of the firms were quite small and the bulk had less than ten employees. Yet, they were all obviously making some contribution to development or they would not be there.

Given the vital role they played, it is instructive to know what sort of people the small entrepreneurs were, for they represented the vast majority and were also the ones whose originally modest efforts sometimes grew into larger concerns. According to one excellent study, although there was an early predominance of refugee elements, most of them were from neighboring Canton province or born in Hong Kong. Relatively few had an upper class background and the rest had parents who were artisans, workers or peasants. Hardly any were the offspring of entrepreneurs and their previous experience was in subordinate posts of existing companies. Going out on their own was a big step. But it was taken despite the fact that, on the whole, they were young, with a meager education and little access to capital.[8]

That they could succeed was a tribute to their ability, determination and hard work. It was also a tribute to free enterprise, since there were hardly any government or commercial constraints to block them. It was simple enough to set up a company, anybody could do it, and almost all sectors were open to newcomers. There were relatively few large firms which might try to control specific products or markets and, given the dynamic situation, they could rarely do so for long. This, in a practical sense, is what opportunity is all about and it was seldom lacking in the Colony. Yet, along with easy entry and

Turning toys into a massive export industry

Credit: HKTDC

chances of gain, there were also possibilities of loss and failure in the rough-and-tumble competition. While this was regrettable, and painfully felt by those who failed, it was this discipline which toughened up the entrepreneurs as a class and selected those who were fittest, in one way or another, and could survive. They then tended to upgrade and expand their operations.

This mixture of opportunity and risk also characterized the labor scene. With unemployment running as high as 10–15% in the 1950s, people were desperate to get a job and did not quibble about the hours and conditions or even the pay. This made it easier for entrepreneurs to recruit any necessary staff and use them quite lavishly in labor-intensive chores. For a decade and more, wages hardly rose since there were always more workers including youngsters and fresh refugees. By the late 1960s, however, the market was getting a bit tighter and employers had to offer better pay and conditions, while the government regulated hours somewhat. The law of supply and demand was now favoring the labor force and it benefited substantially. Yet, each time new batches of refugees arrived or business slumped, as in the early 1980s, there would be a spurt of unemployment and wages would stagnate until labor costs became competitive. Then, more could be sold, more could be produced, more workers could be hired, and pay scales would rise again.

While the government could not prevent trade unions, it certainly did not encourage them and ethnic divisions, ineptitude of trade union leaders and individualism of the rank and file kept labor rather disorganized. This made it look as if the workers were terribly weak and could never impose their will on management.[9] The only weapon they had was the right to sell their labor to whoever they wished. In times of high unemployment, this was not very helpful. However, when business picked up, they could readily move from one company to another, wherever they got the best pay, or nicest conditions or friendliest atmosphere.[10] Job-hopping was not a sign of disloyalty so much as a message to employers that the time had come to offer more and those who did had little trouble holding on to old workers and attracting new ones. It thus fulfilled an important function for the workers, management and even the economy in general. Without this mobility, it would not have been possible to staff new ventures and thereby diversify or to react to passing opportunities and quickly expand.

One could hardly imagine a poorer place than Hong Kong when it emerged from the war and was swamped with refugees. With people living from hand to mouth for the larger part, it was hard enough for them to scrape together the wherewithal merely to survive. How then could they ever amass the huge sums that were necessary to restore and develop the economy?[11]

Once again, it was certainly not from the government that this could be expected. Its tax intake was not very big at the outset and, for reasons of principle, it did not regard the accumulation and allocation of capital as among its proper functions. There were no state banks or special funds for businessmen. It did not advise the commercial banks on what loans to make. And it did not subsidize ventures no matter how promising they might conceivably be. It just built the basic infrastructure and provided a certain number of general, social and economic services, for which it usually charged at cost. Admittedly, there were more of those in later years and government expenditure slowly crept up to 18% of gross domestic product, a bit high for the Colony but low anywhere else.

In return, by running a lean administration, the government did not have to collect very high taxes or any customs duties. In fact, many residents paid absolutely no income tax and others were taxed quite lightly. Even the corporate tax was only a lenient 15% during the 1960s and into the 1970s, and a hardly excessive 17% thereafter, one of the lowest in the world. (Actually, it was so low that normal tax rates in Hong Kong were frequently more advantageous in the long run than favorable tax treatment elsewhere.) This meant that the state's biggest contribution was probably to leave individuals and companies with the money they needed to launch or expand enterprises.

Even then, it would seem that actual and potential entrepreneurs would need seed money and occasional credit, clearly a task for the banks. Due to the existence of the entrepot trade, there was a rather extensive network of commercial banks, merchant banks, finance companies and so on. Alas, they did not have much money to lend in the earlier period because people did not have much money to save. This was gradually corrected and, by the 1980s, the banking system was awash with funds. The other problem, however, was not so easy to remedy since most of the loans were directed to the more familiar operations of the already well-established trading firms. Proportionately less went into industry or services and there was little inclination to lend to such unknowns as most struggling entrepreneurs were. They had to tap less respectable, and more costly, financial institutions.[12]

In an age when any less developed country can go about collecting low-interest loans, grants and technical assistance from the international community, Hong Kong was conspicuous by its absence. It was poor. But it was not a state. It was just a colony of a motherland which could only afford to offer so much assistance. Loans from Great Britain were precious at the time, as was international charity from benevolent organizations. But it was still just a pittance when divided among the plethoric population. Moreover, the government did not really want foreign loans. It much preferred balancing its accounts and spending less if need be. That is why it also eschewed domestic borrowing. During most of the postwar period it not only managed to make ends meet, it regularly ran a surplus until the early 1980s. Then it had to issue bonds which, given its record and solvency, were not hard to place.[13]

There were only two noteworthy sources of external funds, Overseas Chinese businessmen and Western or Japanese multinationals. No one knew how much Chinese money passed through the Colony, in either direction, since it was never counted. As a relatively safe haven, it must have been substantial. The MNCs later hit upon Hong Kong as an offshore production base or location for regional headquarters. Its relatively cheap labor and low taxes were the main attractions. By 1983, registered foreign investment added up to US$1,000 million although there was doubtlessly more. This capital, and even more so the facilities and technologies, was a valuable contribution.[14] But it was still only a fraction of the total investments.

It is hard to conclude otherwise than that, especially in the early years, most of the capital was generated by the entrepreneurs themselves. They would save their own money bit by bit, and perhaps borrow some more from friends and relatives or moneylenders, and start a firm. Profits would be plowed back, year after year, and the firm would grow. Only then, and still rather exceptionally, would they—or could they—take out loans from a bank or float shares on the stock market. In this way, companies were born and proliferated and gross domestic capital formation rose from about 20% of GDP in the 1960s to 30% in the 1980s. While the levels were on the low side for East Asia, they were still reasonably high and the investors often got more for their money. Unlike some others, the Hong Kong Chinese were never obsessed about owning the very latest machinery or acquiring the very finest technologies. They accepted a bit less, sometimes actually second-hand machines and conventional techniques. But this was usually more than adequate to get the job done well and cheaply. Only when it was not enough did they move up to something better and more costly.

As for Singapore, it was not hard to decide in which direction to develop the economy. There was not much that could be done with agriculture. Worse, the old mainstay, the entrepot trade, was in serious difficulty. This was not very diversified since the Colony had always served as a gateway to China and the vast majority of its re-exports were there. Alas, after the Communists took over the mainland, there was a tendency toward autarky in the People's Republic that left less room for trade. Then, in 1951, the United Nations imposed an embargo due to Chinese intervention in the Korean War. This completely disrupted the entrepot business leaving only domestic exports, which were quite minimal.

Manufacturing was about the only place to turn. As to what type of industry was best, where Hong Kong had its comparative advantage, the choices were equally simple. It had large numbers of unemployed persons who could be hired for exceedingly low wages. And it had little capital. What was more, there was no space for large installations or heavy machinery. The only possibility was clearly labor-intensive light industry. It did not take a government planning agency or academic think tank to come up with that conclusion.

The initiation of the first major industry was partly coincidental, since some of the earliest entrepreneurs were textile manufacturers from Shanghai and elsewhere. They had the knowhow. They also sometimes had the equipment or could acquire it. This sector expanded swiftly as others realized the potential and entered it. From cotton, it spread to wool and synthetics. And a subsidiary branch almost exploded. With material produced locally, it was possible for innumerable tiny workshops to make clothing and accessories. Once it was only cheap underwear and one-dollar ties. But the industry upgraded and gradually went upmarket until Hong Kong became one of the world centers of ready-to-wear fashions and the biggest exporter of garments in general. This was accomplished despite growing restrictions from Great Britain, the European Community and the United States as of the 1960s.

Another early sector was plastics as untold primitive

factories used extrusion molds to make rudimentary articles, often in very short runs. Among these were kitchen utensils and artificial flowers, whose popularity eventually declined. But sales of plastic toys and dolls kept on growing. By the time tastes changed, toy makers were able to adapt by producing metal gadgets with electric motors. They even kept in stride during the electronic game era. In fact, Hong Kong is now the number one exporter of toys. Of course, not everything worked out as well. Wig making underwent an incredible boom that dissipated even more rapidly than it had materialized. What was remarkable was that, thanks to the extraordinary flexibility and versatility of its businessmen, each passing fad could be seized, and then dropped if necessary.

By the 1970s, the electronics industry was doing even better. It began with the production of standard components and assembly of radios. But Hong Kong turned out to be such a good base that American and other multinationals entrusted it with more and more products while locals opened firms to subcontract. Then some of them forged ahead, adopting any new product almost as soon as it appeared and making simpler and cheaper versions. This even applied to some of the latest telecommunications gear and computers. Once chips were used for making digital watches, its makers moved into that branch aggressively and become the number one exporter in quantity.

Aside from some shipbuilding, cement and plastic production, there was little heavy industry. This may have been just as well. For it left more funds for light industry and did not burden manufacturers with high-cost suppliers. Raw materials, intermediate goods and machinery were sought wherever they were the best for the price. This often gave local makers an additional edge over rivals in places where domestic industries were protected or subsidized. With exports reaching as much as 80–90% of output in many lines, the manufacturing sector could expand beyond all expectations. From a mere 1,500 establishments with 90,000 employees in 1950, it distended to nearly 46,000 establishment with 900,000 employees in 1980. While few visitors realized it, Hong Kong had a highly industrialized economy with as much as 31% of GDP coming from manufacturing in 1970 and a bit less at present.

What is most intriguing is that this sector consisted of the very things more ambitious countries tended to shun. It took on slews of petty products with minor markets such as plastic flowers, or flashlights, or binoculars, or batteries and other sundry articles. But they all contributed to turnover. And they increased the economy's resilience since there was never a slump for all of them at the same time and one or another might be enjoying a modest boom. Even the principal products like textiles, garments, toys and radios were usually categorized as "sunset" industries, bound to fade away. Yet, in Hong Kong, they continued thriving. Textiles and garments, for example, increased almost twenty-fold in value from 1960 to 1980.

The fact that there was no targeting of industry or incentives to direct entrepreneurs there made it much easier for any other activity to emerge. As soon as opportunities arose, as soon as entrepreneurs figured out how to benefit from them, new ventures were initiated. This was not very hard for tourism since travel agencies required rather small staffs and modest finances. As the number of tourists multiplied, more and more hotels went up, some connected with international chains and others opened by local firms which eventually spread their own networks abroad. Given its convenient location on most Oriental routes, and ultimately again as a gateway to China, Hong Kong profited and reached 2.8 million tourists by 1983. Their presence was not only a boon to the tourist trade but business in general as they bought antiques, souvenirs, electronics, 24-hour suits and what not in the world's biggest bargain basement.

Banking also went international. The Hongkong & Shanghai Banking Corp. and others opened branches abroad and foreign banks flocked to Hong Kong as fast as licenses could be granted. By 1983, there were 134 licensed banks and 115 foreign representative offices. This was not the result of any master plan by the government, nor did the banks benefit from any special incentives at first. It was quite enough to service a prosperous and increasingly international business community and

An unbeatable combination:
cheap labor and sophisticated machinery

Credit: HKTDC

enjoy the standard, low tax rates. When offshore earnings were exempted from even that, offshore business mushroomed and reached a level not far from that of Singapore. Thus, both these centers took a place left vacant by Japan which was unable to forgo its love of restrictions.

During these years, trade made a comeback. This was largely due to the rise of export-oriented operations. Much of the industrial production was directed toward the more affluent Western countries or those in nearby Asia. Under the principle of free trade, there were no special incentives or favorable exchange rates. Companies exported because they had to, the home market was simply too tight. And they stayed competitive by enhancing quality and keeping their costs down. Later, when China rejoined the community of nations, the entrepot trade got a fresh wind. But it lagged well behind the even more vigorous domestic trade which held some 65–75% of the total in an export ratio that revolved around 70% of GDP. Meanwhile, imports grew apace, since raw materials, intermediate goods, machinery and even food had to be brought in. The perennial trade deficit was balanced by invisible earnings and capital inflows.

The Colony never developed general trading firms. Only the British *hongs* engaged in a relatively broad range of activities, while countless trading companies were almost hole-in-the-wall affairs. This was partially because some were breakaways from larger companies. But it also arose because many local manufacturers looked after their own sales, personally traveling abroad to find clients rather than letting anyone else get in between. Many of the foreign buyers, major department stores or mail-order houses, also set up their own purchasing offices. While the *sogo shosha* came, they did not dominate the market by any means, handling mainly the trade with Japan. Individualism and specialization seemed to mesh better with the mentality of the people and the mood of free enterprise. But this did not keep Hong Kong from exporting three times more per person than Japan.

Where businessmen really succeeded in a big way, much to the surprise of doubting onlookers, was in shipping. Some of the old British firms had their own shipping lines which waxed or more often waned with the times. The real impetus, however, came from complete unknowns. These were sometimes refugees from Shanghai, occasionally with no background in shipping but a liking for movable assets. They realized that, by manning ships with British officers but Chinese and other Asian seamen, it was possible to keep costs low. They were also adept at buying and selling vessels at the right time. In this way, gigantic shipping lines were built up by tycoons like Y. K Pao and C. Y. Tung. All in all, Hong Kong's fleet was probably the world's second largest. No one really knew just how big it was since most of the ships were registered abroad and flew flags of convenience.[15]

Thus, in one way or another, with no preconceived notions or fixed plans, the people of Hong Kong put together a uniquely versatile and adaptable economy. Things did not always go well and it was shaken by many untoward events, the trade embargo, oil crises and protectionism.[16] It sometimes even looked as if the Colony might perish. But growth continued unabated. During the 1950s, a period of great turbulence, it showed a reasonable rate of 5–6% a year. From 1961 to 1973, this shot up to 9%. In the decade after the oil crisis, expansion was harder and growth slipped to about 8%. Given its size, its overpopulation, its lack of resources, and its vulnerability, this sort of performance was extremely impressive and probably made Hong Kong the most astonishing "miracle" of them all.

Still, it may be asked, what about the people? What did they get out of this? According to the statistics and visible evidence, they also experienced notable improvements. Housing, clothing and nourishment were certainly much better. Cars abounded and leisure was spreading. Anyone who really wanted a job could find one. And wages rose to the point where it was impossible to come by cheap labor.[17] What about the gaps, the rich and the poor? These unquestionably also existed, there were plenty of millionaires and some remaining beggars. Not everyone had the same opportunities or knew how to use them. Yet, the inequality was considerably less in Hong Kong, and all of the Five, than most other countries, advanced or developing.[18] A smoothly functioning economy had its own ways of contributing to that.

The only things that could stop this economic dynamo were related more to politics. It stumbled briefly during the Cultural Revolution in China, when riots broke out in the Colony as well and seriously undermined confidence. This was more than overcome when a pragmatic regime arose under Deng Zhao-Ping. However, whatever the intentions of those in Peking, it was natural that the government and ordinary people alike should become increasingly nervous as the year 1997 approached. For, at that date, there was bound to be a major change in status. British rule, and no less significant, the rule of free enterprise and unbridled capitalism, would come to an end.

NOTES

1. For the composition and functions of the Hong Kong Government, see N. J. Miners, *The Government and Politics of Hong Kong*.
2. *Laissez-faire*, and how it worked in Hong Kong, is the subject of Alvin Rabushka, *Hong Kong: A Study in Economic Freedom*, and Jon Woronoff, *Hong Kong: Capitalist Paradise*.
3. Obviously the *laissez-faire* of Hong Kong is not "pure" and it hardly seems necessary to say so. Thus, overemphasizing its deviations is a bit like tilting at windmills, a sport many academics enjoy. See, among others, Nicholas C. Owen, "Economic Policy," in Keith Hopkins (ed.), *Hong Kong: The Industrial Colony*, pp. 141–206.
4. The most comprehensive and detailed analysis of how the economy functions in practice is still Tong-yung Cheng, *The Economy of Hong Kong*.
5. Nothing could surpass the carping and criticism of the *Far Eastern Economic Review* whose generous advice—if followed—would have ruined the economy long ago.
6. More on how the bureaucracy operates, including a case history on the mass transit railway decision, can be found in Peter Harris, *Hong Kong: A Study in Bureaucratic Politics*.
7. Interesting background on policy-making can be gleaned from the Budget Speeches of the various Financial Secretaries. See also C. P. Haddon-Cave, "The Making of Public Policy in Hong Kong," presented to the Mont Pelerin Society, Hong Kong, September 4, 1978.
8. Victor Sit et al, *Small Scale Industry in a Laissez-Faire Economy*.
9. Few places have been more roundly condemned for "exploitation" of labor, as if Hong Kong were somehow singularly evil. The major opus on this is Joe England and John Rear, *Chinese Labour Under British Rule*.
10. It was easy enough to play employers off against one another because business circles were no more organized than labor.
11. The best information on the early period can be obtained from Edward Czczepanik, *The Economic Growth of Hong Kong*.
12. For more details, see Y. C. Jao, "The Financial Structure," in David Lethbridge (ed.), *The Business Environment in Hong Kong*, pp. 159–99.
13. This was a result of circumstances rather than policy. It can be assumed that efforts will be made to return to balanced budgets.
14. See C. L. Hung, "Foreign Investments," in Lethbridge, *op. cit.*, pp. 200–33.
15. The merchant fleet was estimated at 1,410 vessels with 58 million dwt at the end of 1983, second only to Japan.

16. See Victor Mok, "Trade Barriers and Export Promotion," in Tzong-Biau Lin et al, *Hong Kong, Economic, Social and Political Studies in Development,* pp. 297–331.
17. Lack of statistics on income makes it difficult to compare Hong Kong's status. A rough idea, however, can be given by the per capita GDP in 1983 of US $5,123.
18. See Ronald Hsia and Lawrence Chau, *Industrialization, Employment and Income Distribution.*

PART TWO:

THE POLICIES

From their development histories, it should be amply clear that if there was anything that turned these once rather unpromising countries into overachievers it is the policies and strategies they fashioned. Success could not be traced to their natural endowment, which was quite mediocre. It could not be ascribed to availability of capital, for they were rather poor to begin with. It could perhaps be credited to the quality of the leaders and ordinary people. But they only did well when they applied the right policies in the right way, which was not always the case.

This justifies the growing interest in analyzing their efforts in order to determine just which policies were most useful in attaining these formidable results. After all, such policies can be introduced by anyone who so desires. Normally, they could be counted on to improve the performance of others as they did for the Five. By adopting the appropriate methods, there might be considerably more economic "miracles."

Various policies, strategies and techniques have already been selected by observers as crucial to the East Asian success. Some are relatively well known, others less so. Some are regarded as more essential than others. Those which will be dealt with here include especially the methods of promoting industrialization, techniques for raising funds domestically, the approach to technology induction and, most popular of the lot, export orientation.

What is remarkable about this list is that, at first sight, there is nothing remarkable. There are no unsuspected tricks or gimmicks. These are all standard techniques. Planning is the hallmark of the Communist system and "infant industry" methods go back over a century. Technology transfers are constantly occurring and exporting is no more novel an economic function than importing, even when promoted more resolutely.

Yet, despite the fact that the techniques are already quite old, and have been used rather broadly, they did not always produce the desired results. Certainly, they did not create economies which advanced as rapidly and proved nearly as dynamic as those of the "dragons" and "tigers." This would seem to indicate that policies are only "miraculous" when applied well and, alas, that would not seem to have happened very often elsewhere.

One reason why the East Asians succeeded with the very same strategies as others is that they did not simply adopt them as they were. As must be evident, they adapted them to local circumstances and they improved on them by learning how and when they should be used. When imperfections arose, they were willing to make changes. And, if it turned out that a policy was no longer useful, it could even be dropped.

The other reason is that they realized that the biggest problems do not arise at the level of theory or general principles. It is only the practice of any policy that counts. They were therefore exceptionally careful about implementation to see that there was a follow-through and that it was effective. They were also more worried about the countless little details that were often overlooked elsewhere but spelled the difference between success and failure.

While the various techniques and strategies are presented individually, to get a better look at them and grasp how they functioned, they were never used separately or in isolation. It is only as a combination of policies that they appeared or could be effective. And, in working out a suitable mix, it was frequently necessary to tone one down or give greater emphasis to another. This was partly a question of adapting to local circumstances. It could also result from strikingly different ideological options in the various countries.

What is most surprising in East Asia is the extent to which certain policies were given high priority in some places and scarcely existed in others. Similarly, due to differences in economic style, crucial strategies might be pursued with exceptional vigor by some leaders and almost ignored by others. While the goals remained unchanged, it could happen that the government undertook implementation in certain regimes and the private sector in others.

As a matter of fact, the range of approaches which ultimately evolved was amazingly varied. It went from the most *dirigiste* to the most liberal, from the most state dominated to the most *laissez-faire*, from those who tried to force the economy toward specific sectors or activities to those who steadfastly refused to intervene. It included some who sought social goals and others who thought of nothing but economic growth. The spread was about as broad as could be imagined among countries within the capitalist realm.

This shows that, no matter how effective and useful the policies may appear in general, there was no uniformity in how they were employed even within such a small circle as five East Asian countries. For any who would learn from them, this fact is of paramount importance. It is not necessary, or even desirable, to adopt given techniques or strategies—let alone a standard package of policies—but rather to study them and determine which are applicable to one's own situation. This makes borrowing more difficult, since essential choices must be made. But the chances of finding an appropriate solution are greatly enhanced.

Some may be tempted to assume that the key to success in wielding these policies is to exercise outstanding virtuosity and finesse. It is necessary to figure out how they work and then undertake the proper fine-tuning. Surely, to some extent, this is true and it is essential to know more about how the policies function than is generally the case. But there are some things which are just as decisive in explaining the "miracles" in East Asia.

One is commitment. It is quite impossible to introduce policies which require far-reaching changes in the status quo and make substantial demands on the nation without the leaders showing sufficient determination. It is no more feasible to carry out the policies without a good deal of support from the people, and this implies that they also muster a positive will. Will does not mean that they submissively accept the decisions or passively participate in the efforts but that they show initiative, drive and a readiness to sacrifice. No country can succeed without that, no matter how wise its policies.

On the other hand, there are certain circumstances in the present-day world which are incredibly helpful in accelerating the development process. The reason some policies have worked, and others not, is that the former were more in tune with the times and took greater advantage of the possibilities which have arisen. They made the process more manageable and dynamic than ever before, for those who understood them. And they sharply increased the odds of succeeding.

The policies, the will and the circumstances must all be considered when assessing the economic "miracles" and trying to replicate them.

6

Where There's A Will . . .

Economic development and, even more so, well-being and affluence are certainly goals which appeal to most countries and are quickly hoisted to a position of high priority. However, in many places they remain little more than abstract ideas and receive little more than lip service. Time passes, and there is much talk of the need for advancement, but close to nothing is done. For, aside from ritual praise of these goals, there is no deep-felt or far-reaching commitment and people find it hard to summon the will for what is, even in the luckiest nations, a truly daunting challenge.

Thus, before considering the various policies and strategies adopted in East Asia to attain these goals, it is necessary to understand why these five countries mustered the essential commitment and will. For this, as for everything else in the development process, there were very great differences in approach, so much so that it might be felt that some of the leaders or peoples overdid their zeal or did not manifest enough. Yet, in the end, they were all within an acceptable range and demonstrated the variations that are possible.

When studying the experiences of any given country, many observers almost automatically look to the top first. They consider the policies and philosophies, the statements and actions of the national leaders. This is particularly apt, or so it seems, when dealing with countries known for extensive central control and strong rulers. That is the case of all Five at various times, as demonstrated by a Park Chung Hee, a Chiang Kai-Shek, or a Lee Kuan Yew. In Japan, the leadership has been more by consensus, but not one of the whole population, and what the inner circle decided was usually implemented. Hong Kong, lest it be forgotten, is still a Crown Colony.

Among these various leaders, some possessed a deep personal commitment to economic development. The most pronounced was probably that of Korea's Park, who was born the younger son of a poor farmer and knew intimately the misery of the countryside.[1] Most others only had a more distant and impersonal acquaintance with poverty, many actually being from the upper classes. But they were pushed in the same direction by patriotism or pride, wanting their country to be recognized for its economic success.

There were other reasons as well, not as often mentioned, but surely as compelling. When leaders came to power by means other than popular elections, it was necessary to provide legitimation in some way, few better than improving the economic status of the nation and living standards of the people. In East Asia, perhaps more noticeably than elsewhere, there was a very definite tradeoff between political advancement and economic progress, with the populace more willing to accept gains with the latter as compensation for slower movement toward the former. For those who had failed earlier, as for the Kuomintang, the economic challenge was more acute.

Yet, despite a solidly-based commitment to economic development, even in East Asia there were other goals that had to be considered. For Korea and Taiwan, as well as prewar Japan, it was necessary to reinforce the defense posture against clearly defined and openly threatening

Activitist leadership: President Chun in the rice paddies

Credit: KOIS

enemies. It was also hoped to raise national consciousness in the face of present or past humiliations from Western powers or, for the Four, from Imperial Japan. There was always some concern with social issues, such as education, housing, health and welfare, etc. In Singapore, in the earlier days, this was seen as particularly pressing.

Whatever their value, these goals were bound to detract in some manner from economic development as resources and manpower were drained away. The strength of the commitment was therefore proven by the willingness to downgrade all other aims—no matter how urgent or imperative—and give economic activities the top priority. The decision was not easy, and often it required external pressure (such as American advice and then refusal to grant more free funds), but it was clearly taken.[2]

The path to the decision, however, was not always

straight. Economic development was highly regarded in its own right, but it could also be presented as a mediate goal, since it was a key to all others. If the economy fared poorly, then there would not be enough funds for military might or social uplift and the country could hardly improve its status or the people their well-being. However, if the economy could be strengthened by *temporarily* sacrificing these other things, then in a somewhat more distant future, when the country was richer, the remaining goals could more readily be attained. This roundabout reasoning which was often used by the leaders, and carefully explained to their followers, resulted in a broader commitment that was actually firmer for being less categorical.

Taking a more subdued and sustained line was doubtlessly the best tack. For, over the course of many years, it was necessary to uphold the priority for economic development and this could only be done by showing that it was a foundation for most other valid aims. Otherwise, the country would probably lurch from priority to priority as one area or another appealed to the leaders or masses or, worse, try to make everything a priority. In addition, it was wiser to maintain a somewhat slower but steadier pace rather than encourage periodic spurts or great leaps forward which would result in impressive peaks of activity followed by inevitable troughs and create confusion and instability.

Alas, the commitment of the leaders—no matter how authentic and unshakable—was not enough to get the countries very far along the path to development. Their pledges had to be converted into acts and, for that, the personal writ of even the most absolute ruler never reached quite far enough. It was necessary to establish administrative machinery which could carry on the basic activities of any national bureaucracy and, in addition, play a decisive role in economic matters. If not, the Five would have been as "soft" as a hundred other states and would have achieved as little as they.

East Asia, in some ways fortunately, inherited a lengthy bureaucratic tradition. It sprang from ancient empires and centralized states as well as the pervasive philosophy of Confucianism, which provided moral support. But none of this had been of much help in economic undertakings in the past. Nor could the bureaucracy be quickly turned around or harnassed to the new goal of economic development. In fact, an inbred reluctance to take novel actions, the respect of hierarchy, and fear of assuming responsibility repeatedly got in the way. Once pointed in the right direction, however, the bureaucratic tradition was of more use.

Obtaining bureaucratic commitment to the economic priority was far from easy and took decades to be fully accomplished. This was done only partially by introducing incentives for those who displayed wise decisions and useful actions, incentives which had to be sufficient to compensate for the safer solution of holding back and making no mistakes. This took the form of promotions, commendations and medals, but also the possibility of moving into one of the state-run corporations or the government. On the other hand, those who did less than was expected could be downgraded or discarded. A final category, which proved too venal, might face even worse penalties.

Actually, the most effective method of reforming the bureaucracy was quite simply to change the people in it. Older bureaucrats, with little or no concern for economic matters, were retired out early or kicked upstairs. Younger, better educated and more dynamic bureaucrats were taken in and gradually became a majority. Among them some were specifically trained in economics or useful technical subjects, the so-called "technocrats." Their status rose individually and collectively as economic issues became uppermost. In places where the economic ministries or planning agencies enjoyed some predominance, they could exert increasing influence over all other, more traditional ministries and agencies.[3]

While proper leadership was important in maintaining the commitment, a no less crucial element was money. The finest words and the loftiest sentiments would have accomplished little if not backed up by the necessary funds. What is truly remarkable about the East Asian Five is that they did, as is so vulgarly said, "put their money where their mouth is." The funding of developmental programs grew steadily as a share of national expenditures, even when this cut into seemingly vital defense or apparently more laudable social expenditures. The national budget was further supplemented by other forms of financing, through state banks and other institutions, by means of voluntary or forced saving.

Although it took strong leaders to impose a commitment on the bureaucracy and allocate greater funds for developmental purposes, it would be very mistaken to assume that strength, let alone ruthlessness, is the key to success. The world has always been full of strong and determined rulers, many of whom were considerably more tyrannical and despotic than any who arose in East Asia. Such leaders have often proclaimed economic development as a priority goal, sometimes they even tried to do something about it, but none of them succeeded by brute force. On the other hand, a place like Hong Kong where the colonial masters purposely restricted their intervention in the economy could push ahead.

One explanation for this is that there is a limit to what even the toughest leader can do. At most, he can give orders and perhaps impose his will on his assistants and part of the administration. But he is hardly in a position to reach the right decisions on his own, he needs external expertise for that. And, while he can expect some obedience from the state's servants, he will find it much harder to wring any compliance out of the mass of the people. The other explanation is that, should he try to do so, it would quickly appear to be counterproductive. Excessive pressure from above would only result in those down below following instructions even when they were wrong and failing to come up with their own efforts and initiatives. In short, it would stifle rather than stimulate the very sort of reactions that are essential for economic progress.

It is therefore preferable to impose restraints on the power of the leaders, whether individuals or groups, so that more leeway can be left for the other vital participants, businessmen, workers, merchants, farmers, teachers and so on. This can be done basically by establishing a public sector and a private sector, and leaving the average citizen pretty much free to act as he deems fit within his own realm. If the state still has to intervene in the private sector, for one reason or another, it can be more effective by using "carrots" than "sticks." While this requires a bit more intelligence and subtlety of the leadership, it is certainly worth the effort.

Thus, even when the man of destiny appears center stage, he is but one of the economic actors. No matter how important his role, and he could probably destroy the economy single-handedly if he wished, he cannot create a flourishing economy without the aid of a vast cast of supporting actors and even greater throngs of extras and walk-ons. It is therefore necessary to consider with even greater care the rest of the population including those in quite ordinary positions.

It is repeatedly claimed that East Asia was in a very advantageous position because the population was imbued with Confucian values. Due to the traditional upbringing and education, people were trained for or almost spontaneously engaged in certain types of action that were conducive to the tasks at hand. The Confucian ethic, according to Herman Kahn, was instrumental in "fostering a dedicated, motivated, responsible, and educated citizenry and a sense of commitment, organizational identity and institutional loyalty."[4]

There is no doubt that the reputed Confucian "virtues" were of much help in economic development. But it would be very naive to assume that they explain everything. After all, the Confucian ethos was even stronger in bygone centuries when pitifully little economic progress was achieved. Moreover, in the view of most experts, there were also Confucian "vices" which hindered the appropriate behavior for modern economic enterprise, such as hesitation to break with tradition, lack of initiative or imagination and generalized passivity and submissiveness.[5] If Confucianism was of use during the present development process, it is largely because it has been much modified and manipulated, the useful characteristics purposely exalted and the more harmful ones toned down.

In addition, it was often the actual material conditions of the people rather than any moral principles which encouraged them to be so "virtuous". Life in Meiji-day Japan, and even postwar Korea or Taiwan, was terribly harsh. Farmers labored long hours for a rather meager harvest, much of which was paid to the landlords or government while little remained for them. Hunger, and sometimes actual starvation, was more than just a memory. It occurred until very recent times and encouraged people to work that much harder. Those who lost their land and drifted to the towns and cities were often in even worse straits since they had no source of sustenance and encountered a shortage of jobs. They were scarcely in a position to quibble about the terms or show any laxity in their work will.

Despite all this, the East Asians managed to set aside some money and accumulate savings. They postponed their paltry rewards and painstakingly expanded their pitiful reserves. But this was not due only to some homespun Confucian morality. Thriftiness was necessary in olden times to have something to fall back on. If the harvest were bad, or if the job were lost, there had to be something standing between them and utter disaster. Even in postwar Japan, where things were considerably better, it was necessary to put money aside to pay for a home, to get a proper education for the children, and to provide for life after retirement. Without such savings, it was not certain one could really get by.

Yet, even when these useful characteristics arose out of traditional philosophies and customs or sheer necessity, they were never quite exempt from other influences. The most important by far were patently economic. Most of the actions were clearly and strongly affected by market forces even before a modern economy evolved. While people worked hard under most circumstances, they definitely worked harder when the rewards were greater. More money for vegetables than rice or for construction work than farming determined what they would do. Higher wages in one region than the next triggered massive migrations. Better pay in a given company or profession led to suitable shifts.

For all their frugality, the people were not fools. When inflation was low, they saved more readily. When inflation flared up, they quickly spent what they had accumulated and could even engage in dissaving. If the interest rate in the banks was not high enough, they would lend money on their own or put it in the kerb market. Or they would buy real estate. The amount of savings was clearly linked to the real interest rate even for very untutored people. Nor, for all their dedication, were they heros. They would not stick to their job, let alone make special efforts or come up with useful ideas, just because it was good for the company and the country. It had to be good for them as well.

That is why the assorted virtues could more readily be harnessed to the economy. It also explains why it was so important to use "carrots" as opposed to "sticks". People were in an admirable position to figure out what was good for them and to adapt their behavior accordingly. And they were not sloth when it came to finding incredibly intricate and convoluted ways of getting around the rules. While it would have been possible to force them to work harder, or oblige them to save more, or press them to show greater initiative, it was far easier to make it worth their while.

This need to offer incentives, to win their support, only increased later on when the economy improved somewhat. The traditional virtues were already fraying as each new generation had a notably different upbringing and the Confucian ethos weakened. When the threat of going hungry or homeless receded, there was less compulsion and the push had to be replaced by a pull. Eventually, most of the incentives had to be material and almost directly convertible into yen, or won, or dollars. Ultimately, among those who were reasonably well-off, even monetary rewards were somewhat disdained and people would simply not work as hard or ably as desired or save as much as wanted.

To maintain the work ethic, and the related virtues, it

was necessary to supplement the material rewards with moral encouragement of one sort or another. The oldest, most traditional, was an appeal to patriotism. In some places, the appeals never ended. But it was often less the positive call than a deep-seated urge to show the Westerners, or the Japanese, that Orientals, or Japan's former colonies, could accomplish wonders that drove them most. On a more personal level, there was a petty rivalry among individuals and families to show that they had achieved more than the next. Keeping up with the Kims, or the Suzukis, or the Changs, was as prevalent and perhaps more frantic than keeping up with the Joneses. And companies worked themselves to a frazzle to be one-up on the competitors.

The preservation of the work ethic was not always spontaneous. Often it was contrived. And it was most carefully and artificially cultivated where it mattered most, in the companies. Company executives, especially the founders, were extremely concerned about how their staff performed and they did not shun any stratagem to see that they made the grade. They blandished "carrots" more than any government and they used, or tried to use, a "stick" whenever possible. They pushed their workers on to extraordinary efforts by dangling better wages or special bonuses before their noses while doing their best not to give more than the next as that could ruin them.

The most prominent form of management in early years, and still very prevalent today, was paternalistic in which the owner worked with a relatively small staff on a rather intimate basis. Some of the personnel actually consisted of family members, who could obviously be pushed harder. The ordinary employees were somewhat subdued by such an environment and felt compelled to work as much as the rest. But they also enjoyed the closer relations, the periodic kindnesses, and the little favors or fringe benefits that were provided. Perhaps, just as much, they preferred avoiding the larger, more modern companies where things were too impersonal and precisely regulated.

Modern management, which eventually spread through Asia as well, consisted more of an exchange of services against money with a cold calculation on both sides of what it got for what it gave. However, by running larger factories in a more efficient manner, it was possible to earn more and thus safely pay more to the labor force. It was also possible to engage any number of foremen, supervisors, and productivity specialists to see that the workers did as much as possible in the allotted time.

However, it was not the modern Western management that squeezed that last bit of commitment from the workers. The Japanese have the honor, such as it is, of

Activist leadership:
Hyundai's Chairman Chung inspecting a construction site

Credit: Hundai

devising a system that draws employees so deeply into the company that they are forced to give almost limitlessly for the good of both the company and themselves. By providing better wages, greater status, and all sorts of fringe benefits, the leading Japanese firms attracted eager personnel. Since social security was inadequate, and the company pension essential, they held on to them. By linking wages and promotion to years of service, they made it ever harder to think of leaving. In return, they obtained a normal day's work, plus considerable overtime, plus contributions to quality control and suggestions, and even the right to impose the company's social life over that of the individual's private existence.[6]

While the company expected, and often extracted, very considerable dedication from the workers, it would be unfair to assume that this was purely gratuitous. The entrepreneurs had to discipline the workers because they were also coming under tremendous pressure, this time from relatively impersonal but no less powerful forces. Companies were being disciplined by the market which made them produce their goods at lower prices and yet with better quality if they wished to survive. With new companies regularly springing up, the pressure was unrelenting. And inability to shape up resulted not merely in loss of a job, as for a worker, but loss of the invested capital, perhaps liability for debts, and loss of face.

No matter how painful this situation was for both management and labor, it would be a bit simplistic to sum it all up as rank exploitation by cruel capitalists or "the system." An entrepreneur accepted the risks when establishing a company and could just as well, and probably more readily, have sought a job elsewhere. Employees knew that they would have a rough time in whatever job they took, but they could at least choose their employers to some extent. They did not hesitate to enter a sector, profession, or company that appealed to them more than others. Nor did they hesitate to leave it if they later felt they had been mistaken.

Although labor was not sufficiently organized to agitate for workers' rights as a class, each individual worker nonetheless preserved the ultimate recourse of quitting and going somewhere else. That will explain the prevalence of job-hopping, especially among the young. This, by the way, is not only a safety valve for the workers. In an expanding economy where labor is ever harder to come by, it is also an amazingly effective way of keeping management in line.

But it would be artificial and restrictive to consider the rise of these five economies purely in their own terms and by referring only to what is specific to the region. They were all part of a much broader movement that was sweeping the world and arousing them from an earlier slumber. For centuries, indeed millennia, Asian economies like most others had only grown fitfully and marginally due to one hazard or another. There was no conscious or sustained effort to raise them from one economic level to another, although some rulers naturally found their own position enhanced if they could sweat more out of their subjects. Confucianism, for all its virtues, assumed stability and order and actually worked against general economic improvement. Buddhism, with its otherworldliness and fatalism, was even worse.

It was not until the industrial revolution in England and the emergence of Western civilization that much attention was paid to how economies could be systematically improved. It was also only then that people, in some circles at least, adopted the previously implausible idea that societies should be judged by their progress. Those which ranked rather low were discredited and found worthy merely of tutorship by higher cultures. That was the fate of Korea and China, but not Japan which launched into a frenzy of activity, more to show the foreigners what it could accomplish and avoid control than for the intrinsic merits. After the Pacific War, however, other parts of the region also felt an urge to develop.

It was not only they. Around the world economic development became a crusade which was praised and promoted by both the poor and backward nations and the rich and advanced. Individually, over a hundred so-called "developing countries" formally proclaimed economic progress as a priority aim. Jointly, in the United Nations and related agencies, they launched one "development decade" after another. From something rare, economic advancement became the most popular and widespread policy in the world and any country which did not at least pay it lip service was seriously discredited.

In such an atmosphere, national leaders had little choice but to include economic development in their list of goals even if they had no special liking or inclination for it. Indeed, those who would have much preferred evading it were forced to adopt the goal as well and at least make symbolic gestures in that direction. Those who were seriously concerned, on the other hand, found their own wishes emphatically backed by national and international bodies and a rising tide of developmentism. That certainly strengthened the position of the more dynamic leaders and made it much easier for them to impose this as a priority.

No less significant is that, among the many goals which any leader could propose, there were very few which appealed to his fellow citizens quite as much as economic development. It was not without difficulties and required considerable discipline and sacrifice, but certainly less than any military adventure or political campaign. In return, it offered very welcome benefits in terms of higher wages, better working conditions, more comfort and leisure, some security for old age, and so on. There were very few who could resist that in the name of some pristine purity and the vast majority sought nothing more.

Thus, when one speaks of the leadership imposing its will on the people and making them put in long hours of hard work, it is not for something these people did not want. Quite to the contrary, even when the leaders did not raise such demands most ordinary citizens were willing to make these sacrifices themselves solely for the material rewards involved. Turning the personal, somewhat self-centered strivings of individuals into a higher and broader national movement for improvement and renewal added a moral element which some found comforting and others could exploit. The only hitch was that now the leaders had to deliver the goods. If people worked and sacrificed as they had been asked to, but the economic results did not come, then the leadership could be in deep trouble.

As noted, in these five countries, the economic upswing did come. And this, more than any government pressure or stirring appeals from the leaders, is what created the pull that caused people to throw themselves willingly into the crusade for development. As the economy expanded, suddenly countless opportunities arose that had hardly been dreamed of before. There were more chances than ever for someone with money, or intelligence, or muscles, or perseverance to make good. New industries were launched, new companies were founded and staffed, new jobs and entirely new professions were emerging. It was finally possible to trade the old life, with which one was not particularly satisfied, for something that was new and hopefully better.

This only accelerated the process of change. Literally millions of East Asians were moving in directions that to them at least looked like onward and upward. (That those directions were also useful for the economy was hardly noticed.) Vast hordes of youngsters from the rural districts, where they were often superfluous, went to the cities where they could find work. Simple peasants were becoming industrial operatives and high school graduates got office jobs. Girls could do a stint on the assembly line until they got married. People who had never run a company, perhaps never even worked for anyone, were now opening small establishments that with time might grow. Entrepreneurs who got the hang of things in one sector tried another. All of them were eagerly educating their children so that they could do better yet.

Outside observers will bemoan the "inhuman" conditions of East Asia's early "sweat shops" and crowded offices. True, they were beastly compared to what existed in the affluent West or what might be desired more ideally. But they were usually a vast improvement over life in the paddy fields. It took far more toil to grow rice and conditions were considerably more grueling, out in the sun or rain, slogging around in the mud, and not even certain that a drought or flood, cold spell or pests, would not destroy the harvest. It was also less soul-destroying than looking for work day after day and knowing that nothing attractive was available for semi-educated school leavers. As for the women, who were certainly less well treated, few foremen were as strict and demanding as the average mother-in-law.

No matter how apparently hard or demeaning the task,

it could be safely assumed that whoever was accomplishing it thought he or she was in a somewhat better position. Indeed, it would be presumptuous to conclude anything else. Few human beings are so stupid or reckless as to leave a job they dislike for one that is even more unpleasant. Rather, they carefully calculate what is in their interest and pursue it as best they can. Each time they move, they aspire to some sort of advancement. This is what makes the ferment and agitation of a period of growth so exciting to those concerned. It is this possibility of upgrading and self-realization which explains much of their hard work and also why they suddenly become more imaginative and innovative.

In a period of expansion, with new companies founded regularly and some of them growing spectacularly, they also tend to forget a bit of their petty egoism and accept to throw in their lot with one entrepreneur or another. While the more drab or mean cannot draw or hold on to employees, budding captains of industry or financial magnates have no trouble attracting masses of workers. They can instill a faith in their company which will lead many subordinates to work more than money could buy in order to help the company grow. Beyond this, there is often a vague yet pervasive feeling of helping the country rise as well. This breeds special forms of nationalism and patriotism which push the people a wee bit further and also give them a feeling of doing more than just looking after themselves.

This is what has occurred throughout East Asia. And, in this kind of context, economic development becomes not just an empty word or a distant dream but patent and almost palpable reality. Then there is not much need for the national leaders to brandish artificial and paltry incentives. It is the economy itself which offers all the inducements that are necessary and provides the rewards that make people strive. Moreover, with enough growth, they do not work grudgingly or sullenly. So much is happening and so much is possible that they inadvertently get carried away by a strange exhilaration that draws them into further rounds of activity that could never have been conceived of, let alone decreed.

This is extremely important to remember, especially for those who think of economics as a dismal science. It is, admittedly, very dreary when things don't work and improvement is so marginal that one barely notices. It is worse when an economy which once functioned well slows down and enters a marked decline. However, when things suddenly fall into place and the economy takes off, it is the most exciting science that exists. This is an atmosphere which breeds "tigers" and "dragons."

*   *   *

While it would be exceedingly pleasant to end on such a positive note, it would be intellectually dishonest to echo the official spokesmen or naive academics and journalists who infer that there is something almost "miraculous" about the East Asian population that explains the extraordinary upsurge. There is no doubt that people work hard, put in long hours, show imagination and drive. They do so to earn a living, or rise socially, or because they have some concern for their companies and nations. But they are not paragons of virtue and they cannot be automatically assumed to perform properly. More specifically, there are slews of pettifogging bureaucrats, narrow-minded politicians, lazy workers, incompetent entrepreneurs and national leaders of indifferent caliber. The best that can be said—and that happens to be enough—is that the average level in all categories has been sufficiently high to spur the economy, although never so high it could not be attained by others.

NOTES

1. See Park Chung Hee, *The Country, The Revolution And I.*
2. What happens when other things get in the way, as in the case of Syngman Rhee (ruling over the very same Korea), is traced in Joungwon A. Kim, *Divided Korea, the Politics of Development.*
3. The renovation of key personnel was most systematic and successful in Korea. See In-Joung Whang, "Elite Change and Program Change in the Korean Government, 1955–67," in *Korean Journal of Public Administration*, April 1969.
4. Herman Kahn, "East Asia's Four Young Tigers," *Modern Asia*, August 1979, p. 65.
5. See Bun Woong Kim, "The Korean Political Psyche and Administration" and "Confucianism and Administrative Development Intervention," in Bun Woong Kim and Wha Joon Rho (eds.), *Korean Public Bureaucracy*, pp. 117–45.
6. See Jon Woronoff, *Japan: The Coming Social Crisis.*

7

Diverse Faces of Capitalism

There is no doubt that all five countries showed a very firm commitment to economic development and aroused about as much will to succeed as could be expected. This was certainly to the good and is highly praiseworthy. Otherwise, it is very unlikely that much would have been achieved. Yet, it is equally clear that commitment and will alone would not have resulted in much economic development. People in East Asia had always worked hard, under one impulsion or compulsion or another, but they had never accomplished any exceptional upswing, let alone an economic "miracle."

It is therefore not possible to explain their recent economic history, as some simplistic or misguided "experts" on the region like to do, by purely social or moral phenomena.[1] It is necessary to delve into other aspects of their development process and ascertain why it was only this time that growth was so rapid and effective. This means one must take a good look at the underlying economic system that was adopted and see how it affected the inhabitants as economic actors and participants in the development process. In a sense, it is necessary to determine why, in addition to working hard, they were also working smart.

In a world plagued with "isms," the choice of which regime to adopt is more complex than it used to be. The primary options are capitalism, socialism and communism. But some nations have tried to combine them whereas others rejected the lot and retreated into autarky and isolationism. While one would assume that the Five must eventually settle for capitalism, that decision was not as simple or clear-cut as it might have seemed. There were numerous historical, political, cultural, practical and other factors that nudged certain leaders in diverging directions.

Obviously, all five countries were members of the "free world" which ritually pledged support of "liberalism" in economics and naturally chose "capitalism" as the basic system. As it happens, all five were even more fervently members of this broader community due to certain historical events. South Korea had fought a bloody war to throw back an invasion by the Communists, Taiwan was beleaguered by Communist China, and Japan was clearly in the American camp. Hong Kong had a huge refugee population and Singapore's government was worried about possibilities of subversion.

Under these conditions, it was hard to imagine any other decision. The more one compared oneself to the enemies, the more liberalism and capitalism appeared to be the only proper ideological choices. In addition, if one was pragmatic, as most of the leaders were, it was soon apparent that the potential economic benefits of capitalism were much greater than what could be attained by communism or even moderate socialism. Intent as they were on promoting development, they could not help noticing that the liberal economies were growing much faster and giving their peoples more of the good things of life.

The domestic political situation was also such that the leaders could hardly tamper with existing property rights, with the sole exception of farm land, if they wished to maintain broad support among the population. Also, the less the government meddled in the economic affairs of the people, the less irritation and resistance it was likely to arouse. Even where the citizens were relatively orderly and disciplined, they had traditionally had better relations with governments that let them go their own way without interfering too much.

All of these factors pointed irresistibly toward the maintenance of capitalism as the economic system. And, on the whole, it was preserved. Just what capitalism was may not have been crystal clear to everyone, whether in the elite or among the masses, but it certainly entailed two rather distinctive components.

The first condition was that private ownership of property and especially of the means of production be protected. Land, houses, factories, mines and so on were normally owned by individuals or corporations formed by them and only under exceptional circumstances, and with due compensation, could they be taken away. Moreover, the state was expected to restrict itself with regard to ownership of property and, even more so, any means of production.

The second essential feature was a bit harder to convey. Basically, it implied that the state would not intervene to decide how the economy functioned but would leave the crucial decisions to the free play of market forces and the autonomous and spontaneous decisions of the various economic actors as to how to respond to them. It would not try to influence events in one direction or another or pressure people into, or prevent them from, behaving other than in ways they regarded as fit.

This meant that certain natural yet invisible "economic laws" would prevail over conscious and arbitrary decisions of the powers-that-be. Comparative advantage would determine which production factors would be used and in which combinations, market equilibria would decide the prices for goods, wages, interest rates and so on. Entrepreneurs would move into one sector or another on the basis of potential gains and workers would sell their labor where it brought the best remuneration.

Relatively impersonal market forces would not only fix the price of shoes or the wage for a bricklayer, they would accomplish some more intricate operations. They would decide, for example, whether a country should place stress on textiles or steel by offering better returns for one product or the other. Goods would be sold at home or abroad depending on the prices they fetched. Even more crucially, they would determine which entrepreneurs should rise or fall because successful ones would have reacted more wisely to the market signals.

This is roughly the system to which all five countries, under their successive leaders, were committed. But this does not mean that they particularly liked it, or at any rate all of it, and it does not mean that they were willing to accept it in all its particulars. As a matter of fact, there was only one place that was willing to play the game by the strictest rules, namely Hong Kong. Elsewhere, there were other influences at work.

In the four other countries there were very mixed feelings about the capitalist system. As might be expected of "dragon" economies, many of the political leaders were activists and not so inclined to leave things to chance. While they praised the aspects of free enterprise, individual responsibility and an abundance of opportunity, this may have been partially lip service. For, in the political sphere, they had forcefully created regimes that were strikingly different. It was usually one in which the leader, often with an elite bureaucracy, took most of the decisions and expected rather meek compliance from the people. Some of them were almost Confucian-style rulers and it was hard for them not to expect their will to be done in such an important area as economic progress.

Moreover, they had serious doubts about the ability of the people, the common and ordinary people, to adapt to what looked like a very complicated system. After all, few of their citizens had ever been engaged in commerce and hardly any were familiar with industry. How should simple peasants and tradesmen or their offspring know how to navigate in the complex world of market forces? How could they, or indeed anybody, know exactly what the market signals indicated or be able to adjust their behavior rapidly enough? Equilibria were fine, for those who benefited, but many others would get hurt and eventually come to the state for redress.

It was not even as if the leaders could be blamed for that sort of thinking. The people, the common and ordinary people, were also a little bit perplexed about how things worked and were not always willing to bow to market forces. In fact, many of the first generation businessmen systematically sought real or artificial monopolies where they would be safe. Others pressed for tariff and similar protection behind which they could grow. And there was a constant barrage on the government to help this venture, or to prevent damage to the other, or to build essential infrastructure for one project or another.[2]

The people, even more than the government, tended to conceive of economic progress mainly in terms of the affluence and ease it could bring. They would look toward more advanced countries and insist that they have the same kind of living conditions. The state should provide better housing, it should add proper amenities, it should open schools and hospitals and preferably subsidize them. Finally, it should provide the safety net of health and unemployment insurance, social security and old age pensions. None of these people were militating for socialism, heaven forbid! They simply wanted what was increasingly regarded as right and proper for enlightened societies.

This will explain why the "capitalist" regimes that were installed in the five countries varied so considerably. The span from state-dominated economies in Korea and Taiwan, to a mixed one in Japan, and more liberal entities in Singapore and Hong Kong, was incredibly vast. Indeed, there was cause to wonder whether certain regimes did not occasionally go too far.

In Korea and Taiwan, there was substantial state ownership of property, which is secondary, but also of means of production, which is a more striking deviation. They had literally dozens of production facilities under their control and the public sector represented a notable share of total output. Some of these were basic services like power, post and telecommunications, railroads and so on that were often state-run elsewhere. But there was a more serious breach when they went into purely industrial operations like steelmaking, shipbuilding or petrochemicals.

When it comes to intervention in the workings of the economy, they were even more at variance with classical capitalism. Korea ran what could fairly be regarded as a form of "state capitalism." This was a command economy where many of the essential decisions of private businessmen were strongly influenced by the state, when it did not simply give orders or act on its own.[3] That was basically the purpose of planning and targeting, when it was decided from above which sectors were the appropriate ones to enter or whether to make greater efforts at exporting. Such exercises in Taiwan were somewhat looser and freer, and in Japan and Singapore yet more so. But they still implied flagrant tampering with the market forces because they consisted not only of official urging or private persuasion but concrete, and sometimes almost compelling, inducements to move in the desired direction.

What was in some ways even more delicate, and also further removed from pure *laissez-faire*, were the individual measures directed not at a given sector or practice but specific companies. The close relations which arose between certain political leaders or bureaucrats and certain businessmen most definitely gave the latter substantial advantages. Korea's policy of "backing winners" meant that once selected entrepreneurs had withstood the test of the market place long enough they would no longer have to worry if they followed the state's instructions. In Japan and Taiwan, such particularistic relations existed as well, but more often in the interest of the businesses concerned.

The Singapore government, while sharing some of the proclivities of more domineering states, did limit both its commercial operations and intervention. Its plans and guidelines were largely indicative, its incentives relatively secondary, and the top leadership only intervened in vital cases. Japan was even stricter on keeping out of commercial activities, aside from the increasingly few public corporations it ran. Planning became so amorphous as to be almost meaningless. But active backing of specific industries and projects was very widespread and often decisive.[4]

Hong Kong, on the other hand, was exceptionally scrupulous in abiding by both particulars. It held only the property that was necessary for its own operations or to raise revenue and engaged in no commercial activities aside from very basic public services like water and sanitation. The government did its best to avoid influencing ordinary business dealings one way or the other. Even when pressed by the business community or special interests, it tried not to intervene and placed its faith in the market forces to restore order in due course. Thus, it was the purest upholder of the creed which was the least typical of the Five.

This provides a very broad range of "capitalist" economies. In fact, the gap could hardly be wider than between Korea's *dirigiste* economy and the almost pristine *laissez-faire* of Hong Kong. Yet, all of them were solidly on the capitalist side of the fence and even those who went furthest could not be mistaken for communists or even socialists. No matter how it was restricted or influenced, there was always an extremely energetic and aggressive private sector which managed to take the lead. Entrepreneurs accumulated most of the capital and made most of the decisions. While they had one eye on the plan, the other was on the balance sheet. And the feedback from business to government was substantial.

At the same time, although this sort of reflection is rarely made, they were all truly "capitalist" in another sense. It is sometimes felt that an absence of state control or intervention is enough to qualify as capitalist and under this dispensation dozens of developing countries in the Third World slip into that category. Yet, as Hong Kong showed, non-intervention cannot be mistaken for indifference and the state must do everything it can—within certain limits—to see that the economy is progressing smoothly. It must provide certain fundamental things which are indispensable, whether concrete infrastructure, essential social institutions or maintenance of law and order. This is what distinguishes it, and all Five, from places which are not so much liberal as poorly organized, "soft" or anarchic.

The skimpiest description of the Five countries is quite

Hong Kong does not neglect physical planning

Credit: GIS

enough to show that "capitalism" is a very broad term that can cover a considerable variety of practices. Rather than a specific model, it would seem to be a theme on which many variations are possible. One of the most intriguing conclusions from studying the East Asian Five is therefore that, despite these remarkable differences, they were all able to make a go of economic development. They all managed to expand and diversify the economy, increase employment and income, and attain very impressive growth rates.

If one were to stop at this point, it could perhaps be argued that it really does not matter much which variation is chosen and that it is all a question of taste. In some countries, the rulers are stronger and wish to control as much as they can. In others, they are less dynamic or more circumspect and leave economic affairs more to the people. Equally plausible is the idea that in some more backward countries, those having the least familiarity with a modern economy, the state has to intervene to make up for deficiencies in the economic maturity of the population or to take greater advantage of limited financial and human resources. It may also be preferable to have a more collective or centralized approach in countries whose people have a long and abiding tradition of cooperation while highly individualistic people should be given greater leeway.[5]

There is doubtlessly a grain of truth in this. It would be foolish to forget the existence of deep-rooted customs and traditions arising from the culture or religion. And it would be pointless to ignore the inevitable influence of the personality of the leaders. Like it or not, they will mold the basic institutions, whether capitalist or communist, and make them look like something very different from the textbook model of how things are supposed to be done. If the system still works, so much the better. Since all five economies have been outstanding successes it might seem petty and quibbling to push ahead and seek a more "ideal" format.

Nevertheless, there are some intriguing trends which cannot be ignored. They are particularly significant since they all gravitate in the same direction.

It has been hypothesized, and often persuasively argued, that communism and socialism are much simpler systems than capitalism. The state, which is at the center of things, is in a far better position than a multitude of individuals widely dispersed about the country to know what is going on and take the best decisions. In addition, it has the foremost machinery and wisest personnel.[6] If they decide such an industry is useful, they are more likely to be right. If they promote it, this industry is more likely to see the light of day. If they want to boost exports, and take strong measures for that, exports are bound to multiply. And so on. The lesser economic actors, with a partial knowledge of the facts and considering only their own interests, could hardly adopt a policy that is beneficial to the nation as a whole and can be accomplished as efficiently.

Unfortunately, it has turned out not to be so easy for the state and its leaders to know what is going on throughout the nation or to influence this. Statistics are often sparse and unreliable, so the starting point is already a matter of conjecture. Is is hard to know what natural resources are available, who possesses which skills and can work at which tasks, and what industries stand a chance of success. If the products are to be exported, there is even greater uncertainty about potential markets and the likely competition. Thus, promoting specific sectors is very risky since the conditions may not be ripe. If financial assistance, protective barriers or manipulation of the market are used to compensate for any inherent lacks, the sector may succeed in a very artificial and costly manner.

When it comes to the details, things are even more involved. It is not only a question of launching a given industry but of shaping it to fit the needs of a myriad of other industries which it supplies or depends on. In consumer branches, it is incredibly difficult to figure out how many of what product, of what size, or color, at what price, etc. will find acceptance among the masses of buyers. The best place for getting this sort of data is never the center but rather the periphery, among those who sell the goods and should be able to feed back the information. That, alas, goes against the prevailing current of directives being channeled from the center out and, in more cases than not, from the top down as well.

Finally, running an economy is not only a question of producing what is desired and getting it to the customers.

No matter how unpalatable this may be to some, it is equally necessary to make a profit out of it. Profits, although hardly as uplifting as nation building, are the essential lubricant of an economy since they are the source of wages for the workers, taxes for the government, further investment or earnings for the entrepreneurs. Profits, among other things, are also the primary market signals for most of the crucial economic decisions. Yet, it has turned out that politicians and bureaucrats are uncommonly poor at developing a feel for profits or even the need to avoid deficits and losses.

These various considerations are not theoretical by any means. The worst examples naturally come from the communist countries where production is usually inadequate, although sometimes excessive, since it has been impossible to produce what was desired. But even among the Five, the four more *dirigiste* countries, despite their overall positive performance, have made mistakes of this sort. The mistakes were proportionately more numerous in those countries which went the furthest toward state control and direction, namely Korea, Taiwan and Japan.

Planning has occasionally resulted in sectors that were too large, whether run by the state or private companies. This was the case for petrochemicals throughout the region and shipbuilding in Korea and Japan. This excess capacity, by the way, depressed the prices in these industries and resulted in losses or a need of subsidies. Other sectors were stunted because they had inadequate access to credit. They were usually related to consumer goods and services and sometimes housing. More significantly, there has been growing criticism of the performance of many of the state and semi-state corporations in Korea and Taiwan while the Japan National Railways is a complete mess.[7]

Meanwhile, and somewhat to the chagrin of the government, it turned out that capitalism was not such a complicated system that it could not be applied by ordinary people. The market signals, which had to be obeyed, were unexpectedly clear and persuasive. Usually, they were easer to fathom than the rather convoluted legislation and nebulous guidelines. Moreover, the penalty for not following them was not an admonition or fine but financial disaster. Those who guessed right were generously rewarded.

Market signals affected the entrepreneurs by indicating which sectors showed greater promise. Those in which production was still inadequate offered better returns on investment than those which were already crowded. If a particular product became popular, one could do extremely well. If the products of a given manufacturer were cheaper, or of higher quality, or delivery dates were regularly met, he would tend to prosper. If not, he would either have to improve his performance or disappear. When labor was cheap and machinery expensive, simple cost calculations drove him to use more of the former. If the relationship altered, rising wages for labor would encourage him to buy more machinery. If he could earn more in foreign countries than at home, he would export.

Laborers also followed the market signals.[8] For them, the most salient ones were the wages for alternative work. If rice commanded a good price, the farmer would grow that. If he earned more for vegetables, he would put more of his land into truck gardening. When factories sprang up and offered good wages, he might work there part-time and some of his children would move to the city. There, they would get unskilled work in a factory or, if educated, clerical work in an office, taking the type that offered the best rewards. When their skills improved, they would climb upward in the same company or elsewhere. They might even think of starting their own firm if they saw a chance of getting ahead.

When seen at this practical level, the market signals were exceedingly plain and convincing. If anything, it sometimes seemed that they were much too clear and emphatic and could actually be disruptive. They could lead to too many entrepreneurs rushing into a more promising sector. And this happened. But only the more successful stayed. Or, they could lead to a lot of job-hopping. And this also happened, especially in earlier years. But it was important then to have a lot of mobility so that new companies could be formed and new sectors opened. Finally, it might happen that the labor force would lose its zeal for hard work and think more of rewards. This, too, was a concomitant of the process. Still, was there any reason why people should not seek a better life?

The state's continuing troubles and periodic blunders and a growing business sense among the people wrought a gradual change in the system. It was reluctantly admitted that it was not so easy for planners to pick winners among industries. And it was considerably more difficult for bureaucrats to run the actual production facilities. This led to a perceptible downgrading of planning in Korea, which was made increasingly indicative and where the once almost sacrosanct targets were no longer obligatory. The same process had already taken place in Taiwan and Japan with much less fanfare, since the authorities had not gone as far to begin with.[9]

There was also a trend toward privatization of industry. Some state corporations had done reasonably well and could be maintained. Others provided basic inputs for many downstream producers and had to be upheld at any cost. But more and more entities were sold off to private entrepreneurs or individual shareholders.

In some ways, the most crucial step has been to relax the control on the commercial banks which makes the whole machinery for funding business more liberal. Only in cases where losses would be disastrous, or the government had already invested too much, were there moves toward new acquisitions. Thus, the public sector had reached its crest and was ebbing.

The other side of this turnabout is somewhat less discernable but no less significant. It involves the power relationship between the government and the private sector. It also stemmed from the increasing ability and drive of the entrepreneurs. As their companies grew, and could do quite nicely alone, the advantages of accepting government tutelage no longer outweighed the disadvantages. By now, they knew what to do on their own and did not need anyone else's advice. Meanwhile, the politicians (and even bureaucrats) discovered that they could make enemies just as well as friends by helping some and indirectly hurting—or at least slighting—others. The best way to maintain decent relations all around was to keep out of the hurly-burly of business as much as possible.

The outcome was a more open and balanced partnership between the government (basically the political leadership and top bureaucracy) and business circles. There was a shift away from a Korea, Inc. where the state was plainly in charge and toward a Japan, Inc. in which the business community was slightly predominant. But, if present trends continue, it could eventually result in a situation where the two parties are not so closely entwined and in which it really is the market forces that determine most of the essential economic actions. This is a clear alignment on the position of Hong Kong and Singapore which had only become marginally more interventionist in the meantime.

Thus, the capitalist option has become even firmer

than it was at the outset. State ownership and intervention have receded. The private sector has definitely advanced. And market signals presently enjoy the same sort of respect that was once reserved for catchy slogans about a strong industry making a strong country or exports being the highest form of economic endeavor. With this, the gaps between these five initially very different regimes are closing with a movement toward more liberalism rather than less. Henceforth, the "miracles" should be more spontaneous and less contrived.

NOTES

1. For a particularly good (bad) example, see Herman Kahn, *World Economic Development: 1979 and Beyond.*
2. While this is a very general phenomenon, a curious manifestation was the rise of what were called the "political capitalists" in Korea. See Kyong-Dong Kim, *Man and Society in Korean Economic Growth*, pp., 67–80.
3. The government-business relationship in Korea is particularly well documented. See, among others, Leroy P. Jones and Il SaKong, *Government, Business and Entrepreneurship.*
4. It is a pity that more does not exist on the government-business relationship in Japan. An inkling of what goes on can be gained from Jon Woronoff, *Inside Japan, Inc.*
5. Such views are naturally espoused primarily by the leaders and their supporters. They are best illustrated by the writings of Park Chung Hee, including *The Country, The Revolution And I.*
6. The paradigm of the elite organization is Japan's Ministry of International Trade and Industry. On its political (but not economic) role, see Chalmers Johnson, *MITI And The Japanese Miracle.*
7. Stories of these troubles appear regularly in the local and regional newspapers and magazines such as *Asian Business, Asian Wall Street Journal, Business Korea* and *Far Eastern Economic Review.*
8. How this operates in Korea, and doubtlessly the other four, is analyzed in Sookon Kim, "Employment, Wages and Manpower Policies in Korea," Seoul, Korea Development Institute, 1982.
9. Nothing has reduced the government's clout more than the inability to offer financial support. See Yukio Noguchi, "The Government-Business Relationship in Japan: The Changing Role of Fiscal Resources," in Kozo Yamamura (ed.), *Policy and Trade Issues of the Japanese Economy*, pp. 123–42.

8

Conjuring Up Industries

Picking capitalism, and establishing the corresponding machinery, was a very big step. But it would have led nowhere if the Five were not able to use the system properly. Capitalism is not a magic formula that merely has to be uttered or a sacred principle that just has to be invoked for an economy to flourish. That it is no panacea has been proven incontrovertibly by the majority of those who supposedly practice it. Rather, the onus lies with those who proclaim capitalism to subject themselves to its rules.

Unlike socialism or communism, capitalism was initially nothing more than an acceptance of seemingly natural "laws" which operated best when least interfered with by external influences, such as the arbitrary action of governments or collusion among owners of essential inputs, producers, or workers. It involved a respect for market forces which indicated what should be done and when. The most noticeable signal, and the spring for most efforts, was profit. By seeking profit, the economic actors could contribute not only to their own well-being but the greater prosperity of mankind. To make the ideology more palatable, when faced by the noble sentiments of the other "isms," the accent was placed on freedom, as in free enterprise and free trade. But there was no freedom to ignore or disobey the market signals if one hoped to succeed.

Within this framework, it was necessary for politicians, bureaucrats, businessmen, farmers, workers, consumers, in short, everyone, to determine what they should do and how. In the economist's jargon, this meant to seek their comparative advantage. In simpler terms, it meant doing what one is best at, this best being defined as what brings the greatest return. Every person can do some things better than others and also some things better than other people. In like manner, every country, rich or poor, advanced or backward, can do some things better than other things and also, even for the worst off, it can do some things better than other countries. This depends basically on its endowment of various production factors. They must be carefully considered to find the most promising directions.

For some, it may be hard to determine which way to turn since they have so many opportunities. In the case of the Five, the situation was painfully clear. In each one of these countries, land was in terribly short supply and in some places the climate was not very good either. They had very little mineral wealth or sources of energy. They were quite poor, possessing scant capital and unable or unwilling to borrow much more. The only factor they had in any abundance was labor. If anything, it was often overabundant and grossly underutilized.

With this combination of factors, it was perfectly obvious that, with the sole exception of Taiwan, there was not much point in specializing in agriculture. They could only go so far due to population pressure and other limitations. Even if farming were developed further, and there was certainly some room for improvement, sooner rather than later the law of diminishing returns would set in. Mining, aside from some few ores in some scattered places, was even less encouraging. Services, especially those which used considerable labor, were a possibility and many, probably far too many people were already engaged in that sector. But their contribution was increasingly marginal.

By process of elimination, the only field which offered much potential was industry. That was partly for the rather limp reason that so few articles were manufactured locally at the outset that any increment was welcome. There was nowhere to go but up and even quite awkward efforts brought gratifying progress. The intrinsically more important reason was that industry was able to absorb some of the excess labor. Also, certain specific branches were able to put labor to more intensive use and therefore showed even greater promise than otherwise.

The introduction of labor-intensive manufacturing was the reasoned conclusion of professional economists and planners when they considered the fate of East Asia. It was a proposal that even the most unenlightened politicians could understand and the concept was so clear that most governments eventually adopted it formally. Meanwhile, without any particular prompting, budding entrepreneurs had figured this out for themselves and were launching one simple product after another. This made the solution not only evident but generally acceptable.

Still, even then, it was not so easy to pursue this comparative advantage rationally. Low cost labor, more disparagingly called "cheap labor," has never been a popular asset. While no one would hesitate to mine ores, drill for oil, farm fertile and well-watered fields, or engage in sophisticated manufacturing, there has always been—and probably always will be—a strong stigma against making cheap labor the basis of an economy. Despite the dire need and abject poverty, many national leaders and local businessmen tried to avoid this and lay a different foundation for growth. Each time they did, it crumbled while more benighted efforts that were based on this one abundant factor managed to rise up.

It was only by admitting the value of cheap labor, and avoiding the temptations to tread other, more appealing or dignified paths, that the fledgling "tigers" and "dragons" got started. This applies to every one of them, including Japan, whose economy was as primitive and labor-intensive as could be imagined during the early period of development about a century ago and was still rather dependent on labor even in the first and second decade of postwar growth. In the other Four, it is possible even now to visit factories which are overflowing with workers and rather short on equipment . . . although this is a much rarer view than before.

While most chroniclers of East Asia's economic rise quickly pass over this introductory period and regard it with some embarrassment, it is essential to pause a good moment and consider it at length if one is ever to understand how the reputed "miracles" came about. For, at their inception, they were most definitely miracles of cheap labor and little more.[1] As indicated, the countries possessed very few other assets. More significantly, it is impossible to impute the success, as is so often done, to cheap *and* well-trained, experienced, or disciplined workers.

When economic development began to unfold, the workers throughout the factories of East Asia hardly merited that name. They were overwhelmingly of peasant extraction and thus had no prior acquaintance with an industrial economy. Those who, like the daughters of poorer *samurai* or *yongban* and the children of former tradesmen or merchants, could lay claim to some greater education or familiarity with business, still had no experience in an industrial context. And their skills were not overly useful, anyway. For, all that was really asked of the first batches of factory hands was that they should be able to master some very rudimentary tasks, often just a few motions that were repeated endlessly, and then endure the incredibly harsh conditions and tiring hours. This, not all could do. And the mobility of workers and turnover of personnel were extremely high.[2]

It was this willingness to accept hard, tedious, lengthy service which represented one of the desired assets of the early labor force. The other was that it should be cheap. That was ensured by various circumstances. The population was already exceedingly large, and growing too rapidly to be absorbed in the traditional farming sector. Indeed, due to improvements there, the more common situation was one of rural exodus with untold thousands of peasants flocking to the city to seek work. They were not very demanding, given the generally low level of income throughout the country and an ability nonethless to survive at such a modest level. To this, of course, must be added the fact that workers were highly dependent on management, terribly grateful to get any job, and unorganized and unable to agitate for better conditions.

This gave East Asian labor forces a formidable, if not particularly laudable, advantage over their counterparts in the more advanced countries . . . and not the other way around. After all, workers in Meiji-day Japan and in Korea, Taiwan, Hong Kong and Singapore not so long ago, were only paid about one-eighth as much. This made them only one eighth as costly which meant that for exactly the same money it was possible to get eight times as much work out of them. Or more. For, in truth, they put in more hours a week, more days a year, and also toiled much harder during every one of those hours than the better paid and better organized workers in the West. The real differential was probably closer to ten, fifteen or even twenty.

What manufacturers in more advanced countries had going for them, and could largely compensate for the considerable disadvantage in labor costs, was more machinery. This machinery was obviously much more productive and it made Western workers more efficient. If the man-machine combination could do, say, twenty or thirty times as much work (since we must consider the cost of buying the machine), then the advanced countries could still win out. But, if the differential were not as great, or machinery could not be so easily used, or Asian companies bought the same machinery or equipment

Garments still remain highly labor-intensive

Credit: HKTDC

almost as good, the competitive edge would shift back in their direction.

The trick therefore is not just to use labor lavishly because it is cheap but to use it where labor is decisive. It is necessary to select industries that are particularly labor-intensive and, in other sectors, to find specific processes or operations that need more labor than the rest. While some authorities complain that this is increasingly difficult, if not impossible, there have always been such opportunities and they will continue to exist in the future. Those who find them can make a go of it even if their only asset is "cheap labor."[3]

When the Japanese first got started, back in Meiji days, one major source of earnings was silk production. The silk worms had to be raised and raw silk separated from the cocoon with incredibly delicate and time-consuming care. This was soon overshadowed by textile production, initially on very simple hand and then power looms. Obviously, silk produciton is unlikely to induce the birth of another economy today. But many products still require tremendous hand work. Among them are most of the crafts as well as footwear, toys, plastic articles, tableware, furniture and so on. While textiles are now heavily automated, some branches are not. And garments still constitute a huge area in which labor is extremely important due to the unquenchable urge for changing fashions and distinctiveness. Such products therefore remain vital elements of industry in contemporary Hong Kong, Taiwan or Korea.

This is not the end of the line by far.[4] It is not only a question of making a number of specific products which require plentiful labor. Assembly of just about everything is highly labor-intensive. It is necessary to put together dozens, hundreds, even thousands of components to make items as varied as radios and televisions, motorcycles and automobiles, machine tools and sewing machines. For this reason alone, the assembly portion may be transferred to countries with low labor costs or they can launch production on their own by importing knock-down kits. Of course, they may be excluded or become uncompetitive where the processes can be mechanized, automated or robotized. But that is not always so easy. And it is pointless where the production runs are relatively small.

What is most intriguing about the Five, however, is that they did not limit themselves to those sectors where cheaper labor has a striking advantage or stick to assembly-line work and production of fashion-oriented or short-run articles. They used its merits to break into many other sectors one would think they could never enter. This they did by exploiting the one or two crucial elements in a much larger operation in which they seemingly had no special advantage.

There is no more fascinating example of this than the Korean shipbuilding industry. Modern ships are such intricate products that, at the outset, the Koreans only had the capability to make the steel body and some of the cruder equipment. But this did not hold them back. They simply purchased the engine and more complex gear from Japan or Europe. Yet, the savings on the labor-intensive body work was enough for them to undercut Japanese and European shipyards. For electronics, despite their technological limitations, the NICs could even manufacture highly sophisticated articles. They made many of the standard components and assembled ordinary products, both more cheaply than Japan or America. All that was missing were a few special parts, which could readily be procured abroad.

The intelligent use of cheap labor was thus enough to get the East Asians not only into a number of simple product lines but some rather advanced ones as well. Still, there was a limit to how far it would take them. The reason the development process, originally sparked by cheap labor, could continue so long is that they were able to continue adapting to the changing factor endowment and comparative advantage rather than cling to their original positions.

While all five countries remained poor in land and natural resources, their economic growth permitted them to acquire another production factor which was previously exceedingly scarce, namely capital. Some of the money that was earned on manufactured goods could be pumped back into the companies in order to expand and also to upgrade. Additional machinery was bought which meant that the same workers could now accomplish much more than before without working nearly as hard. Indeed, the increase in plant and equipment was extraordinary. In some sectors, the capital stock was soon so great that Japan was able to supersede just about every country in the world. Even the NICs, in those sectors which interested them most, had equipment that was among the best.[5]

This resulted in a gradual, but very noticeable and relatively rapid shift from labor-intensive to capital-intensive production. By further improving the educational system in their countries, having their workers attend school longer or engage in more on-the-job training, the technical level could also be enhanced. This made the salient feature of East Asian workers much less cheapness than ability. They were finally becoming the well-trained, experienced and disciplined workers which their managers doted on and admiring foreigners finally recognized. That provided the necessary basis for the simultaneous shift from labor-intensive to technology-intensive industry.

Although part of this movement sprang from the lofty ambitions of the local government or business circles, it was hardly a contrived or artificial process. The changes in the industrial base paralleled the changes in comparative advantage. Even if more machinery could be purchased because companies earned enough money, the move was much more a consequence of the growing awareness that labor was losing its edge. It was no longer possible to rely solely on cheap labor to compete. For one, labor in all five countries had become increasingly expensive. Japanese workers earned about as much as those in some parts of Europe, if not yet as much as American or German workers. And even those in the NICs had moved from a mere eighth to about a quarter or a third of the level in advanced countries. At the same time, they were facing competition from even poorer countries in the Third World which were really cheap.

The only way to compete effectively was to decrease the amount of labor and increase the amount of capital correspondingly. This also required an elevation of the technological level. And it implied another form of upgrading which was just as crucial and difficult, an improvement in quality. Selling more sophisticated goods, goods which were costly enough that one wanted better design, greater reliability, longer durability, or the like, more attention had to be paid to how carefully goods were produced. In this process as well the East Asians did very nicely. Japan became renowned for its fine quality. While the same could less often be said of the others, they were making notable headway.

While all five countries were similar in accepting the need to adapt to comparative advantage, and then reshape the economy as comparative advantage itself changed, there were noteworthy differences in how they did this. For some, it was largely spontaneous and left to the individual entrepreneurs to worry about. In others, it was felt that some degree of guidance or intervention, this emanating from the government, would help expedite the transition. It was this latter trend, and the various policies and institutions that characterized it, which was most often seen as typical and distinctive in East Asia and was also frequently assumed to be the true source of the "miracle."

In the more controlled or guided economies, there was a strong inclination to feel that it was impossible to count essentially on market forces and the flair of local entrepreneurs to determine the actual comparative advantage. They were, or so it seemed, too few and too inexperienced to know much about such things. Even if they could figure out a positive combination for their own companies, it was far from certain that all of their isolated and self-centered decisions would add up to the correct policy for the nation as a whole. Furthermore, they might be too weak or too poor to act on their hunches whereas, by bringing the greater power of the state to bear, a more vigorous stance could be taken.

This was already sufficient cause, in the view of the authorities, to have more of the decisions as well as the broader framework provided by the government, most often in the form of action by groups of technocrats or bureaucrats. But there was a further concept that eventually clinched the argument and made the state feel it must take the lead. While, assuming everything went well, it might be conceivable for entrepreneurs to correctly gauge the existing comparative advantage on the basis of the market signals, it was out of the question for them to guess what the future comparative advantage would be. To profit from a "dynamic" comparative advantage as opposed to a mere static one, it was wiser to trust in the broader and higher vision possessed by the national leadership.

Reasoning of this sort was very prominent in Korea, which went furthest along the road of state guidance during the Park era. In Taiwan, under the Kuomintang, it was also quite popular . . . in government circles at least. A similar tack, although naturally less formalized and structured, prevailed in some areas during Japan's early industrialization. Prior to and during the Pacific War, the state controlled the economy in its smallest details. This influence did not entirely disappear during reconstruction and government direction, real or apparent, has survived in one form or another to the present day. Even Singapore was not fully immune from the temptation, although it remained more liberal on the whole.

These countries therefore created a superstructure which arrogated the right—or duty—to take a rather wide range of economic decisions in the place of the entrepreneurs. The specific institutions created and the precise policies differed considerably from one case to the next, but there was a reasonably broad consensus on what had to be done. The approach usually consisted of three elements: planning, industrial policy, and targeting.

Korea, Taiwan and Japan all established economic planning bodies of one sort or another. The effectiveness of this machinery varied considerably over time but the general impression is that planning was most influential in Korea, less so in Taiwan, and of uncertain significance in Japan. The reason for these differences arose partly from the scope of the plans, going into greater detail in the former than the latter, being relatively compulsory in the former and quite indicative in the latter. Equally important was the fact that in Korea and Taiwan the planning body was near the top of the administrative hierarchy and enjoyed considerable authority, while in Japan it was much lower in the pecking order.

There is no doubt that planning played a useful role. It was able to mobilize resources, financial and other, and direct them toward some of the more desirable purposes, such as were laid down in the respective plans. It was possible to avoid much overlapping and duplication, prevent unfortunate gaps and bottlenecks, and expand the economic base. Even when the plans were not strictly enforced, they did serve as a guideline or at least an indication to all concerned of what the goals were and where the economy should be heading.[6]

While overall planning was significant, an even sharper focus and more concentrated efforts were mounted specifically for industrialization. Since manufacturing was to be the leading growth sector, it had to receive higher priority in terms of funds, manpower, and so on. Thus, beyond the plan, there were other operations undertaken to encourage the sector and which were gradually comprised in the idea of an industrial policy. This arose from formal programs and much more informal cooperation between bureaucrats and businessmen.[7]

Industrial policy went into very great detail. It specified not only which narrower branches of industry but often exactly which products should be encouraged to differing degrees. Whether openly or more covertly, it sometimes also concluded which companies should partake in a sector and what their respective roles should be. Industrial policy was partly accomplished by the planning body. But it was directed and controlled even more by the ministry in charge of industry. This ascendancy was unmistakable in Japan where the Ministry of International Trade and Industry bluntly pushed the Economic Planning Agency aside.

One of the most crucial issues of industrial policy was whether that state itself should create and foster industries or whether this should be done by the private sector. Here, there was a parting of the ways between Korea and Taiwan, which let the state initiate and sometimes dominate such key sectors as oil refining, petrochemicals, steel and shipbuilding. In Japan, like the more liberal economies, the state left almost all of the actual investment and management of such ventures to private companies. This naturally diminished the state's role and made its influence more indirect.

Industrial policy could theoretically have applied to all industries indiscriminately, without stressing any one in particular. However, since the purpose of the whole exercise was to give a sharp impetus to certain key sectors, it was not surprising that it established priorities. Taking this a step further, another strategy evolved which was ultimately called "targeting." This time, the government or planners would pick one or more specific areas on which very strong emphasis would be placed in order to bring about a decisive breakthrough. After it was achieved, the focus would be moved to other areas unless, as for electronics, there were so many individual products that one after the other was targeted.[8]

While planning and industrial policy were both oriented toward the future, fostering sectors which did not yet have but should eventually possess a comparative advantage, in targeting the idea of "dynamic" comparative advantage was most drastic. The areas chosen were rarely those which had been entered by local entrepreneurs because they felt they still did not have the necessary capital, manpower or technology. Yet the state deemed that, according to its projections, it would be possible to sustain them later on. Rather than waiting for a natural—but slower—process to occur, it was willing to throw its full weight behind a major assault on the given branch or product.

Thanks to planning, industrial policy and targeting, there is no doubt that the three countries concerned made remarkable progress, especially in their priority fields. They also managed to put together economies that were broader and deeper than would have been feasible if the task were left to private businessmen alone. Their success is so patent and visible that there is not much sense in attempting to prove it.

What is more imperative, and more controversial, is to show that for all its advantages this development path also had drawbacks and disadvantages. For, as must be obvious, it is not so easy to determine comparative advantage, not even for the government with all its technocrats, bureaucrats, planners and advisors. Worse, once the policies start influencing the flows of funds and personnel, it is extremely difficult to even perceive what the comparative advantage is. In trying to anticipate it, the real prices and values of things are concealed or distorted and the market signals are masked or go on at the wrong times.[9]

Negative results can take two forms. It is possible to invest, not just moderately but very heavily, in sectors that did not and perhaps never will possess a comparative advantage. Or, not quite as bad, it is possible to invest in more suitable sectors too early or too much. In the first instance, much of the investment is wasted. This happened for metal refining and petrochemicals in all three countries, where the industries had to be cut back almost as soon as they were built up. Otherwise, there could be varying degrees of overcapacity, as for Japan's steel industry, Korea's machine tool project and shipbuilding throughout the region.

The other form is much harder to detect, although it may be equally detrimental. That is a lack of investment in those areas which were not targeted. When most of the resources and talent are directed toward some few sectors, it is unavoidable that less is left over for the others. Some of them may have been just as promising, but the planners did not realize this. With inadequate resources to develop, they never materialized and were never missed. Helping rising sectors also works against those which are assumed to be losing their comparative advantage since they are starved of funds prematurely and decline faster than necessary. More generally, this can

The labor-intensive end of shipbuilding

Credit: China Shipbuilding

result in a "dual structure" which is divided, among other things, between priority and non-priority industries and between favored and neglected companies.[10]

For such reasons, the countries which had opted for substantial state involvement eventually realized that it was not so easy to outguess the market or predict the trends. They gradually relaxed their controls and made the plans ever more indicative. Rather than promote specific branches, they found it wiser to back research and development or manpower improvement which could be of use to the whole economy and then let the private sector decide which ones to tackle. In addition, they increasingly sought prior advice and subsequent feedback from actual businessmen so as to correct their overly theoretical or academic visions of the future.

This enhanced the role of the entrepreneur, who was the primary thinker and doer in the liberal economies, whether Singapore or more markedly Hong Kong. However, before considering the situation there, it is essential to stress that even in the more state-dominated economies and even at the peak of their control there were always entrepreneurs who functioned pretty much on their own. They ignored or paid only superficial attention to what the government proposed and invested in what they thought would bring the best return. This they did with their own funds or what they could borrow. It was actually only a minority of entrepreneurs who followed the government's lead very actively. And even they would not get drawn into projects which they thought had no prospects.

The entrepreneurial spirit and a concern for market signals never disappeared from East Asia. Throughout the region, myriads of individuals decided whether it was better to work for someone else or go out on their own. They picked the sectors they felt would succeed and in which they had, or could acquire, the necessary knowhow and equipment. They hired and trained personnel, made and sold products, and prospered or vanished. If one sector turned out to be particularly rewarding, more entrepreneurs would come in. If another lost its comparative advantage, it would shrink as companies went under or shifted into other lines.

To regard this as disorderly and anarchic would be more than mistaken. Each one of these entrepreneurs was a planner in his own right, intensely concerned with reading the market signals and studying the economy to tell whether he would fare well or poorly with his venture. Since this was usually his money, and not that of the state, he was probably even more careful than the most conscientious technocrat or politician. His decisions, while certainly self-centered and lacking a broader view, were nonetheless integrated in the bigger picture by the market itself. If he did not adopt a factor combination that made him competitive, he would quickly disappear. If he did not produce something that was desired by the consumers, his disappearance would be even swifter.

Although many entrepreneurs withdrew, there were always new ones to replace them. And, from this continuous influx of businessmen, it was eventually possible to bring forth some who were particularly competent or dynamic. After floating their first venture successfully, they might undertake a second and third. Some even lauched several dozen and created whole groups of companies, a number of which were consolidated as *zaibatsu* and later *keiretsu* in Japan and *chaebol* in Korea. Within these groups there was often a degree of planning, industrial policy and targeting that could put the government's amateurish efforts to shame. The group founders and their assistants were much more aware of which articles could be produced at a profit, not only then, but in another few years and even further off. They did not hesitate to invest in these new sectors and promote them. While the outstanding business leaders were only a small minority, they were more influential than their number would suggest and they provided examples for the broader ranks of rising executives.

Certainly, there was still much waste involved. Those who guessed wrong, or were too weak to survive the competition, or were just unlucky, did fail and lose their funds. But this was a loss for the individuals who had made mistakes as opposed to a loss for the population as a whole when those who arrogated the right to take essential decisions proved wrong. Moreover, the disappearance of isolated companies which went bankrupt was less disruptive than the collapse of a whole sector which had been poorly chosen from above. Besides, the visible losses of these individuals were usually less extensive than the invisible losses of companies and sectors that were kept alive artificially by government backing.

Admittedly, counting on entrepreneurs to build a deep and broad economy was somewhat more misplaced. They would not go into sectors which were deemed "good" for the economy or nation but only those which were good for them . . . because they could make a profit. In some instances, due to linkages or fear of foreign dependence, an argument could be made for creating an industry whether or not it was dictated by market forces. But in most other cases, the liberal economies managed to enter pretty much the same advanced industries as the command economies. They may have arrived later, and been a bit slower, but they got there. Meanwhile, older sectors which the more aggressive planners had written off, and then helped destroy, managed to flourish where they did not face such disadvantages.

It is hard to say in any abstract manner which path was

superior, since there were pluses and minuses for both. But it was evident that planning, industrial policy and targeting occasionally went too far and that those who engaged in them felt that it was necessary to rely more on the market signals. Those where everything was left to free enterprise periodically felt that a bit of guidance from above would not hurt, especially Singapore. Thus, one can perhaps seek a middle point between the contrasting approaches. In so doing, it should be remembered that neither group was really at an extreme. The liberal economies did maintain a modicum of order and discipline and even those who went furthest toward state control never entirely forsook the market or rejected comparative advantage. If not for this, there is little chance that the world would have witnessed any "miracles" in East Asia.

NOTES

1. This *also* applies to Japan. For the wage structure in Meiji Days, see Takafusa Nakamura, *Economic Growth in Prewar Japan*, pp. 112–36.

2. Again, while still sufficiently evident in the NICs, this *also* applied to Japan during the whole prewar period. See Mikio Sumiya, "The Development of Japanese Labour Relations," in *The Developing Economies*, Tokyo, Institute of Asian Economic Affairs, December 1966, pp. 499–515.

3. It is dismaying how rarely academics study the role of wages in development, if it is not to condemn exploitation. It would appear that what is uppermost in the minds of all economic actors is of little concern to them.

4. More precisely, this does not have to be the end of the line. For most developing countries and unimaginative planners, these other possibilities rarely materialized.

5. On the upgrading of the textile industry in Korea, see Yung Bong Kim, "The Growth and Structural Change of Textile Industry," in Chong Kee Park (ed.), *Macroeconomic and Industrial Development in Korea*, pp. 185–276.

6. Amazingly little of value is written about planning in Japan and Taiwan, for good reason. For planning in Korea, see Leroy P. Jones and Il Sakong, *Government, Business and Entrepreneurship in Economic Development*, pp. 38-140.

7. More exists on Japanese industrial policy, although its existence was recently denied by the government. See, among others, Miyohei Shinohara, *Industrial Growth, Trade, and Dynamic Patterns in the Japanese Economy*, pp. 21-56

8. Targeting is even more vehemently denied and most studies were done by foreigners. They include Jack Baranson, *The Japanese Challenge to the United States*, and Daniel I. Okimoto et al, *Competitive Edge, The Semiconductor Industry in the U.S. and Japan*.

9. For a comprehensive analysis of this, see Wontack Hong, *Trade, Distortions and Employment Growth in Korea*, pp. 146-205.

10. There are numerous studies of the "dual structure" in Japan, including Takafusa Nakamura, *Economic Growth in Prewar Japan*, pp. 213-31, and *The Postwar Japanese Economy*, pp. 151-206. Those on Korea and Taiwan are yet to be written.

9

Upgrading Exports

Probably no strategy is associated more intimately with the success of the East Asian Five than export orientation. While their rise as manufacturers was notable, it was nothing compared to the speed with which they emerged, virtually out of nowhere, to become some of the most aggressive and competitive exporters of a growing range of products. This achievement was all the more impressive since few other developing countries ever got very far and most seemed unwilling to even try.

Just how export-oriented they are can be shown by the figures for exports as a share of gross national product, which starts with a low 13% for Japan but quickly rises to 34% for Korea, 49% for Taiwan, 78% for Hong Kong and 134% for Singapore. This was in the early 1980s. In other periods, the figures were sometimes even more considerable.

The fact that the lower figures are no more than the levels of exports in some European countries does not signify that exporting was unimportant even for Japan. It is not so much a question of how much is traded but what, and how vital, these exports may be. Very little of the trade in East Asia consists of similar products exchanged between neighboring countries with relatively permeable borders and which could be done without. Rather, the East Asians sell their exports in order to obtain raw materials, foodstuffs and capital goods without which they could not continue producing or, to be perfectly frank, simply survive.

The exceptionally high figures for Hong Kong and Singapore, however, are a bit misleading. They consist of both domestic exports and re-exports, goods imported from one country and later exported to another, sometimes after a degree of processing. In Hong Kong, this derives from its function as a gateway to China. For Singapore, it is part of the long entrepot tradition in which goods were assembled for distribution throughout the region. Limited only to domestic exports, the figures would be 50% for Hong Kong and 85% for Singapore, high but less spectacular.

Still, the crucial factor is by no means the amount of exports as a share of production but the impact exports have on economic development. For all of these countries, exports have been a leading, and sometimes even the primary, source of growth. The initial takeoff only came after exports started rising and the rapid economic growth was led by even more rapid export growth. Whenever exports soared, the economies climbed as a whole. And, when they fell there was a serious slump.[1]

The Five are sometimes praised for having invented this extraordinary strategy of export orientation. But they do not really deserve the credit for inventing anything. Exporting has always been a normal economic response to certain situations and it was circumstances, more than anything else, that first made them turn in that direction. The countries were so resource-poor, and occasionally short of food, that they had to import. In fact, they regularly imported more than they could pay for during the first postwar decade. This could only be done because of American aid and some reserves of foreign exchange, both of which were rapidly dwindling by the late 1950s. If they did not do something to earn more convertible currency they would be ruined. Thus, they were strongly pushed toward exporting.

Their first timid gestures were not even to adopt exporting as a policy option but to finally remove some of the obstacles to exports which had arisen during the initial period of import substitution and with the overvaluation of their currency. And this they did not even do on their own so much as at the urging of American AID officials or consultants from international agencies. Still, in retrospect, this was a decisive step for they began moving away from import substitution which had long been propagated as not only the best but almost the only way in which a developing country could progress.

At first, none of them really had high hopes for export orientation as a development strategy. In Japan, it was only desired to export some more of the traditional, prewar manufactures like textiles and garments. In Taiwan, when the idea of switching to exports (and simultaneously reducing support of import substitutes) was mooted, most of the businessmen were incredulous. They felt that the fledgling industries would be crushed while the country sold a bit more of its farm produce and processed foods. Korea, coming at a time when the others had already demonstrated a certain effectiveness of the policy, only thought in terms of exporting some very rudimentary products of its light industry. No one, certainly no one whose words have endured, conceived of export orientation as a dynamic, forward-looking strategy that could be applied to a very broad range of goods.[2]

Yet, that is what it turned out to be under the influence of the East Asian "tigers." Actually, it may be the fact that the practice materialized before the theory that was so precious in making it work. Without clear precedents or formal rules, the efforts were more spontaneous and imaginative. Businessmen and bureaucrats proceeded by trial and error. While the mistakes were painful and costly, there is no doubt that the benefits once discovered were exploited to the hilt. They are what gave the "tigers" their teeth.

While it was promptly realized that much could be gained from this novel strategy of export orientation, it took some time to realize just how positive and benefical it could be. The merits mentioned here are the most decisive. But others exist. As for possible demerits, that will be dealt with later.

The most obvious advantage is that production of certain articles could be increased many times over. Even the larger of the Five had relatively small domestic markets at first and there were very strict limits to how much could be sold. However, when exports turned the whole world, or much of it, into a potential market, there were almost no practical limits to sales. This, at any rate, is how things looked to the rather minuscule manufacturers which existed then. From year to year, exports did grow, permitting—and actually inducing—a vast increase in output.

But this was just the start. For, since they could now produce in larger quantities, it was possible to think of enhancing scale. The desire to gain more economies of scale, and operate to the optimum scale, became almost an obsession with rising entrepreneurs. While they did not always succeed, those who pulled ahead managed to erect factories as big, and sometimes bigger, than those of foreign rivals. The increases in scale allowed them to boost productivity. This could be done through an improved organization and utilization of labor or by introducing more machinery, which made sense with the larger output. Eventually some companies attained not only scale but degrees of efficiency that enabled them to compete almost anywhere.

The rapid expansion in production and scale had even deeper influences. With so many units flowing out of the factory, and a vested interest in keeping ahead in a narrow field, there was an increased specialization and an accelerated accumulation of knowhow about the given product line. This made it possible to move along the learning curve more swiftly, and to get much further, than would ever be expected of a developing country. With a greater stake in the sector, businessmen would strive to enhance technological proficiency. They might even make serious efforts at research and development and pass from copying to innovation, and sometimes even to creative invention, because they were moving into the forefront and had to do more of their own.

Another crucial effect, one which is too often overlooked, is that by producing largely for external markets the more responsive companies were encouraged to improve quality and control costs. As long as they were selling to local consumers on a protected market, it was possible to get away with shoddy goods and exorbitant prices. Indeed, that was a primary drawback of import substitution in many countries. This could obviously not be done abroad where the customers had a wide choice of goods and were being courted by many eager sellers. Exporting was only possible if makers supplied merchandise that was better or cheaper than their competitors, a harsh but salutary discipline. It was also a discipline which eventually spread to the economy as a whole since export-oriented manufacturers could not tolerate excessive support or protection of other sectors.

Export orientation has often been praised as an outward-looking strategy. That is not only because the goods are destined for overseas markets, although that is what was originally meant. In other significant ways it drew businessmen into wider circles that influenced them positively. Merely by seeking customers abroad, it was necessary to know more about trends and fashions in more advanced countries, as concerned the specific product and more broadly. This led to a familiarity with other related products, new machinery and techniques, different ways of combining production factors, and so on. Quite generally, businessmen could see how a modern company was run and adapt their own management practices back home. They could also find out what was going on in advanced economies and identify new products or sectors to try later.[3]

Export orientation not only had benefits for the overall economy and specific entrepreneurs, one of its greatest contributions was to the labor force. That is because the exports that did best contained the production factor which was relatively cheapest and, in the case of all Five, during the earlier period at least, this was labor. Exports included a proportionately larger labor content than most products made locally and, as exports began to grow, it was exactly these sectors which expanded to absorb even more labor. While barely noticeable at first, the effect was cumulative and eventually reached the point where most of the unemployed, as well as many who were formerly not in the labor force, were working and the economy reached full employment. Thereafter, growth of the export-oriented sectors stimulated higher wages.[4]

This goes to show that a major, if somewhat more diffuse, advantage of export orientation was to enhance an already existing comparative advantage. Labor was clearly the abundant production factor domestically, and the best products to launch even under the old strategy of import substitution were also labor-intensive. But production levels could never have risen as high as when cheap labor in East Asia was allowed to replace more expensive labor in the West, not only on their own markets but around the world. By making extensive use of this comparative advantage, the Five were able to give a tremendous boost to their economies. Thus, no matter how "miraculous" it looked, the foundation was very real and very natural.

Where the Five deserve considerably more credit than for supposedly inventing export orientation and benefiting from it is pioneering the practical aspects and making the strategy work. While the theory is apparently simple and straightforward, the actual implementation was far from easy. In fact, it was so hard that, aside from the small band of "tigers," there have not been many others which succeeded.

Looking back, it does not seem that the planners and economists who rejected export orientation actually questioned the validity of exporting as an alternative to production for the domestic market or that they denied the existence of a considerable comparative advantage for labor. In fact, they clearly urged exports of raw materials or agricultural produce where they existed and expected modest sales of traditional crafts or simple articles from light industry. But they could hardly conceive of backward countries producing large quantities of manufactured goods that could compete with those of far more industrialized nations. To be perfectly frank, this did not look very feasible to anybody at the time!

Yet, even in the initial phase, there were openings. While the early East Asian goods were often second-rate, and could hardly sell on quality, they were cheap enough to sell on price. The items which used the most labor were appreciably cheaper and were able to penetrate a number of second-rate markets. They could be sold to other developing countries where the consumers were far less demanding or quite simply lacked the money to buy anything else. Or they could be sold to less affluent segments of more advanced countries, such as the poorer working classes, disadvantaged minorities, or youngsters who were not yet earning a salary. In fact, there even turned out to be a special niche for shoddy goods, such as paper lanterns, plastic flowers, and dinky toys. This gradually expanded to embrace tacky wristwatches, costume jewellery, and so on, for those who did not wish to keep them very long anyway.

This is what might be called the "easy" stage of export orientation since the markets were there and just had to be tapped. It was much harder to penetrate more serious sectors where the demand for quality would be much greater. Yet, even there, it was a big mistake to assume that quality is everything, as some self-satisfied domestic companies foolishly did. Goods rarely sell on quality alone, just as they rarely sell on price alone. There must be an attractive combination of price and quality, good enough quality for the price, which makes wares priceworthy enough to win acceptance in much broader circles. East Asian businessmen, at least those who made it, usually found a suitable combination of quality and price, one which could vary tremendously as they worked their way upmarket, improving quality and also boosting prices. In fact, soon it was impossible to find cheap Oriental trinkets outside of Chinatown and, instead, those clever Orientals were selling manufactured articles of all sorts that were as good or better than could be produced in the West.

Success through export orientation therefore has two essential sources. One is the various advantages which were mentioned first, and which any country could benefit from. The other, even more vital, is the ability to produce articles that are good and cheap enough to penetrate foreign markets and then to continue refining quality without raising the prices too fast. How that was done is described elsewhere and is part of the more general explanation of why the East Asian economies advanced. But, if it had not been done, their attempt at export orientation would have been a lamentable failure, probably a much bigger flop than sticking to import substitution. And any country which wishes to switch strategies would be wise to remember that it is not as easy as it looks.

While the early steps toward export orientation derived from circumstances, and the first efforts at exporting were relatively spontaneous, it did not take long for the strategy to become considerably more structured in certain countries, especially Japan, Korea and Taiwan. This represented a move toward a policy that is sufficiently distinctive to be called export *promotion*.

The export promotion measures adopted by the governments were not terribly different in nature from those used to promote industrialization in general. And sometimes they actually supplemented them, giving companies which encouraged exports double support. There were rebates of duties on raw materials, intermediate goods and machinery needed for export production, easier access to bank loans for the company and perhaps credit for the purchasers, sometimes also favorable exchange rates and rights to restricted imports or priority in use of scarce foreign exchange, and a broad range of tax breaks on investment for and profits from exports. Direct subsidies were rarely granted but a tendency to keep the national currency undervalued was more widespread. In addition, in Korea and the others to a lesser extent, exporting was elevated to a patriotic duty with the best exporters reaping praise and rewards.[5]

These measures were extremely effective in increasing exports; there is no doubt about that. The only problem is that in some cases they may have been too effective. While, in most cases, export goods did have a sufficient comparative advantage to justify the effort, some goods could only be exported at all, or to the extent they were, because they were supported in one way or another. This implied an invisible, but no less real loss for the economy. More broadly, excessive stress on exporting led to undue neglect of other sectors, whether farming or services or even manufacturing of goods primarily for domestic use. Besides, the more a country exported, the more it depended on continued exports for its economic standing. This made it more sensitive to sudden changes in the international climate and vulnerable to pressure from major suppliers or purchasers.

Only the Hong Kong government was aware of the pitfalls of export promotion, especially if vigorously pursued. It therefore stuck to a policy of strict neutrality as concerns the destination of goods. There were no special incentives to export and exporters had to get normal credit from the banks. Profits were taxed equally. And no one was berated for concentrating on the domestic market, although even there exporting tended to receive somewhat higher status. In Singapore, although the government made no secret of its desire to encourage exports, it maintained a more liberal position. There were relatively few incentives, aside from tax breaks, and that over a limited number of years. But the local businessmen were always looking for sales, and foreign markets were big and often bountiful.

Thus, despite the fundamental differences, it could hardly be said that those which strongly promoted exports did notably better than those which merely encouraged or approved of it. Proportionately, Hong Kong and Singapore exported much more than the others, although this was partly because they are so small and commercial. Doubtlessly, they could have sold even more with stronger backing. But those additional sales might not have been worth the effort and resulting distortions.

The differences in approach derived partly from differing economic policies. They also reflected cultural and historical factors since Japan, Korea and Taiwan had much less familiarity with exporting and businessmen probably had to be persuaded by official policy and palpable incentives to make the effort. With a modest domestic market, they could at least hope to get by without exporting. In the two city-states, there was no internal market to speak of and the only promising places for selling goods were external markets. By interrupting the entrepot circuits, they could readily replace foreign imports with their own goods and then have them exported. And, since they could count on no backing, they would only launch products for which they were inherently competitive.

No less striking variations arose in the actual marketing of exports. In Japan and Korea, and to a lesser extent Taiwan, it was official policy to promote the rise of large-scale trading ventures to concentrate and strengthen the activities. They are typified by the general trading companies known as *sogo shosha* in Japan and *chonghap sangsa* in Korea. These organizations, with their huge staffs, are able to handle literally thousands of products, from the smallest to the biggest. They also have far-flung networks of overseas offices and ready access to financial support. While stress is primarily on exports, they also engage in substantial importing and domestic distribution which helps to sustain such large companies and gives them added solidity. What is more, imports can occasionally subsidize exports.[6]

In Hong Kong and Singapore, such highly structured operations do not exist, although one does find the remnants of the old British and European trading houses known variously as *hongs* or agencies. Even in Taiwan, the attempt at forming general trading companies only progressed fitfully with few indigenous units arising. Instead, there has been a marked dispersion of the trading function among various, often quite small units. There is an endless proliferation of trading companies, some consisting of only one or two persons and run out of rented space or the trader's home. There are some slightly larger units which, as soon as they begin expanding also tend to split up as employees or partners go off on their own. Rather than control the distribution channels, the traders are often circumvented by suppliers and buyers. Most local manufacturers of any size, and the size can be quite puny, would wish to handle their own sales even if it means just an annual trip abroad or sporadic correspondence. Meanwhile, some major buyers have set up permanent offices to purchase goods regularly while smaller operators visit East Asia once or twice a year to look at the merchandise and sign contracts.

Once again, although the methods vary tremendously, it could hardly be said that one is clearly superior to the other. The flow of exports from all five countries has continued smoothly, whether expedited by a few large or many small traders. What this proves could hardly be stated with pinpoint precision. But it would seem that, as before, it is partially a question of taste and a result of cultural factors. The more strictly organized and group-oriented countries clearly prefer larger ventures. Nor is there any doubt that the existence of *zaibatsu* and

Producing more watches than Hong Kong can use

Credit: HKTDC

chaebol was instrumental in the rapid rise of *sogo shosha* and *chonghap sangsa*. In more individualistic and open communities, it is quite natural that smaller, more variegated agents should emerge. What they lack in structural solidity and organizational ability they make up for by flexibility and speed.

The most intriguing difference, however, is even more noteworthy and also economically relevant. The Koreans and Japanese, whether in government or private circles, have tended to see exports much more in terms of volume or quantity of trade. Targets are specified in numbers of units sold, or tons shipped, although this takes the form of overall value of exports as well. Companies, both manufacturers and traders, are very concerned about their share of the market or of total exports. This does not seem to interest the Chinese anywhere near as much. Of course, the government keeps a record of the quantity and value of shipments. But the individual businessmen, manufacturers and traders are decidedly more concerned about the profit they make than what their ranking or market share may be.

This, too, has definite cultural roots. The Chinese are traditionally more commercially-minded. The three economies are run as much by merchants as by manufacturers. There is also a deep respect for wealth. The Japanese and Korean economies were never quite as mercenary and money never contributed as prominently to status. The economies were built up as much by political figures and bureaucrats as actual entrepreneurs, and the leading businessmen are production-minded manufacturers. For the greater glory of the state (and enhanced scale), exports are expanded as much as possible. But this makes it hard to cultivate profits since, the lower the price, the more is sold. No such compulsion exists in Taiwan, Hong Kong or Singapore and everything is done to squeeze the most profit out of each deal even if, at the end of the year, less is sold. This tends to make Japan and Korea more productive . . . and less fruitful. The economies are powerful, but people certainly do not gain as much from a like effort as their subtler neighbors.

While there are conspicuous contrasts regarding export promotion, trading and profit, they are certainly less essential than the similarity of approach. All five countries, whether within government circles, the business community, or even the general population, realized the importance of exporting for economic growth. They all made strenuous exertions, even if not always in the same way. And this has enabled them to benefit handsomely from a strategy that others had neglected or failed to apply properly.

Still, no matter how successful export orientation has been so far, there is no guarantee that it will be as effective in the future. Any strategy is only suitable in specific circumstances. When circumstances change, so should the strategy. It should never become so habitual or automatic that this is forgotten.

There are two decisive circumstances which explain why the five countries were able to do so well. One, which is to their credit, is that they continued honing their competitive edge and could thereby export more from year to year. The other, more fortuitous, is that world trade continued growing rapidly and thus the potential market for their goods kept swelling. While there is every reason to believe that the Five can further enhance their competitive strength, and theoretically sell more exports than before, the world trade situation has changed perceptibly. Trade is no longer as bouyant and has, on occasion, become very sluggish.[7] In addition, protectionism has increased and much of it is generally directed against products sold by East Asians when not against one or the other of them specifically.[8]

Under such conditions, exporting is not as wise a policy. It will be harder to expand exports quite simply because trade is growing less and each gain for the Five would probably signify a loss for others. It would be even riskier to sell aggressively in markets where domestic industries are suffering and unemployment is substantial. Any such attempt could be counterproductive with more restrictions imposed than before. While a natural propensity to export would be understandable, special measures to promote exports would smack of beggar-thy-neighbor tactics and result in a nasty backlash. It would be much safer, and probably more beneficial in the long run, to increase exports more gently and perhaps even slower than circumstances might permit.[9]

In some countries, it would be advisable to go even further in eliminating the almost blind bias in favor of exports that has arisen over the years. By giving top priority to exporting, and then skewing the economy in that direction, planners and businessmen have often forgotten the advantages of importing. In their own self-interest, it should be remembered that importing cheaper industrial inputs makes it possible to produce more cheaply and either export more or make a bigger profit out of it. More selflessly, it is also possible to improve the living standards of their population by bringing costs down, an especially popular tack at a time when wages will be rising less smartly. Finally, in the mutual interest, importing more from other countries will give them the wherewithal to buy more manufactured goods from East Asia.

NOTES

1. For the contribution of exports to growth, see Edward K. Y. Chen, *Hyper-growth in Asian Economies*, pp. 109–28, Wontack Hong, *Trade, Distortions and Employment Growth in Korea*, pp. 5–35, Shirley W. Y. Kuo, *The Taiwan Economy in Transition*, pp. 135–80, and Tzong Biau Lin and Yin Ping Ho, "Export-Oriented Growth and Industrial Diversification in Hong Kong," in Wontack Hong and Lawrence B. Krause (eds.), *Trade and Growth of the Advanced Developing Countries in the Pacific Basin*, pp. 69–128
2. While most of the misgivings were only mentioned in private conversations or the press of the time, the reluctance and hesitation can be easily sensed. The lack of enthusiasm was even more noticeable. See Gustav Ranis, "Industrial Development," in Walter Galenson (ed.), *Economic Growth and Structural Change in Taiwan*, p. 219, and Samuel P. S. Ho, *Economic Development in Taiwan*, p. 119.
3. Some of these precious, if impalpable, advantages are described in Larry Westphal et al, *Korean Industrial Competence: Where It Came From.*
4. Studies on the employment effect of export orientation include Gary S. Fields, *The Labor Market and Export-Led Growth, Hong,*

op. cit., pp. 206–51, Kuo, *op. cit.*, pp. 135–74, and Tzong Biau-Lin and Mei-chiang Lin, "Exports and Employment in Hong Kong," in Tzong-Biau Lin et al, *Hong Kong, Economic, Social and Political Studies in Development*, pp. 225–74.

5. For more on general policies and specific measures, see Bela Belassa, *Development Strategies in Semi-Industrial Economies*, Michael R. Czinkota, *Export Promotion, The Public and Private Sector Interaction*, Hong, *op. cit.*, pp. 36–145, and Kuo, *op. cit.*, pp. 297–310.

6. See Kunio Yoshihara, *Sogo Shosha*, and Alexander K. Young, *The Sogo Shosha, Japan's Multinational Trading Companies*.

7. Trade growth worldwide slumped from an annual range of 5–10% in the 1960s and 1970s to 0–5% by the 1980s.

8. See Jon Woronoff, *World Trade War*.

9. For suggestions on how best to adjust, see Neil McMullen, *The Newly Industrializing Countries: Adjusting to Success*, Louis Turner and Neil McMullen, *The Newly Industrializing Countries: Trade and Adjustment*, and David Yoffie and Robert Keohane, "Responding to the 'New Protectionism': Strategies for the ADCs," in Hong and Krause, *op. cit.*, pp. 560–94.

10

Downgrading Imports

Although it was clearly overshadowed by export orientation, there is not the slightest doubt that the East Asian
Five also made extensive use of import substitution. This
is the strategy they began with. It was pursued intermittently even in the midst of the export boom. And they
have come back to it increasingly as the economy
matured.[1] While planners and economists have repeatedly criticized the failings of such an inward-looking approach, they were never blind to its advantages. Local
businessmen were even more fascinated by certain
aspects.

Indeed, it does not make much sense to seek economic
progress without looking into the possibilities of import
substitution. There are a vast number of products which
are so obviously needed in any developing country that
local purchasers are willing to spend their hard-earned
money on imports. Some of these articles could surely be
produced domestically and this would save the economy
foreign exchange that is needed for more essential purposes. If the shift is not made spontaneously, faced with
mounting trade deficits the government may have to introduce a more forceful policy to conserve funds and
nurture industry. It will then select, or have local entrepreneurs select, the products which can most readily
be produced locally and do what it can to facilitate the
process.

It would be rather ludicrous to claim that now that export orientation has proven to be more effective it is futile or wasteful to bother about imports. After all, no matter how much a country exports it will be hard to collect enough foreign exchange to pay for vital capital goods, raw materials and those remaining imports it does not choose to replace. In addition, a good many products do not really lend themselves to international trade because they are very fragile, perishable or bulky. Most of these items can also be promoted by roughly the same measures. Finally, some industries are regarded as essential to sustain a modern economy, and they will be pursued come what may. All this can spread the economy more broadly and make it more resilient than an excessive dependence on exports.

While both import substitution and export orientation are valid strategies, the former was originally more appealing since it appeared to be a particularly "easy" path to development. The products which were recommended to backward countries were reasonably simple and could be manufactured without too much machinery. The technologies were generally known and widely available. Quite ordinary people, working in ordinary ways, would be able to do the job. Moreover, most of the articles were rather common objects of consumption even in poorer societies, which meant that a ready market existed. This alone should have been enough to justify production. But, if a further push were needed, it should not cost the state that much. And, if there were a danger that nascent domestic producers might be crushed by cheaper or better imports, they could simply be cut off. This seemed to be a delightfully workable formula.

In many cases, the inherent advantages of the operation were perfectly adequate to attract eager entrepreneurs and much of the import substitution was spontaneous. But ambitious governments often felt that the movement was not swift or sweeping enough, and their businessmen usually agreed. Throughout the Third World, and also in Japan, Korea and Taiwan, the state intervened to see that the strategy was followed more energetically. It also introduced a broad array of measures to enhance the chances of success.[2]

One series of measures was adopted to establish and promote the new industries. Entrepreneurs were granted low-interest loans and had access to the necessary foreign exchange, sometimes at favorable rates. They were permitted to import essential equipment and license technologies. These items were granted accelerated depreciation. It could even happen that companies would obtain cheaper public land and special infrastructure. In the case of entities owned or supported by the state, these advantages could be even greater while certain costs would be directly subsidized and losses written off.

The other side of the arrangement was to protect these "infant industries" from outside competition until they were strong enough to get by on their own. This consisted of high tariffs on competing products (but not the necessary inputs) and, on occasion, the tariffs could be almost prohibitive. Even more radically, there could be quotas or outright bans on imports. To protect their people from predatory multinationals which might wish to produce locally, some governments reserved specific sectors in which foreigners could not invest or at least had to enter joint ventures.

These measures, which were clearly discriminatory, were not generally approved of by the more advanced nations, although they tended to tolerate their existence in genuine developing countries. When Japan, followed by Korea and Taiwan, found such methods too crude or came under pressure from their trading partners, they switched to considerably more indirect and subtle—but hardly less effective—methods. Rather than having the state subsidize a project, this task might be taken over by a state-related corporation such as NTT or China Steel. National laboratories might do valuable research work and hand it over to private companies for a pittance. After the formal trade barriers were lowered, the bureaucrats might still urge local companies to "buy national" and see to it that the government led the way.[3]

However, it ultimately turned out that import substitution was not so simple as it seemed. Even when following most of the rules, it was rare that truly efficient and productive industries arose and all too often imports remained better and cheaper than local products. A number of more serious snags and outright abuses arose which gave the strategy a very bad reputation.

The most evident limitation to import substitution, one that had always been conceded, was that backward countries often had a very small domestic market. This was due more to the low purchasing power than the size of the population. While some of the bigger economies were able to muster a sufficient clientele to justify numerous projects, relatively cramped ones found it hard to reach an acceptable scale. Moreover, they were bound to saturate whatever market they had rather soon. For that reason, even if a country did reasonably well, it could not hope to get very far purely on import substitution.

Far less evident were the difficulties of manufacturing even the more rudimentary products that were selected for these schemes. In countries with scarcely any industrial experience, there was a frustrating lack of knowhow among businessmen and skills among workers. The goods turned out were frequently quite shoddy, sometimes even defective and unusable. But, or so it was argued, these were just teething pains and the "infant" industry would surely improve its performance with more experience. This meant that, to overcome these handicaps, the government was often tempted, and then pressured, to expand and strengthen its supportive and protective measures.

This turned out to be a grievous blunder in more cases than not. For, by promoting and protecting ventures, it was no longer necessary for them to strive to succeed. Companies could sell their output on a highly protected market where competing products were much more costly and sometimes simply not available. No matter how poorly made, or expensive, anyone who really needed those articles had to buy them from local sources. With some of their costs artificially reduced and prices artificially elevated, even incompetent companies could do quite well financially. As long as this situation lasted, entrepreneurs saw no compelling reason to make serious efforts to improve. Worse, with support and protection almost guaranteeing success, they began to choose new projects more carelessly, with little concern as to whether or not there was, or would eventually be, a comparative advantage. Under these circumstances, it is evident why many of the "infant" industries never grew up and some should never have been born to begin with.

The most insidious aspect, and in the long run the most pernicious for the country, was that these misguided attempts at import substitution could easily degenerate into a system of collusion and corruption. The important thing was no longer to come up with a promising idea but to have it endorsed by the government and then obtain a concession to work that industry locally. This was all the more valuable for *de facto* monopolies. The next step was to seek appropriate support to reduce the starting costs and preferably finance the project with external funds. Then, once the goods were being produced, efforts were made to raise protection to levels that ensured a good return. If worst came to worst, and the project was really a flop, work began on a bail-out or perhaps to transfer it to the public sector with the entrepreneur receiving due compensation. Obviously, for each of these transactions, bribes had to be paid to bureaucrats and politicians which encouraged the rise of both dishonest businessmen and unscrupulous officials and governments.

This will explain the very spotty results of import substitution. It was much more difficult than assumed to create sound and viable industries on exiguous markets, and with inexperienced manufacturers, although it was far from impossible. But even the existence of flourishing projects might not be so good for the economy as a whole if they were unduly subsidized or protected. For then any apparent "success" of the owners, and the sponsoring authorities, was offset by losses to the consumers and taxpayers. The hidden loss was that much greater if the projects tended to skew the economy in the wrong direction or engender a pervasive atmosphere of corruption.

Thus, while those engaging in export orientation reared "tigers," the practitioners of import substitution frequently bred "white elephants." Even in those East Asian countries which firmly supported import substitution, there were problems with businessmen abusing monopoly positions to amass great wealth and buy favors. Not all the projects, especially in the earlier period, were valid. And later on the promotion of strategic sectors was strong enough to result in some impractical or overambitious projects. While corruption was curtailed, collusion proved harder to suppress.

Still, on the whole, import substitution went well in

East Asia. It was probably as big a success as one can find for the strategy anywhere. Far from rejecting the method, it was used more wisely and inserted in a broader context. This enabled the Five to derive more of the benefits and avoid some of the drawbacks.

One way to accomplish this was to exercise greater caution in applying the various supportive and protective measures. Certainly, they were used. But much less lavishly than in other developing countries and the conditions imposed on those who received backing were stricter. Loans were harder to come by and interest rates not that much better. It was clear that the principal and interest had to be paid back, and the borrowers knew it. In the choice of protective measures, there was a preference for tariffs which only offered partial protection as opposed to quotas and bans. Efforts were made to keep the differential moderate. This meant that entrepreneurs had to achieve a reasonable level of efficiency and their prices could not be that much higher than those of foreign competitors.

Another tactic was the clever use of competition. Even in industries that were protected, whenever scale was less essential the government tried to avoid monopolies by having several companies established. While they may have been less productive in theory, in practice they were forced to fight for the same clientele and the ones which became most efficient would win larger market shares. Their rivals could hardly afford to be squeezed out and were also obliged to upgrade. In sectors where it was impossible to do this, with only one steel mill or power company, attempts were made to parallel the situation in similar sectors of more advanced countries and hold them to those higher standards.

Moreover, the protection intially offered was only temporary. It would gradually be eliminated so that the local producers would eventually have to adjust to world conditions. If it looked as if a specific company or even a whole sector was not shaping up properly, it was possible to let in foreign imports to encourage them. This meant that, from the outset, most entrepreneurs knew that they could enjoy a privileged position for a limited period of time and that they had to improve their performance before the support and protection were withdrawn. They could not afford to rest on their laurels.

Placed under such pressure, the businessmen reacted much more positively than their counterparts in countries where support and protection determined success or failure. They certainly chose their projects with considerably more care. They also made more strenuous efforts to increase productivity and enhance quality. One

Producing more shoes than Koreans can wear

Credit: KOTRA

of the rewards of this was to earn profits which could be plowed back into the original operation. Another was to obtain government backing for further ventures since they had proven their ability. This made it much easier for the government as well because it could now entrust more complex projects to more experienced entrepreneurs who already had some working capital, production facilities and trained personnel. Meanwhile, and this was rare in the developing world, the government might punish businessmen who failed by withdrawing the incentives, calling back the loans and transferring the projects to others who looked more promising.

This helps to explain why such ventures did so much better in places like Korea, Taiwan and Japan. But it is no less intriguing to ask why these governments adopted a very different approach that made the entrepreneurs keep their nose to the grindstone. One of the reasons is that the leaders were aware, or had been warned, of the potential abuses. They had seen how giving in to pleas for support and protection had harmed other economies. They even saw how it hurt their own, this being most striking in pre-Park Korea. Thus, they were more determined to avoid the pitfalls. They were also exceedingly ambitious and wanted to accomplish so much that, given the state's limited resources, it was very difficult to back individual projects too generously and funds allocated to the first batch were expected back promptly to launch a second and third series. Moreover, the early switch from import substitution to export orientation as the predominant strategy meant that any support could not last too long.

But the more resolute and intelligent role of the state did not emanate purely from the wisdom of its leaders. It was essential for them to accomplish the greater task of nation building and lax pursuit of import substitution was clearly not the way. More specifically, they were bound to be criticized for anything that could be regarded as unfair support of one sector by businessmen in all the others while helping out specific companies created resentment among those which received no aid, namely the vast majority. Any hint of mismanagement or corruption in ventures which enjoyed special favor could erupt into scandals that even strong governments did not relish. Once the state began promoting exports, there was a new source of pressure since trading partners would no longer tolerate excessive protection and demanded a liberalization that exposed import substitutes increasingly to competition.

Whatever the causes, it again becomes obvious that success was not a result of suspending the economic laws or exercising a magical intervention of the state so much as by proceeding as judiciously and moderately as possible. The more exactly companies or planners gauged their actual or potential comparative advantage, the more likely they were to prosper. The less extreme the support and the protection, the more likely it was that entrepreneurs would take the right decisions to begin with and later make the necessary efforts to improve quality and productivity. And, for one reason or another, it turned out that the shorter the interference in the market and the faster the return to market signals, the more viable an operation would be.

This resolves the seeming paradox that Singapore and Hong Kong also witnessed the rise of many of the same industries although they had not particularly stressed import substitution and offered rather few special measures in the former and absolutely none in the latter. All they did, as for everything else, was to allow entrepreneurs to consider their abilities and the existing opportunities and decide on their own whether to go ahead. This often meant that a demand would arise which could not be met immediately and tight supplies of such a product would push the price up. This was the crucial market signal. It attracted imports. It also attracted entrepreneurs who thought they could make the same goods cheaply enough to replace the imports. If they could, then they won. If not, it was their loss and not the state's.

That they could pull it off so often was partially attributable to the ability of the local entrepreneurs to combine the various production factors in such a way as to benefit from cheaper labor at first. Once in the market, however, they proceeded to enhance productivity and quality by introducing better machinery, technologies and managerial techniques. If they could do this well enough to get into export markets, they could certainly do it repeatedly on the home market. Moreover, even without artificial protection, they enjoyed certain natural advantages due to proximity and knowledge of the market. They did not incur the huge shipping costs which bore heavily on large and bulky goods. By dealing with local buyers regularly, they knew precisely what was wanted and could adapt to changing needs more readily. Of course, they could also deliver the goods much faster.

This spontaneous import substitution, such as occurred anywhere, was gradually superseded throughout East Asia by a much more systematic approach. Companies would select, target if you will, articles which they felt could just as easily be produced locally. They would then acquire the necessary machinery, technologies and expertise. If this were a more complex field, they might bring in a foreign partner. That is how particularly dynamic entrepreneurs set up one venture after another and created whole groups of companies. Assemblers would take another tack, gradually establishing subsidiaries to produce one part or component after the other. If they did not want to do this on their own, they might ask friends or former employees to set up such operations and promise to buy their output. Traders and wholesalers, once they had created a market for some imported good, might ask the foreign manufacturer to take up local production or do that on their own or through a related company.

In these cases, in addition to any natural comparative advantage, the assemblers or distributors might actually subsidize and protect their subsidiaries and subcontractors until they became competitive. Established groups would also do the same thing for new members. Such measures, when undertaken in the private sector, were followed through much more rigorously since no company was willing to finance another for long. It was assumed that eventually the local products would be much cheaper, and just as good, as imports. So they pressed their subsidiaries and subcontractors very hard to shape up. Nor did they shun the ultimate sanction of dissolving an unsuccessful venture or ceasing orders to suppliers that could not make the grade. Since this sort of promotion was carried on by private companies and not the government, there was much less room for criticism from abroad.

There is one last reason why import substitution was probably so much more effective in East Asia. Contrary to what is often supposed, there is no contradiction or incompatability between import substitution and export orientation. If anything, they are complementary. Some industries or products are more amenable to the former approach, others to the latter. To construct a well-rounded industrial base it was almost inevitable to use both at one point or another.

Moreover, each of the strategies could be applied to certain sectors at different times and in different ways. It was not at all unusual to initiate an industry under the standard import substitution policies and bring it to maturity only to find that it was then capable of taking up exporting. If it showed promise, it might well be supported by the standard export promotion paraphernalia. This is what happened to Japan's steel industry, Korea's cement industry, and Taiwan's textile industry, all of which originally arose to meet domestic needs and then expanded into exports.

On the other hand, some products had to start with an outward bias because the domestic market was either too small or too poor. The Japanese and Koreans initially made television sets for Americans since their own people could not afford them and Taiwan's refrigerators and air-conditioners were certainly not for the locals at first. But, by increasing the scale of production it was possible to bring costs down to the point where the goods could also be sold readily on the domestic market.

Frequently, smart businessmen played both markets. When demand was lively abroad, they tended to cultivate the foreign markets which were more affluent and could absorb more consumer goods. When things were slack, they turned to the domestic market to unload what remained, sometimes at a discount. On the other hand, basic industries tended to count on domestic sales for their essential business and then sell whatever surplus there might be on foreign markets, sometimes at dumping prices since fixed costs were already covered. By combining both markets, it was possible to boost scale and efficiency more than on just one of them.

These various factors made it possible for the Five to get much more out of import substitution than many countries which made it their principal or sole strategy. This can be seen not only from the success in specific projects but the amazing number of industries which were eventually fostered. Whereas most developing countries only conceived of a narrow range of products as being suitable for import substitution, East Asia showed that the range was quite extensive.

What are generally regarded as candidates for import substitution are a motley assortment of rather primitive articles which can be produced with modest amounts of capital and by relatively unskilled personnel using rather common technologies. Most of them are labor-intensive, although not all. One batch consists of standard items of light industry such as bicycles, hand tools and rudimentary farm implements, ordinary electrical appliances and machinery, and so on. Somewhat more elaborate are basic chemicals and fertilizer, cement and plywood, or processed foods. Textiles also come under this heading. This is what might be classified as "first" stage or "easy" import substitution.[4]

The "second" stage is a big step forward, one it was formerly assumed might never be taken by most developing countries. It involves more highly capital and technology-intensive industries and required considerable industrial capability. But many of the difficulties were lessened by foreign engineering firms which were increasingly able to deliver turnkey plants with everything neatly arranged for the buyer. They also offered suitable training and technical backup. This made it much easier to proceed to more advanced industries such as fine chemicals and petrochemicals, plastics and synthetic fibers, steel and other metals. Even extremely complex assembly industries became feasible once foreign makers were willing to provide knock-down kits which merely had to be put together locally. This paved the way for "production" of many electrical and electronics articles as well as motorcycles and even automobiles.

This metamorphosis of import substitution was already so startling that many observers failed to notice another one which is even more extraordinary in certain ways. The "third" stage consists of two very different, but closely related, elements. One is increased local production of intermediate goods, both the materials needed for downstream production and essential components of assembly line goods. Part of this is a refinement of the basic industries, further processing the fibers, plastics, chemicals, steel forms, metal blanks and so on needed by local manufacturers. The rest consists of mass producing untold thousands of parts such as motors, coils, batteries, brakes, spark plugs and so on to replace what originally came in the kits. The other element is production of capital goods, the machinery and tools needed to manufacture. This can go as far as erection of completed facilities and whole plants.[5]

A "fourth" stage might also be mentioned, although it has hardly been recognized yet. Most authorities think of import substitution as taking place almost exclusively in the manufacturing sector. But there are definite openings for farmers to grow new crops, such as exotic fruits and vegetables, or livestock, which had earlier been imported. More impalpable, but no less real, are the replacement or supplementing of foreign imports in the tertiary sector. This time it includes "products" such as rented cars, credit cards or comic books and services like fast foods, bowling alleys or travel agencies. As a matter of fact, whole branches can be imitated and absorbed including essential ones like banking, insurance, advertising, shipping, tourism and so on.

What is really intriguing is that very few countries aside from the Five have gotten as far as the third stage, and not many even reached the second. Most remained stuck in the first phase and gave up after that. As it happens, the Five also switched to export orientation when the possibilities of the "easy" phase had been exhausted. This did not take terribly long since the range of goods was relatively limited and the domestic markets were quite small. If further progress were to be made, it was necessary to look elsewhere and thus the export drives were launched. But they returned to import substitution again and again as new possibilities cropped up.

One reason why the Five could proceed so far is that, all this while, the market had been growing and maturing. The population itself only increased slowly. But purchasing power expanded rapidly in keeping with the economy, more than doubling each decade. This created a much bigger demand within the manufacturing sector for the basic metals and chemicals of the second phase and then the intermediate and capital goods of the third phase. Meanwhile, people were becoming more affluent and could afford more luxurious consumer goods, some of which had originally been largely for export. The other essential change was that, over the years, capital had accumulated, the organizational ability of companies improved, there were many more skilled workers, technicians and managers. This meant that commercial ventures which would once have been out of reach could be launched more surely and efficiently.

It was this successful progression of the economy, much of which is owed to export growth, which enabled the five countries to proceed from one stage to the next. Obviously, although presented separately, the stages were not isolated from one another but rather closely interrelated. They also tended to overlap with each new one beginning before the others were completed. But there were definite periods when one or another was more prominent. For the NICs, the first phase arose in the 1950s and early 1960s, the second in the late 1960s and 1970s, and the third and fourth will evolve over the

1980s. For Japan, the periods were much earlier, with some first phase growth in the Meiji era and the others arising a good decade or more before they appeared in the NICs.

While it was always conceded that import substitution could play a useful role, it was long held in low esteem. It was therefore less popular and less overtly encouraged than export orientation.[6] But these priorities are now being reversed, due less to any sudden appeal of the strategy than the alarming spread of protectionism. Whether they want to or not, the Five will find it harder to penetrate external markets and have to fall back on their own much more. This *may* give import substitution another chance to prove itself.

NOTES

1. So little has been written about import substitution in East Asia that it is becoming suspicious given its manifest influence. There is some mention of a first phase before export promotion began, and than almost complete silence. But a careful reading of any economic history will reveal its continued existence.
2. See Bela Belassa, *Development Strategies in Semi-Industrial Economies.*
3. See Jon Woronoff, *World Trade War.*
4. There is some reference to "easy" import substitution in studies of early industrialization such as Samuel P. S. Ho, *Economic Development of Taiwan*, Kwang Suk Kim and Michael Roemer, *Growth and Structural Transformation in Korea*, and Takafusa Nakamura, *Economic Growth in Prewar Japan.*
5. This phase is described in Woronoff, *Korea's Economy: Man-Made Miracle*, pp. 157–74.
6. For a contribution to the debate on which strategy is "better," see Anne O. Krueger, "Export-Led Industrial Growth Reconsidered," in Wontack Hong and Lawrence B. Krause (eds.), *Trade and Growth of the Advanced Developing Countries in the Pacific Basin*, pp. 3–34.

11

Technological Leapfrogging

There is no doubt that technology has been decisive in enabling the Five to progress as rapidly as they did.[1] Yet, the full impact of technology has only slowly been realized. While it was once hardly even considered among the various basic requirements for economic growth, like capital and labor, or raw materials, it has come to be accepted as almost indispensable. But this recognition, and the essential follow-up, were not as widely spread or effective as might be assumed. Only in East Asia, once again, were the achievements truly spectacular.

What is most striking about Japan's growth, and later that of the Four, is how quickly they sensed the decisive role that technology could play. In fact, without exaggeration, it was conceded more than intuitively by the Japanese over a century ago when they contemplated the first visiting Westerners. Surely, or so they felt, these crude "barbarians" were in no way superior to Japanese as concerned essential human qualities. All that made them better, if the word could be grudgingly used, was their more advanced science and techniques.

While it was only formulated somewhat later, the Chinese and Koreans also realized early on that much could be learned from the West when it came to modern science and industry. On the whole, they were also desirous of attaining what the Japanese sought, namely, in a slight paraphrase, "Western technology, Eastern spirit." But they were not quick enough about it during the late nineteenth century, or they underestimated the "barbarians" more than the Japanese had, and they fell prey to the colonial powers, including a resurgent Japan. When autonomous development could finally resume after the war, it was evident that the value of modern technology would not be missed.

However, a passive admiration or distant longing for technology would not help. It was necessary to acquire the essential knowhow and put it to use. This was not so easy for countries with a limited familiarity with the vast progress that had been made overseas. And, from the start, it was clear that the process of acquisition would be neither simple nor inexpensive. In addition, it was necessary to determine which techniques were likely to be most helpful in order to avoid wasting time and squandering money.

Selecting technology was always a very serious matter for the Japanese, even in the earliest times. Special missions were sent abroad in Meiji days. Subsequently, overseas offices of the trading companies or government agencies kept an eye out for noteworthy inventions which might be of use. The holders of the relevant patents and rights were contacted and efforts made to acquire them for Japan. At home, factories were established under foreign supervision and key expatriate staff hired to run them. Meanwhile, foreign teachers were brought to educate future generations of technicians, engineers and scientists. Not all of the projects were a success, but certainly enough were for Japan to move ahead rapidly.

This process, which had been piecemeal and sporadic in prewar days, became incredibly systematic and institutionalized after the war. While the country was considerably more advanced, concentration on military production had distracted most companies from developing technologies that could be used for consumer products. They soon found that, in the meanwhile, the West had accumulated a tremendous store of knowledge which could be tapped. Again, the interest was there and Japanese companies scoured the technical and professional literature to see what was available and who could be approached to obtain any desirable technologies.

The crucial constraint was manifestly not a lack of interest but a shortage of money to acquire this knowhow. After its defeat, the country was dreadfully poor and most of the funds were needed for essential reconstruction and restoration of facilities. Yet, some money could be set aside for inducing technologies. Since the government agencies, and especially the Ministry of International Trade and Industry and Ministry of Finance, controlled the access to foreign exchange, they tended to sit in on the decisions. Thus, the more general targeting exercise was paralleled by another one targeting the specific technologies that could do the most good. There was much comparing of alternative methods for accomplishing the same ends and finally a decision to choose one or the other, or perhaps all, so that Japan could really find out which was better and know more about the technical possibilities in general.

While the bureaucrats were usually conscientious in their activities of collecting information and then screening applications, they were not really equipped to assess the technical value and, often more important, the prospects of commercial utilization. This led them to overlook some valuable technologies until forced to come back to them by businessmen, as for Sony's development of transistors. So the exercise was only a genuine success because there was tremendous input from the private sector. And the whole operation became vastly more efficient and productive when the regulations were withdrawn and companies could simply license the know-how they wanted.[2]

The Japanese method of acquiring knowhow was later adopted by the Koreans with characteristic vigor. Korea had fallen much further behind than the Japanese and, when its economic development finally began in earnest, there was an even greater reservoir of desirable technologies to pick from. Since they had pitifully few technicians or experienced businessmen, the initial steps had to be taken by the government. Bureaucrats working out plans for specific sectors went much further in evaluating the various technologies that could be used. A special Ministry of Science and Technology was established. Only later were the rising companies in a position to decide on their own, still with the prior approval of the authorities until quite recently.

The approach in the other countries has varied, with Taiwan sometimes closer to Japan and Korea but also showing greater similarities with the very different attitude in Singapore and especially Hong Kong. There, there was hardly any intervention from the bureaucracy in the choice of technologies, just as the choice of scale, products or financing was regarded as being among the basic matters for individual entrepreneurs to decide. Realizing that improved technologies could help them produce more effectively, or get ahead of domestic or foreign competitors, there were many businessmen who travelled abroad and acquired the necessary expertise. But the process was clearly less structured and less compulsive.

Those enamored of technology would assume that the former, more aggressive policy was most effective. In some ways, as concerns quantity and perhaps quality, they would be right. When it comes to suitability, the outcome is more equivocal. For, the desire to induce technologies could hardly be separated from the urge to acquire the latest, most productive and most sophisticated ones. That they were terribly expensive is only the first problem. Far more important is what has come to be known as the need for "appropriate" technology. Most of the available knowhow had been developed by highly advanced countries, with an entirely different factor endowment. They were usually rich in capital and stressed features that saved labor, the complete opposite of what should be done in a country which has vast reserves of unemployed or inexpensive workers.

This means that, by selecting advanced technologies, Japan and Korea were accentuating the gaps between the technological levels of certain industries and companies. They were also making it harder to absorb labor. This

Appropriate automobile technology in Korea

Credit: KOTRA

could result in considerable waste and distortion and give unfair advantages to those who benefited from government support. On the other hand, it did make it possible to make more rapid headway and, at specific points, be as productive as the most advanced companies in the world. Then, by using cheaper labor for the remaining jobs, an otherwise backward country could actually gain a competitive edge over the leaders.

What has been adopted in Hong Kong, Singapore and Taiwan comes much closer to appropriate technology. It was acquired by individual businessmen with their own funds. This meant that, rather than take a big leap forward at broad intervals, the tendency was for a more gradual and even upgrading of the technology of the whole sector. The move followed, rather than anticipating, changes in comparative advantage and each step merely used a bit more capital and a bit less labor than the previous. This approach also simplified the learning process drastically since the same staff could be used with minor adjustments and retraining. The chances of a serious breakdown, as when imported machinery or techniques simply did not work in the new context, were almost insignificant.

Pushing ahead to the most sophisticated technologies, for all its theoretical advantages, was always a very risky proposition for practical reasons. Absorbing the know-how required extensive preparation of the people who would use it, and who rarely had any prior exposure to the tasks. It is hard to imagine how many things can go wrong when a backward country takes the big step into a new sector or switches from the traditional to a more modern production system. While rarely noted, many things went wrong in East Asia as well, although somewhat less than elsewhere.

In this connection, it is worthwhile recalling that

technologies can be induced in various ways. Some of them are considerably easier than others as regards a smooth and effective transfer. But they may have implications that make them less popular in some places. The purest form of technology is a bundle of concepts, formulas, processes, designs and the like which are novel or unique. While that is usually what occurs to mind first, it is the rarest type. It happens much more often that technology is embodied in an individual machine, a set of machinery or a whole plant which incorporates special techniques or turns out a special product.

East Asian businessmen were constantly on the lookout for helpful technologies they could acquire from more experienced companies. They would then contact the proprietor, negotiate a price (usully paid in royalties or similar fees) and enter into a formal licensing agreement. The technology would be transferred to them under careful supervision and every effort made to have it function properly. This was not the simplest method since it required considerable technical ability on the part of the licensee. But it was preferred by Japan, and also Korea, because it was not necessary to accept all sorts of related equipment which they felt could be made locally. And they did not want more dependence on the licensor than neccessary. Two thousand such agreements were concluded annually in Japan during the 1960s, and several hundred a year in Korea and Taiwan, with the levels only beginning to decline recently.

Of course, not all businessmen felt they could afford such royalties, and not all technologies were open for acquisition by just anyone. Some companies adopted less legitimate means of obtaining what they wanted, the most common being reverse engineering. They would buy a sample of a product they wished to make, take it apart to see how it worked, and then try to replicate it on their own. To steer clear of patent and other laws, they might make minor alterations. If they were particularly adept, they would actually improve on the original, patent it, and compete against the inventor. Improper as it may have been, that is how many Japanese companies got started and now counterfeiters in the NICs follow the same path to produce not only ordinary articles but even high tech items.

But the bulk of the transfer took the form of buying machinery that was generally on the market and was known to possess better characteristics. Up-to-date technologies were embodied in the machinery and, to enhance productivity or improve quality, manufacturers simply had to change over to more recent models. This was not particularly difficult since they already knew the trade and the machinery came equipped with instruction manuals. As a matter of fact, the newer machinery was often easier to use and required less actual skills of the operator than old. Since entrepreneurs in all five countries were very keen about moving upmarket, or simply staying in business, they did not hesitate to keep in step and their stock of plant and equipment is markedly better than in other places of the same economic stage.

Inducing advanced technology by encouraging foreign investment had some definite advantages. It was possible to obtain, at one and the same time, both the knowhow and the capital. If a multinational set up a local operation, there was no doubt that it would bring in technology it was quite familiar with, if not the very latest, then certainly something that would do the trick. The transfer would naturally be smooth since it was undertaken within the company. The company would also make every effort to be a commercial success and upgrade its technology over the years. These were adequate reasons for Hong Kong, Singapore and Taiwan to welcome investments in general and those which included new technologies even more warmly. In fact, such projects were extremely numerous and leading sectors such as synthetic fibers, petrochemicals, electronics and machinery were largely initiated by foreign investors.[3]

Japan, partially followed by Korea, had no doubt that technology could be obtained in this manner or that it could be more readily absorbed. But they were afraid that the multinationals would not allow the knowhow to spread to other companies in the branch or even to nationals on their own staff. There was even greater concern that such multinationals, with more advanced technologies and greater financial backing, would be able to dominate their respective sectors, preventing the rise of local firms. While a bit contradictory, they were also worried about what would happen if for some unknown reason the foreigners decided to pull out. This led to more restrictive policies in which efforts were made by the government to delink technology and investment. By making investment difficult, if not impossible, multinationals were forced to give up on the market or enter through licensing agreements or perhaps joint ventures.

Thus, the divergencies among the five were notable. While all the methods were used by all of them, and everyone bought machinery without second thoughts, Japan and Korea clearly preferred taking just the technology and applying it themselves while Taiwan, Singapore and Hong Kong were more willing to let foreign companies invest and bring their technologies with them.

As for so many other facets, it would be hard to prove that one approach was conclusively better than the other. Once again, the choice was probably more a question of cultural attitudes than economic rationale. There is also the contributing factor that the smaller city-states could hardly even think in terms of technological autonomy. But each side seemed to get what it wanted. Japan and Korea got their technologies and an indigenous base while the others obtained more abundant flows of investment plus technology. While the former had to pay the price, the latter not only got the knowhow for free, the investors put up substantial sums to integrate them in the economy. True, the multinationals did dominate certain sectors. But these were all new sectors which had been vacant to begin with. And, to the surprise of many, local firms were actually learning the techniques and squeezing into the same sectors. As long as the economy flourished, it was very unlikely that the investors would withdraw and even in a downturn they were tied to the market by the money and effort they had already sunk in. On the other hand, the Three were less likely to become inventors of fresh technology like Japan and Korea.

Obviously, outside technology is of no use unless it takes. Most developing countries behave as if the advanced countries were somehow responsible for the smooth transfer. If the results are not as positive as expected, they hastily place the blame on the suppliers. No matter how comprehensible this reaction may be, as with any other commodity, the onus is actually on the buyer as much, and in this particular case usually more so, than the original source. Even if it were not, it is patently in the recipient's best interest to make the transfer as successful as possible.

It is up to those screening potential technologies to select the right one, namely such as can be effectively transplanted into an economy with very different endowments and preconditions. This study, as hinted, can only be partly technical. It is even more important to consider whether the investment is suitable in terms of potential sales of any goods that are produced or savings that arise from enhanced productivity. This is a very complex calculation. It should include indirect costs like supporting infrastructure, necessary revamping of facilities, and retraining of personnel. Since they have cheaper labor, it cannot simply be assumed that if the technology made sense in developed countries it would also be purposeful in developing countries. If, in addition, the new technology requires greater scale, it would be highly advisable to check that markets will exist for the expanded output. That is why such decisions are more likely to be right when businessmen, as opposed to bureaucrats, are in charge. It is to the credit of all five countries that they realized this.

The chances of an advanced technology being firmly grafted onto a backward economy are extremely slim unless the society is prepared for it. This preparation takes various forms, none of them more essential than education. But it has to be the right education, not just any education! Most developing countries find it easier and cheaper, as well as more uplifting, to offer general and liberal courses. The East Asians, with their Confucian heritage, were also tempted to move in that direction and actually did at first. In the meanwhile, the need for more appropriate vocational and technical training was recognized and the school system slanted that way. Korea probably went furthest in encouraging technical education and praising working with one's hands as well as one's brain. But the others were not far behind in expanding vocational schools, creating polytechnics and adding engineering departments to the universities.[4]

Although such academic education was precious, it was still rather abstract and had to be supplemented by on-the-job training which became a characteristic feature of the Japanese companies. Their in-house training consists of both formal lessons and more informal practical work. The idea was taken up with great enthusiasm in Korea, where companies had to introduce such training or pay a fine and where the larger groups established regular technical schools. Of course, this sort of effort only made sense where companies had a relatively stable work force so that an investment in training would pay off over the years. In Chinese companies, it did not make much sense to offer more than very rudimentary instructions on how to do the specific chores since labor mobility was so high. That, in fact, was one of the worst drawbacks of the phenomenon of job-hopping.

While the general context is important, the transfer of technology is a very specific thing in which no two cases are the same. That will explain why companies engaged in such careful planning prior to the actual transference. The physical site had to cleared, requisite facilities erected, suitable infrastructure installed and essential utilities connected. People had to be trained for their future tasks, usually by sending them to the supplier's workshops or a similar operation somewhere else. During a transitional period, it might be necessary to employ foreign engineers or supervisors. None of this could be treated lightly since failure at any stage could be disastrous. Just how seriously this need was taken was exemplified by POSCO where the physical preparations took years and training lasted months, so that there would be no hitch once the steel mill was ready to run.[5]

But one cannot just stop at this point. Technology transfer is not simply a question of acquiring, in packaged form, the knowledge of others. Knowhow itself is a precious asset and the ability to apply it well, and improve on it, spells the difference between propelling one's own economy and being pulled along by others. This was duly recognized in all five countries, although better articulated in some, through the growing stress on research and development.

R&D, though not adequately realized, is not just a useful activity for advanced countries. It plays a crucial role in those just beginning industrialization, even if most of the stress is on development. It is often necessary to adapt any product to local needs by changing the size, appearance or materials used. Production techniques are even more in need of adjustment, so they can be executed by workers with different skills and experiences. Even mechanical processes, while broadly applicable, can also be modified in some particulars to use local raw materials, existing equipment, and so on. This sort of adaptation makes any technology distinctly more "appropriate" than it would otherwise be.

While many regard Japan and the NICs as nations of copiers, at least at the outset, it is not generally appreciated just how dificult copying can be. This already requires no mean R&D capabilities. The ability to improve on what has been borrowed, and make innovations in the technologies of others, is even more arduous. Yet, that level has long since been reached. Now, all five countries are rising to the far more challenging task of creating their own products, production techniques and technologies. This shifts the stress to research and applied sciences as well as eventually basic and pure sciences.

The causes for this progression are self-evident. Over the years, at a breathtaking pace, more and more of the existing knowhow has been assimilated in one way or another. There is not that much more in the accumulated store of knowledge that can be absorbed by Japan, and the NICs are gradually approaching that point as well. Meanwhile, those who have created the technologies

Appropriate automobile technology in Japan

Credit: Mazda

have finally realized just how precious they are and are no longer as willing to license them to others. The Five will have to count on their own efforts more than ever in order to sustain their advance into technology-intensive sectors.

Various methods have been adopted to promote the rise of indigenous research and development. Not surprisingly, the state quickly became the primary promoter throughout the region, and went to unusual lengths in Japan, Korea and Taiwan. Admitting the tremendous costs involved, and the dearth of researchers, the governments established special institutes to carry on research in a growing range of disciplines. Those in Japan were most numerous and best endowed, existing not only at the national but also prefectural level. The Korean Advanced Institute of Science and Technology (KAIST) and

Taiwan's Industrial Technology Research Institute (ITRI), and their related bodies, were exceptionally elaborate for developing countries. Rather than work on abstruse topics, every effort was made to have them deal with practical technical problems and bottlenecks of local companies. Making government-sponsored research even more project-oriented, Japan's Ministry of International Trade and Industry mounted a number of spectacular programs, the best known of which were to develop very large-scale integrated circuits and now a "fifth generation" computer.

Meanwhile, the government urged the private sector to expand its own R&D activities. This was not left to verbal encouragement by any means, since generous tax write-offs were permitted for these expenditures. Even without such incentives, ambitious companies were actively beefing up their capabilities because, as noted, they needed this simply to absorb and improve on existing technology. Then, as they advanced, even greater exertions were made to catch up with foreign competitors and keep ahead of domestic ones. By the 1980s, Japan's research and development expenditures were approaching the best levels in the West (almost 3% of GNP) while Korea and Taiwan were trying hard to reach Japan's old level (2%).

Whereas most of this involved following the path blazed by Western countries, in one vital respect it was an Asian country which took the lead. Technological upgrading could not just be something for researchers in laboratories, because much of the actual work was going on in the factory. And, if the only ones concerned were specialists, they would have a very narrow view. To spread the essential task of improving productivity and quality to the whole staff, the Japanese hit upon the idea of establishing QC Circles.[6] These were small groups of workers who met to discuss, and solve, concrete problems arising in the course of their work. They were also incited to make suggestions. This effort was remarkably useful in pinpointing difficulties and adjusting production techniques or even modifying basic products and technologies. In addition, it enhanced the workers' technical knowledge and participation in the work process. Although it has not been easy, the other East Asians are doing their best to adopt these methods.

There has increasingly been a third partner in this effort, the universities and scientific research institutes, because it will ultimately be necessary to move beyond practical technology and applied science into more basic science. This is the sort of thing governments are poorly equipped to do and companies have little direct interest in. This work is also exceedingly expensive and time consuming and requires exceptionally competent personnel. However, if they are to accomplish something of use to the economy, the scientists must become more aware of practical needs. In order to bring the technical institutes, the companies and the scientists into closer relations, several novel schemes were devised. One is the Academic City in Tsukuba, Japan, and a counterpart in Korea, Daeduk Science Town. But they remain primarily geared to research activities. Commercial purposes are better served at the Hsinchu industrial zone in Taiwan, where high tech companies are concentrated in the proximity of technical institutes and universities whose facilities and staff they can draw on. The small, dispersed "technopolises" may do the same thing in some of Japan's outer prefectures.

This time around, it would seem that there is a definite advantage for countries where the state plays a leading role. It is easier to raise the necessary funds or convince companies to organize their own efforts. And countries

which have large, well-structured companies, like Japan
and Korea, probably have an additional edge since they
can mount massive thrusts to overcome annoying
technological obstacles. This means that Hong Kong and
Singapore would remain more dependent on outside suppliers of technology and absorb a greater share through
the purchase of new machinery. Yet, it would be unwise
to overlook the ability of small businessmen to upgrade
their operations or individuals to engage in self-improve-
ment, especially if their careers depend on it. Finally,
while much of R&D is a collective endeavor, there are
always critical points where individuals with personal
drive and imagination are more likely to make a decisive
breakthough.

While they are not always regarded as such, perhaps
the most significant technologies are not the hard ones
associated with machinery and production but the softer
ones in the field of management. There, too, the Asian
countries found a treasure chest of new methods and
techniques that could be borrowed. . . if they wanted.

To many of the Asians, it was evident that their own
management techniques were none too good. The earliest entrepreneurs were very authoritarian and paternalistic in their methods. They tended to give orders and
expect compliance. They were not very open to counter-
proposals or ideas that worked their way up from
below. Often they tried to handle every last detail of decision-making and implementation and little could
be accomplished if they were not around. They were
particularly bad at delegating authority and institution-
alizing procedures, both of which were sorely needed by
the companies that grew.[7]

It was perfectly natural that businessmen should look
to Western models here as well. This was especially true
of Hong Kong and Singapore where multinationals

abounded and many managers got their first taste of business while dealing with foreigners. But even the most old-fashioned entrepreneurs in Korea and Taiwan sent their children to study business administration in the United States. Somewhat more grudgingly, established companies in Japan sent promising executives off for a few years to earn an MBA. When the youngsters returned with the new-fangled and somewhat alien ideas, they were not always welcome and application of "modern" management was very partial. Still, lip service was paid to the concept of more impersonal, rational and efficient techniques and it was assumed that with time the East Asians would get into step.

However, the resistance to borrowing Western management was much greater than to borrowing Western science and technology. For this time it was necessary to tamper much more with the ways people worked and the relations that existed among them. It was here that the undying urge for "Western technology, Eastern spirit" was strongest. And nowhere was it quite as overpowering as in Japan. The country had long been ethnocentric and had developed its own ways of doing things in an inward-looking society. This was not easy to change and there was no desire to copy others when the Japanese felt they had, or could develop, something far better on their own.

This can account for the very great gaps that do exist between the highly sophisticated techniques which are used for production and the rather traditionalistic techniques that continue to apply to human relations. Naturally, there were changes as the older generation of founders disappeared and family control was weakened. The postwar purges only hastened that and distaste for the way people were treated during the nationalist era resulted in a considerable loosening of formality and some advance in equal treatment. Factory workers were no longer regimented as if they were soldiers and orders were given more courteously. There was much talk of the need for encouraging initiative at lower levels and permitting what was called "bottom-up" management. A lot of this turned out to be mere rhetoric in practice, but certainly the atmosphere was better.

But Japanese customs, or at least some carefully selected ones, still showed through and made Japanese-style management not only very different from Western-style management but almost unique. While it was often characterized by lifetime employment, this is just one aspect of the system. It starts with recruitment straight from school, training within the company and gradual promotion through the ranks, not unlike an apprenticeship system. Both pay and promotion are based more on seniority than elsewhere and this is done deliberately to inculcate greater loyalty. Rather than assign specific jobs to specific individuals hired for their skills, there is a great deal of job rotation and most tasks are handled by small groups. Decision-making is often long and laborious as *ringisho* are circulated containing proposals and have to be approved, and stamped, at each level while those backing a given policy collect supporters through *nemawashi*.[8] The result is supposedly "harmony," but certainly one born more of constraint than spontaneity.[9]

This model was initially rejected as an alternative by the other countries because it was so patently inefficient in many ways and manifestly unmodern. They much preferred the scientific management that was propagated in the West. This implied a more rational use of employees, recruitment for specific skills and payment as a function of ability with promotions going to those who performed best. Workers were hired and fired in keeping with the economic situation and they tended to give no more of themselves than was paid for. Any greater sacrifice had to be coaxed out by incentives. But even then they realized, as was being noticed in the West, that the cruder aspects of the system had to be tempered by a more benign approach to labor relations.

It was only late in the day that some of their leaders began to feel that perhaps Japan had followed the right path while they had taken a wrong turn. That was partially because of Japan's impressive economic progress which it was generally assumed had been made because of—and not despite—its rather archaic management style. It also arose from a new sentiment that East Asians were clearly not Westerners and therefore had no special reason to copy Western models. With a Confucian background, they also longed for a return to supposed attributes like loyalty and harmony that were woefully lacking in places where job-hopping was a widespread phenomenon. But only the Koreans were close enough culturally to move in that direction while the Chinese were distinctly more individualistic and found it hard to adapt to the tighter strictures of Japanese practices.

Thus, despite any differences, all Five were able to master not only the more abstract technologies but also to apply modern production techniques and management systems or to devise their own. That was a major contribution to development throughout the region. Failure to accomplish this would have prevented their rise and forced them back into the ranks of developing countries that never develop.

NOTES

1. For the effects of technical progress on economic growth, see Edward K. Y. Chen, *Hyper-growth in Asian Economies,* pp. 90–108,

and Shirley W. Y. Kuo, *The Taiwan Economy in Transition,* pp. 223–84.

2.   Interesting insight into how Japan adopts and adapts foreign technology can be gained from Makoto Kikuchi, *Japanese Electronics,* Tokyo, Simul Press, 1983.

3.   The effect of investment on technological upgrading and growth is studied in Yung Whee Rhee et al, *Korea's Competitive Edge, Managing the Entry into World Markets,* Denis Fred Simon, *Taiwan, Technology Transfer, and Transnationalism,* and Kunio Yoshihara, *Foreign Investment and Domestic Response: A Study of Singapore's Industrialization.*

4.   The relationship between education and development is dealt with in Solomon B. Levine and Hisashi Kawada, *Human Resources in Japanese Industrial Development,* pp. 22–91, and Noel F. McGinn et al, *Education and Development in Korea.*

5.   Sang Whan Yoh, ''Management of Industrial Projects: The Case of Pohang Iron & Steel Co.,'' Seoul, Korea Development Institute, 1982.

6.   There has been a veritable flood of books on quality control and productivity by Japanese and foreign authors, of very uneven quality on the whole, and far too numerous to mention.

7.   The rather archaic values and methods of first generation managers in East Asia are described in Kyong-Dong Kim, *Man and Society in Korea's Economic Growth,* pp. 43–64, and Robert H. Silin, *Leadership and Values,* pp. 61–94.

8.   Books on Japanese management are also numerous and, if anything, worse on the whole. One useful primer is M. Y. Yoshino, *Japan's Managerial System.*

9.   For some revelations of what is wrong with the system, see Jon Woronoff, *Japan's Wasted Workers* and *Japan: The Coming Economic Crisis.*

12

Age of Neo-Development

In the course of human history, one nation or another has periodically thrown off its lethargy and demonstrated an economic vigor and ability that enabled it to advance at an exceptional speed. Few of these spurts were very long-lasting, and some were related to fortuitous events like foreign conquests or the discovery of precious resources. There have also been more sustained periods of growth which allowed some countries to plod slowly ahead. But it would be nearly impossible to find any other examples of countries with very modest endowments and little indication of economic talent suddenly growing at two and more times the average rate and pressing swiftly onward decade after decade. Yet, that is what happened to the East Asian Five.[1]

Shifting from an agricultural or entrepot base to industrial activity, turning out one product after the other, exporting them to one country after another, constantly boosting produciton and income, maintaining growth rates of 10% or more a year during the booms and not doing so poorly in the downturn, these and other occurrences were enough to attract fervid attention. Even in an age of development, such accomplishments were all too rarely seen. What was more impressive is that they were just surface manifestations of a deeper process of economic transformation and modernization that achieved in mere decades what had once taken generations or centuries.

The distance covered by Japan since the Meiji Restoration, not much more than a century back, was about the same as had been run by Great Britain since the industrial revolution first dawned in the mid-eighteenth century.[2] And it was already drawing even with the United States in many sectors. The other four were actually faster. They clearly parted company with the developing countries, of which they were a not particularly hopeful element just after the war, and soon boasted the title of newly industrialized countries, among the few that really deserved it.[3] For they possessed industries as dynamic as could be found in Northern Europe, another locus of early industrialization, and stronger than those of Southern and Eastern Europe. Yet, they took a mere twenty or thirty years to accomplish this turnabout. It seemed as if history were suddenly accelerating in this one corner of the globe.

Surely, there were adequate reasons to speak of an "economic miracle" in each and every one of the Five. But it would be hasty and misleading to conclude that this emanated solely from something "miraculous" in their policies and strategies. There is one further factor which must be taken into account and without which none of these happenings is understandable. Basically, it can be summed up by stating that the economic context in which countries now evolve has changed so radically that one must speak of "neo-development" to do it justice.

Traditional development was an extremely painstaking and time-consuming process. It is what faced the ancient Egyptians, or Mesopotamians, or Chinese in bygone days. It implied inventing the wheel and the plow, paper and gun powder . . . for the first time. It was almost as dreary and wearying in England when specialization and a division of labor emerged, when great inventions like the power loom and steam engine permitted mechanization. All of these countries were pioneers. So were the United States and Germany later on, when they expanded the range of techniques and inventions. For they had to build vast industries almost from scratch, popularize products that had never been heard of and bring the price down enough to generate mass sales. They also had to conceive of new forms of organization, new styles of management, flourishes like advertising and marketing. None of this was easy while they fashioned what is now commonly regarded as a "modern economy."

All of the countries which appeared on the scene somewhat later, including Meiji Japan and the host of developing countries spawned after the war, were in a completely different position. They were just followers. They simply had to see what had been done by those who went before and imitate it. They did not have to create new products, industries, technologies, production techniques, marketing or managerial methods. This had already been done for them. They simply had to pick from among the vast reservoir of knowledge those items which might help them in their particular situation.

As latecomers, they had an extremely wide choice. This applied even to postwar Japan despite its previous progress. There was still a lot it had not absorbed and which could fill out the economy. For Korea, Taiwan, Hong Kong and Singapore, starting from a much lower point, there was almost no end to what could be gleaned. And they had an added advantage, there was also a Japanese model to follow. This meant that the more recent participants in economic affairs could copy not only the pioneers of traditional development but the pioneer of the process of catching up.

It is only in this framework that the various techniques discussed in this section make sense. They must assume the effects of earlier efforts, and earlier successes, or they would simply be inconceivable. Each one, in its own way, is a means of making the best possible use of this rare mother lode of intangible wealth which is constantly expanded, rather than being depleted, by the actions of mankind. Indeed, the very fact of its existence worked a considerable change of attitudes.

Thus, before reviewing the techniques, it is worthwhile stressing that the mere recognition that one is a follower and not a leader is a precious advantage. This way one can peek over the shoulder of those ahead to see what they are doing. This inspires a very forward-looking approach in which countries can consciously or unconsciously pattern themselves on those which have gotten somewhat further along the path. They can increasingly think not only in terms of what is possible now but what will be possible in the not far distant future when they have reached the same point as their predecessors. And they can decide whether to do things in the same old ways or in new and improved ways.

Rather than endlessly lament the misfortune of being backward, and dwelling on the hardship this entails, people can assume a more positive and future-oriented behavior in which they think and plan for what is coming.[4] Since they have a strong urge to find out, they can project their thoughts forward. They can try to gear their actions and their investments to more distant goals. Instead of taking petty measures for the short-term, they can make far greater efforts for an expected greater return in the longer term.

In such an atmosphere, people can finally start working toward "development." As intimated, this is a relatively new concept since, for millennia, most societies have persistently assumed that things would only change slightly and only rare individuals would obtain notable improvement. But such an attitude is hardly sensible when one can see all around the palpable proof that a country does not have to accept its economic fate and that individuals can better their own lot by acting appropriately.

That there is another lifestyle, one which can be called "developed" in contradistinction to "underdeveloped," is hard to miss in the present circumstances of even very marginal countries. People are surrounded by the gadgets and techniques of other nations. They learn how others live in the cinema, on television, from the press. They may travel abroad. If not, they are very likely to encounter hordes of tourists visiting them quite simply because they are more primitive and quaint. This arouses a desire to bring about improvement, to enjoy the same material benefits (even if one regrets the moral losses) and to become "developed" as well.

By now this desire has become almost as universal as once the urge among barbarians to become "civilized." The need for development has been argued by national leaders of every stripe promising to enhance the lot of their compatriots. It echoes back from the general public in pleas and demands for a better life. The cause has also been institutionalized with organizations and agencies spreading the creed of development and enrolling nations in the crusade. This could not have been demonstrated more eloquently than by declaring the 1960s a "development decade" and then, when that was not enough, adding a second and third decade.[5]

Economic development has also burgeoned into a science of sorts with experts, specialists and consultants who can tell governments what policies to adopt and how to overcome any obstacles. Development economics is taught by learned professors and debated in erudite seminars. Books, just like this one, are written to examine the various strategies applied by one country or another, to compare them and see which accomplished most. This does not mean that foolproof formulas have been found, universal recipes that work every time or even more than once in a while. But the approach to development is far more systematic and serious than it has ever been in the history of mankind.

This atmosphere had several crucial effects. One was to make perfectly clear to the Five that they had fallen behind in certain respects, a message that was received earlier in Japan than among the Koreans and Chinese. The latter bitterly regretted their initial failure and awaited a second chance which came after the war. With so many signs of progress and prosperity about them, and countries around the world proclaiming the goal of material advancement, it was hard for them to do otherwise even if they would. Instead, due to their intense pride and ambition, they threw themselves into the task of development with even greater zeal and dedication than most.

It was no less important for them to realize that one could catch up by adopting the right approach. Economic development was certainly a daunting challenge; it would require tremendous effort and sacrifice. But it was far from impossible. It was only necessary to apply the proper methods and techniques, the contents of which were better known than ever. It was just a question of doing the same things as others who had gone before. These others were mainly Westerners, once blindly admired and then increasingly regarded as not especially superior intellectually, morally or otherwise. If such people could reach the stage of advanced nations, there was no reason why Japanese, Koreans or Chinese could not do the same.

The acceleration of the process, which is a notable contribution of neo-development, helped immensely. It was now possible to boost production rapidly enough to make visible progress in a relatively short time. It was even possible to create more jobs quickly enough for unemployment to be absorbed in short order and then, and this was far more important, for the income levels of workers to rise. Already within a decade, it was conceivable to enjoy some of the promised fruits of development. This made the incentives much more tempting and convincing than government propaganda or promises of the good life to come some day far off when the country was finally advanced.

There has been much talk about the harmony and loyalty, the willingness to sacrifice and postpone rewards that characterized the peoples of East Asia. There is no question but that these features were clearly there and played an important role. But it is not at all certain that the qualities would have been strong enough to carry them through the centuries of painfully slow advance that had been experienced in England and Holland, or even the somewhat faster rise of Germany and the United States. The social gaps might have been stretched, the harmony worn thin and the conflicts which inevitably arise exacerbated to the point that they would have gotten stuck somewhere along the line. They owe it to the fact of being latecomers, who could proceed more smoothly, that their much vaunted virtues were not put to the acid test.

Instilling an urge to succeed, and showing that success was definitely attainable, were not the only advantages for those engaged in neo-development. Even more could be gained by applying some novel strategies that allowed countries to benefit from being followers and not leaders and turned the lag between the two into a highly unexpected and formidable tool.

As noted, the later-developers had the advantage of studying the past progress of other countries which preceded them in economic development. They were able to see how far the front-runners had gotten and, even if they were in no position to copy them yet, this information was still useful. It was also possible to plot what stage many other countries, whether slightly or considerably ahead of them, had reached. This traced a reasonably clear and concrete development path, typified periodically by one country or another, which could show how their own economies should look in the various stages of the progression.

This, more than any abstract econometric model, is what permitted the broader planning that was undertaken consciously in Japan, Korea and Taiwan and intuitively in Singapore and Hong Kong. It was feasible to determine which sectors were predominant in each stage of the growth process. It could be noted which ones should dwindle and which expand as the process unfolded. Even within the three basic sectors, it was possible to pick the specific industries that might take off and pull the economy forward. This also made it much easier to foresee any resulting shifts in employment, savings, spending, etc.

While the planners and politicians might be interested in these broader, macroeconomic parameters, the businessmen were much more concerned about practical matters like how to organize and manage a company. This they could easily find out, often by just buying a book. They were even more curious about the products which might be sold. It was not necessary for them to invent any. They merely had to check which ones were most popular in external markets and manufacture them. By making a somewhat greater effort, they could figure out which products might be popular in their domestic market at that time or some time in the future when the local purchasing power would have increased.

The products that could be taken up by latecomers numbered not just in the hundreds, or thousands, or even tens of thousands. There were literally hundreds of thousands of different articles, some of them finished products, many more parts and components thereof, which an entrepreneur could decide to undertake. Most of these products, the vast majority in fact, were such ordinary and commonplace things by that time that they were not protected by any patent and could readily be made by whoever wanted to. The remaining minority could be licensed, reshaped or simply pirated. Only a small portion were really beyond the reach of developing countries due to proprietary rights or technological complexity. And, in addition to the industrial products, there were new crops for farmers and more services for other businessmen.

The big problem for later-developers was actually to decide just which ones they wanted to produce locally. It was mainly a question of getting the proper factor combination to benefit from the existing endowment, namely abundant labor. As the years passed, the factors would gradually be adjusted and other products could be added using more capital and technology. Of course, even with access to the essential information and instructions, it was never simple to turn out any product efficiently and competitively. But these were certainly less acute problems than faced by the early-developers who had had to create the products to begin with.

It is only on this background that the highly touted

policy of targeting can be understood. In one sense, it was designed to expand the range of products made in the country and to fill out the industrial structure. But, in fact, it was just as much an exercise in narrowing down the vast number of potential projects to those which were most purposeful and could most readily be accomplished. It would have been decidedly unwise to get lost in the endless possibilities of neo-development as concerns product introduction rather than intentionally set some aside for later. Whatever it was, targeting was most definitely not an attempt to dream up completely new products since none of the Five, not even Japan, ever proposed an item that had not already been tested and proven by some more advanced country.

Industrial policy, and targeting within it, had another extremely important function which was also only possible because the countries were followers. Rather than foster industries and products in a haphazard manner, simply because they had become amenable to domestic production and there was a market, products and industries were grouped. They were launched in conjunction with one another in order to take advantage of any possible linkages that existed. This could be forward integration, by establishing steel users to support a nascent steel industry, or backward integration, with a textile plant built to supply the existing garment industry. It could consist of localizing the manufacture of parts for finished articles which were being assembled or making machinery needed by manufacturers. This sort of coordination was extremely helpful in promoting all sectors concerned.

While it was most evident that the latecomers benefited by finding such a wealth of potential products, that is far from the only thing they encountered. Due to the existing structure and circumstances, they had access to many of the essential production factors which may have been lacking in their original endowment.

One of the biggest needs of any developing country, especially those with such meager sources of ready revenue as the Five, is capital. There have always been some supplies of capital available, whether through loans or investment. But the amounts were more restricted a century ago and, as Japan feared and China learned to its discomfiture, it was not always sage to accept such entanglements. Thus, most of the economic pioneers had had to get by largely on whatever funds they had and to accumulate a bit more very slowly and arduously.

This situation changed quite dramatically after the war with the initiation of development aid and other forms of backing for economic recovery and advancement. The most notable sign of this change was the American Marshal Plan in Europe. But Korea, Taiwan and Japan also gained substantially from American largesse during extended periods of time.[6] This greatly eased the postwar distress in all three nations and gave an indispensable impulse to the early phase of development. Singapore and Hong Kong benefited, although not as considerably, from British aid. Since then, the World Bank and its soft loan window, the International Development Association, have offered extensive loans to most of them, although excluding Hong Kong and gradually phasing out the others as they grew. But, they were able to graduate into respectable and regular clients of commercial banks from which they could borrow appreciable sums of money.

Through these methods, it was feasible to raise far more external capital than at any previous point in history. Most of this was on comparatively good terms, some of it actually grants and much of the rest at concessional rates. If anything, it was almost too easy to obtain funds. For, if taken unnecessarily, they were liable to accumulate so rapidly that indebtedness and debt servicing became unwanted burdens. It was equally thinkable to use this money for the wrong things. This does not mean only disreputable purposes but also seemingly admirable ones like building numerous schools or highways. The reason is quite simply that the loans would eventually have to be paid back, with interest, and should therefore go principally into efforts that would make it possible to reimburse them when the time came.

The East Asian Five were unusually short of basic natural resources and, in former times, would doubtlessly have suffered grievously for this lack. It would have been extremely difficult for them to promote many of the industries in which they ultimately became remarkably proficient. The reason is that previously there was not such a lively trade in raw materials and, for what there was, transport costs made the shipment of large quantities over great distances prohibitive. This meant that, for all practical purposes, the only ones which could hope to make steel were countries where both coal and iron ore could be found in relative proximity. It was also impracticable to refine most metals other than near a major source of energy or form petrochemicals far from the supply of gas or naphtha.

This also changed drastically during the latter part of the twentieth century. The progress came due to stepped-up prospection and new mining techniques which produced such massive quantities of ores or oil that they had to be sold abroad. Use of ever larger vessels, which ran on then cheap oil, brought the costs of transport down enormously. By building steel mills or petrochemical complexes along the seaside, and running extremely efficient large-scale operations, it was possible for Japan to become competitive even against the supplier countries. Korea and Taiwan could adopt the same methods. With the sudden rise in oil prices, and also transport costs, it was no longer as easy as it had once been. But the possibilities were at least there if one could keep ahead technologically.

The only production factor of which the Five had an ample supply was labor. This was originally cheap and relatively unskilled labor, which was sufficient during the early phase of development. However, these countries would never have gotten very far if they did not improve and upgrade it over the years. That is arguably their prime achievement since the population was vigorously drilled, trained and educated to ever higher levels. More and more children went to school for increasingly long times. What was even more impressive, a fair number of them were actually taught something useful.

Daewoo's Chairman Kim opening yet another factory

Credit: Daewoo

While this process had been envisaged, and every developing country put stress on education, it was not realized just how far it could go. Korea, according to comparative studies, had an educational system as good as countries twice as rich. Singapore's school system was rapidly approaching the level of those in the West. By the 1980s, Japan was turning out more engineers and technicians, if still less scientists, than the much larger United States and considerably more than any European country. While none of them cultivated much Nobel Prize material, they certainly had the kind of personnel that was going to be needed by the economic structures they were forging.

This rapid transformation was also a consequence of their latecomer status. For, just about everything that is taught in school is part of the common heritage of mankind by now and any nation can train the necessary teachers, adopt suitable textbooks, and make its students work like mad to assimilate the stuff. Admittedly, some subjects are too complex or require exceedingly expensive equipment. But this could often be solved by sending students abroad. It is thus that untold thousands of East Asian technicians, engineers and scientists studied at the best American and European schools. This meant that the precious human resources which it had taken advanced nations centuries to acquire could be quickly replicated in developing countries . . . if they made the effort.

Where the later-developers benefited most, however, was when it came to inducing technology. During the latter half of the twentieth century, there was an incredibly large pool of knowledge that was basically open for any developing country to dip into. There were technologies of all sorts which could be applied to every sector under the sun. There were new crops, farming methods and aids for agriculture. There was no end to the specific technologies for the various industrial branches. It was possible to learn how to run modern services. Even the techniques for planning and developing a whole economy could be picked up.

The government and businessmen of all five countries soon became aware of this and adopted one technology after the other. Often simple technologies were introduced first, then somewhat more complicated ones, and finally the latest that were available. After the technologies in one field had been absorbed, they would move on to the next, and the one after. This made it possible to upgrade time and again, each time taking giant strides in terms of productivity and quality. It was not always easy to assimilate this knowhow, but that was gradually overcome as the school system turned out more graduates and suppliers made up for any lacks.

It is sometimes claimed that it was hard to acquire technologies, this complaint usually being voiced by those who made inadequate efforts. But there was not much sign of undue difficulty in East Asia. Of course, some particularly sensitive technologies might not have been accessible. But most of the others, what could fairly be regarded as "appropriate" to their level, were almost plethoric. They were also very easy to obtain because they quickly became old, conventional or even obsolete as newer methods were devised. Proprietors were happy to get something for them and did not haggle too much over price. If they did, there was usually a competitor who could be tempted to replace them.

Even if the prices looked steep to the companies which had to pay them or the financial bureaucrats who had to approve the agreements, they were not when compared to what they gave the beneficiaries. In some cases, they were able to manufacture certain products for the very first time. In others, they could increase their productivity substantially or turn out products of better quality. This resulted in a tremendous boost in output for the country, more income for the workers, and bigger earnings for the companies. Sales of these products, and profits thereon, made the acquisition of new technologies a very attractive proposition. Otherwise it is hardly likely that this would have been such a popular approach.

But cost was not even the most significant aspect. Where the gains were clearest, and most spectacular, was with regard to time. Previously, it would have taken years, perhaps decades, to improve on whatever indigenous technologies existed. This would have involved abysmal waste as false tracks were followed, products turned out not to be quite adequate, or domestic goods remained more costly than imports. Inducing technology helped avoid all of this. First of all, by going straight to an accepted technology, it was possible to bypass the earlier, less valuable attempts. Secondly, by moving from a low technological level to a much higher one, it was possible to leapfrog ahead.

This explains not only how relatively backward countries were suddenly able to churn out quantities of products as good as those from much more advanced countries. It explains why, on many occasions, it was actually possible to beat them at their own game. Technology acquisition was much cheaper and surer than R & D and, while it did not get a newcomer all the way up front, it brought one very close. With much cheaper labor costs, it did not really matter if the company had a slightly less efficient technology, it was still able to gain a commercial edge and win sales. Thus it was that manufacturers in the Five could eventually compete against those who had developed the technologies to begin with.

There is one additional element which is extremely important in business. That is access to markets. Once again, latecomers had a big advantage in that they did not have to create the market for a new product which was still unknown and unproven. When they began selling standard products they were able to deliver them to the same markets that bought them regularly. These markets could easily be identified. And, as already mentioned, there were effective ways of getting in.

What was more, the very fact that the markets already existed—something any outsider could readily determine—offered a further opportunity to aggressive entrepreneurs. Most earlier companies had started off small, producing enough for the modest sales that were initially obtained, and then gradually expanding as the market grew. All this while, new machnery would be acquired as the need arose, with the more recent equipment being highly efficient but the rest considerably less so. A newcomer could take a very different tack. He could build his production facility immediately to a larger scale, using the latest technologies and machinery, and then produce a particularly fine range of goods at exceptionally low prices. He would then use these strengths to force out the forerunners which were notably less efficient.

It is largely thanks to these multiple advantages of being a later-developer, as much as anything else, that the East Asians were capable of working their economic "miracles." If the possibilities had not existed, there is absolutely no way that they could have developed as rapidly or steadily. Most likely, they would have grown and shown a much better performance than the vast majority of countries. But they would never have been able to make as much progress or to challenge the leaders as soon as they did.

This does not imply that there is something "wrong"

or "improper" about the techniques that were used or simply the fact of benefiting from their late arrival.[7] It would be perfectly senseless to do anything but benefit fully from the past efforts of others in order to advance more surely oneself. Reinventing the wheel, or the motorcycle, or the microwave oven would be ludicrous and futile. Creating new markets rather than penetrating older ones, working on new technologies when plenty already exist, refusing to borrow money at favorable rates would be no less foolhardy.

Basically, all of these things are there to be used and anyone who fails to profit from them has only himself to blame. The purpose of the new techniques is therefore to make the process more effective and fruitful so that the time and effort needed for neo-development can be sharply reduced from what it took to achieve the original development. If anything, the Five should be praised loudly and clearly for having noticed the opportunities and seized them. They deserve special commendation for turning what used to be a rather haphazard approach into one which is much more systematic and for pioneering strategies of neo-development that can be applied more generally.

*   *   *

Just as a footnote, it might be added that, if anything is truly inexplicable and deplorable, then it is that only a handful of countries launched into accelerated growth and not many more. After all, the same factors that encouraged neo-development in East Asia were equally, and sometimes more readily, accessible elsewhere. There were well over a hundred countries which could fit into the category of latecomers and which had every reason to catch up. Most of them made economic development a formal and priority goal of their national policy. Some even drew up plans, targeted priority industries, and mounted ambitious projects. But they clearly did not make the same headway.

It is only on the background of this profusion of failures that the Five may look like—and can justifiedly be regarded as—economic "miracles."

NOTES

1. The average growth of all five countries revolved around 10% during their peak period in the 1960s and 1970s when most other countries were lucky to get 5%.

2. For comparison sake, during the late 1800s and early 1900s, a period of noteworthy progress, England was growing at 2.1%, Germany 2.7% and the United States 4.6% a year. Growth in Japan from the 1880s through the 1930s was about 3-4% a year.

3. As for the developing countries (excluding oil exporters), their growth rates averaged out to some 5% or so during the 1960s and 1970s.

4. This again distinguishes the Five from most other developing countries which tended to look backward and were hardly optimistic about the chances of success, to judge by the resolutions of the United Nations, UNCTAD, the Non-Aligned Group and so on.

5. These further decades were not added because of the smashing success of the first but rather the failure to get very far in ten, twenty and then thirty years.

6. For the impact of aid, which was important but not decisive, see Neil H. Jacoby, *U.S. Aid to Taiwan*, Edward S. Mason et al, *The Economic and Social Modernization of the Republic of Korea*, pp. 165-208, and Tatsuro Uchino, *Japan's Postwar Economy*, pp. 262-6.

7. While there is no need to apologize for benefiting from neo-development, it would be foolish for the Five to ignore this and assume they are truly miracle-workers or that the miracles will be as easy to work once they have caught up.

PART THREE:

THE PROSPECTS

Over recent years, the extraordinary economic vitality of the "tigers"and "dragons" has become unmistakably evident. Such success, as per usual, aroused mixed feelings and a wide variety of reactions. Surprise that any group of countries should be doing so well, and admiration of their ability, were the first, relatively spontaneous responses. But it did not take long for the other countries to wonder what the East Asian phenomenon meant to them. Then it was that the perceptions changed and some of the praise turned into envy and anxiety.

The era in which the Five first got started, the 1950s and 1960s, was one of the most favorable the world economy has ever experienced. Recovery from the war, new inventions, expansion of international trade and a developmental mood backed up by exceptionally generous funding made it the ideal time for any country to develop. While rarely as striking, most countries were able to advance more than in earlier decades. It was hardly noticed that some few were progressing far more rapidly. Anyway, even if they were, this was regarded as a healthy sign and one that should benefit the world as a whole.

Then, in the 1970s, the limits to growth were suddenly noted. The abundant natural resources some of the growth had sprung from, whether among producers or processors, turned out to be less readily available. There was much talk of finiteness and even depletion and less willingness to sell what one had except for a premium. Financial resources had flowed even more freely, as if money were nothing. Perhaps, at the rate it was being printed in some places, this was correct. But eventually the funds ran out and loans had to be repaid, to the acute embarrassment of those who lent or borrowed unwisely. Even trade expansion faltered and sales became sluggish. This came amidst gross overcapacity in some sectors which turned normal trade into fierce struggles to penetrate and conquer markets. Those who lost ended up with seriously ailing and depressed industries.

Meanwhile, many of the initial hopes of global economic prosperity proved to be hollow. The worst showing occurred where progress was needed most, namely in the Third World. Many of the developing countries only managed to expand their economy a mite faster than their population, which left people not much better off than before. The Communist bloc advanced moderately, but not as brilliantly as planned, and the dreams of real affluence receded. Actually, what happened in the advanced nations was most disappointing, as they had such a privileged position that there was every reason to expect solid growth almost indefinitely. However, some went too far in granting social benefits and others overspent on defense. Production, the basis for all these expenditures, was neglected, and they became less competitive.

Only two groups succeeded conspicuously. One was the oil producers and suppliers of other crucial raw materials, especially when genuine or artificial shortages pushed up the prices. The other consisted of more ordinary countries which entered the ranks of industrial producers as junior members of the club. There were just ten on the list of "newly industrialized countries" drawn up by the Organisation for Economic Cooperation and Development: Mexico and Brazil in Latin America; Portugal, Spain, Greece and Yugoslavia in Europe; Korea, Taiwan, Hong Kong and Singapore in Asia.[1] Of them, the East Asians were the least likely candidates, since they had fewer resources, lower starting points, and shorter histories of economic experience. But, after the crises and recession subsided, it was clear that they were the strongest and most resilient of the lot.

The world of the 1980s was thus a very different place.

It no longer seemed that there was enough room for everyone to get ahead. Rather, it looked as if the economic progress of some was stifling or precluding the advancement of others. It could not be avoided that the unheralded and startling rise of Japan and the four NICs should be seen as both an ecouraging and a worrisome phenomenon in other countries. Which of these reactions would prevail depended on what sort of relations they maintained and how closely they interacted with one another. For their Asian neighbors, and for the older economic poles in Europe and North America, the consequences were bound to be significant. But even more remote places would feel some backwash.

The emergence of East Asia has already prompted a number of intriguing questions. The most important for the East Asians is, will they be able to continue their exceptional economic performance or will they slip back into the mass? For those who border them, the question is, will it be possible to benefit from their success? For the older economic powers, there is still an interest in the positive aspects as they ask, will East Asia help create a stronger economic order on a trilateral basis? But there is no less concern as to whether the pressure will continue and make the impact a negative one. Will East Asia become a commercial and technological threat?

This uncertainty about the potential repercussions of a new economic center has already elicited highly varied responses. It has also called forth a number of more complete scenarios. They range very widely from a prediction that a rise of the East must bring a decline of the West to an insistence that there will be close cooperation for mutual benefit, from viewing East Asia as a place of hope and promise to seeing it as a source of danger and disruption. None of this is more than conjecture, a mixture of educated guesses and personal insight, as the next presentations shall also be. But the possible implications are too important to be ignored or dealt with superficially.

In reading the following essays, it might be remembered that the one shape a country's economic trajectory never takes is a straight line. There are ups and downs and longer trends for growth to decelerate. Policies swing one way to avoid unexpected difficulties and another to benefit from unforeseen opportunities. Moreover, no matter how strong an impulse may be, it is never alone and will be affected by other currents and tendencies it encounters and reacts with.

This has to be mentioned in the midst of prognostications which are grotesquely linear and almost fatalistic. There is little point in talking of the inevitable rise of some, fall of others, impending crises that cannot be escaped, conflicts that must erupt and which can have only disastrous results for some, glorious for others. That is the stuff of science fiction, not economic forecasting.

NOTES

1.   OECD, *The Impact of the Newly Industrializing Countries on Production and Trade in Manufactures*, Paris, 1979.

13

New Challenges

To many, the concept of a "miracle" economy seems to contain the idea of an exceptional ease in achieving even the most ambitious goals. Instead, although they got very far, it was hardly with ease that the five countries advanced. They had to continue accomplishing two vital tasks, neither of them particularly simple, namely to work smart and to work hard. They had to find—and apply—the right policies or they would never have gotten anywhere. But, even with those policies, their progress was repeatedly hampered by pitfalls and obstacles, short-comings and mistakes, domestic headaches and foreign imbroglios. Only thus could they grow into their present status.

Yet, while this description would probably be accepted for the start, there is a pervasive feeling that the early portion of the path to development is the toughest. People have no notion of which way to turn at first, but they gradually get their bearings and can then proceed much more smoothly. Such views are further encouraged by the theory of a "takeoff into self-sustained growth." Judging by the examples of the Five, once again, there is no such thing as easy development . . . ever. It is necessary to keep the process going, to find new industries to replace the old, to train workers for different occupations and to seek fresh sources of growth. Mature economies face formidable problems just like young ones, even if they are not exactly the same. In addition, since circumstances are constantly changing, even policies that worked well in the past may not be suitable for the future.

This means that the East Asians will have no respite in the years to come. Basking in their reputation as workers of "miracles" would be about the worst thing they could do. It would be unwise even in the best of times. But the 1980s increasingly look like a particularly troubled period for the whole world. If the Five wish to remain exceptions to the rule, if they want to continue outperforming the rest, they will have to make extraordinary efforts to meet extraordinary challenges.

One of these is particularly obvious, and has been much (if anything, too much) commented on. This is the fact that the raw materials all of these countries depend heavily on have been going up in price. Bereft of adequate sources themselves, and running industries that consume huge amounts of imported raw materials, they were hurt each time prices rose. For just about every commodity there has been a prevailing upward trend, only alleviated by periodic dips, but with no sign of reversing. For some, especially oil, the price hikes have occasionally been sudden and massive and the results almost catastrophic.

The East Asian Five must be complimented on their ability to absorb these price hikes. They have done so in various ways. By revamping production methods or switching to other sources of energy, they were able to conserve the more costly inputs. More significantly, they have also shown a tendency to shed some highly raw material or energy-intensive product lines and shift into others. This was an additional reason for their liking of electronics, machine tools or biotechnology. Yet, despite the abilty to adapt, it could hardly be said that they have come through the difficulties undiminished. With each of these "shocks", the growth rates slumped and some industries were stricken.[1]

While this is considerably less noted, it is no less disturbing that the cost of technology has been rising. Gone are the days when advanced countries would part with their knowhow for a modest price. They now want much bigger licensing fees and preferably a chance to invest and produce themselves within the foreign market. On occasion, they simply refuse to license their technologies.[2] This makes it far more difficult to leapfrog than in the past, so it is not only a question of money but the very possibility of continuing a rapid advance. As for bypassing, it could turn out that some of the Five will be stuck in an older stage while those who actually invent the new technologies move resolutely ahead.

This sort of predicament can also be overcome in various ways. The simplest is by letting in companies which possess the desired knowhow and allowing them to produce locally and perhaps also for export. This is a solution small economies like Singapore and Hong Kong often have to adopt. The others, to some extent at least, are taking the more difficult path. Over the years, enterprising companies have been increasing their own investments in research and development and they are now getting considerably more government support. Yet, no matter how successful they are, it will still be a much more costly process since the sums swallowed up by researchers and laboratories are much larger than those needed to induce existing technologies. Worse, while it is known what those technologies are worth, it is impossible to predict whether or when internal R & D will achieve notable breakthroughs.

What for some time looked considerably more worrisome was that their own principal resource, labor, was not only rising in cost but conceivably being priced out of the market. All five countries had initially depended on the advantages of a moderately priced labor force with more than average skills and work will. This made it possible to produce labor-intensive goods at very competitive rates. With the years, however, wages have risen implacably and invalidated the earlier calculations. The Japanese became worried as their pay packages rose to European levels while the NICs became alarmed as new suppliers of "cheap labor" tried to supplant them.

Yet, this tendency could be countered as well. One method was to improve the quality of the labor force. This was done partly through better formal education and more on-the-job training. A goodly share can be traced to improving the concern for productivity and quality of the individual workers through assorted management techniques. The rest, actually the bulk of the improvement, came from unceasing efforts at mechanization, automation and later robotization which made it possible to keep productivity growing swiftly. While this could be continued in the future, it would naturally be harder and costlier to attain each additional increment. So, the other solution was to move into products with more value added.

There was another side to the labor problem which was far more subtle because it arose out of the sweeping transformations society was undergoing. One aspect is the physical aging of population. Over the years, the once predominantly young work force has been replaced by one with a radically different age composition. With more schooling, few start work as early. With men and women living longer, more older people remain in the work force. And there is an increasing share of people who have retired and must be cared for. The numbers in the NICs are still rather limited, although the demographic trends are already clear. Japan, on the other hand, is expected to have the oldest population in the world by the early twenty-first century.

This greying of the population has very definite economic implications. One is that, due purely to age, there is probably much less vigor and energy available. No matter how hard they are driven, employers will get less actual work out of an aging staff. Since older people have been with the company longer or gotten promotions, they are usually paid more. Where a seniority system prevails, the older the workers, the heavier the wage burden. Equally significant, there will be fewer people working while more are in school or retired, which means a smaller proportion must earn the wherewithal to meet the needs of society at large.[3]

Here, too, there are ways of solving most of these problems which are related indirectly to the general rise in the cost of labor. They consist of boosting productivity even further than in the past. Even more automation or robotization will make it possible to do with fewer workers. Some of the latest developments are clearly pointed in that direction, with an urge not only for highly automated assembly lines but whole "unmanned" factories. By increasing the output of the remaining workers, it can be hoped that they will produce enough to carry the load of those who are not yet or no longer working.

But physical aging is not the only aspect of this trend. There is also a disconcerting weakening of the work ethic, a lessening of the essential will, which can be noticed throughout the region. It has gone furthest in Japan because more generations have grown up in an affluence and comfort that could hardly have been imagined by their predecessors.[4] However, to judge by comments, this is an incipient danger in Singapore or Korea as well. While the situation can still be kept under control by the present leaders even if the youth is less enthusiastic and dedicated, the real crunch will come when it is these very people who have to run the economy.

Solutions here are much harder to find. There are things that can be done on a moral or social level to encourage the younger generations to show the same devotion as their elders. They can be treated to pep talks and company indoctrination. They can be subjected to social pressure or fired for inadequacies. But it is hard to convince others how to behave and, if they do not learn for themselves, they will probably absorb the external

One of Japan's last frontiers: aerospace

Credit: NTT

lessons and preaching very shallowly. Still, while all may not be well, the morale in East Asia remains considerably higher than in the advanced nations. And, in a more sophisticated economy, less time and effort are needed to keep things going anyway.

The greatest threat lies in another, originally unexpected direction. It is perfectly obvious that much of the impulse for growth in these countries came from their access to vastly larger and more affluent overseas markets. Exports played a prominent role in developing industry in general and, in the early years, there seemed to be almost no limit to the possibilities of exporting. After all, there were so many places one could sell to. First came the United States and, for some, the British empire, due to the close relations and a willingness to absorb goods. Then came the rest of Europe, all the easier once common markets were formed. Later there was a boom in the Middle East. Somewhere along the way, goods were also sent to the rest of Asia, Africa, Latin America and even into the Soviet bloc. But, what could come after that?

Not only were there no other conceivable markets, it was increasingly difficult to hold onto those which existed. While they were very pleased to accept cheap manufactured goods in the initial stages, some of the importers changed their mind later on. In the advanced countries, relatively backward sectors were hurt and numerous factories closed down. Developing countries were afraid that imports would crush their own infant industries. This certainly discouraged goods from the Five in the best of times. Then, as the years passed, the situation turned sour in many places and they simply did not have the money to import as much as they would have liked.

Moreover, whereas the Five (and especially Japan) were relatively small economies in a big world when they

first started, it did not take them long to become op-
pressively large exporters. This was strongly accentuated
by a tendency to export a rather narrow range of products in massive amounts for each, leading to sharp
surges. At the same time, some of the importers lost their
own ability to export and were faced with mounting
trade deficits. This put an end to the era of market opening with a form of creeping protectionism that did not
always resort to formal barriers and sometimes put the
onus on the exporter to exercise restraint.[5]

There is no doubt that the present upsurge of protectionism was largely sparked by, and strongly directed
against, the East Asian economies. No one had benefited
more from trade liberalization and now their partners
were worried. They were also annoyed that some of the
Five had markets that were far from open. When international trade flagged during the early 1980s, with occasional improvements but little hope of a return to the
good old days, the room for expansion was distinctly
limited.

This meant that export orientation as a growth strategy, let alone as an essential element in economic policy,
had certainly passed its prime. It was no longer possible
to expect substantial, long-term increases in exports nor
was it even advisable to do so. Indeed, exporting had become somewhat counterproductive. When export campaigns were launched, initially they generated more sales.
But, if they were too successful, this promptly induced
complaints from domestic producers and, with an increasingly short lag, the imposition of more restrictions
or restraint.

Japan is plainly in the worst position. Its exports have
wreaked the most havoc and created the greatest sensitivi-
ty and resistance. There are far more restrictions imposed
on it. Yet, despite the many warnings, the economy has

remained overly dependent on exports. This is not reflected by the share of gross national product, which is quite modest, but the fact that much of its growth has always come from exports while domestic demand played a lesser role. Even now, exports are an essential stimulus. When they are held back, growth slackens significantly.

So far the NICs are better off. This may be explained by the fact that, as much smaller economies with less actual exports (although proportionately more), they are still making a smaller impact on the world trade system. Thus, they still manage to slip through many cracks in the web of restrictions. But it is obvious that the "Gang of Four" is also becoming more of a nuisance with time and barriers are going up against them as well. With greater export-dependence and smaller domestic markets, they can afford this even less than Japan.

Despite any variations, the writing was clearly on the wall by the late 1970s. Export promotion was no longer the fastest and smoothest path to growth. This forcibly shifted interest back to the strategy the Five had long neglected or regarded as inferior, namely import substitution. And they had to pay greater attention to the much broader task of stimulating domestic demand so that it could contribute more to growth. This view was gradually accepted as the correct one and, happily or not, it was felt that a return to the domestic market was essential. But it would not always be easy to create the desired growth there.

One approach is to stimulate the economy by launching major public works each time it becomes sluggish. Such countercyclical policy was applied throughout the region to good purpose, especially in earlier years when so much basic infrastructure was needed. Later on, housing was also promoted in the downturns. But this was only possible when the upturns came soon after and revenue growth was adequate to finance any public spending. By the late 1970s, the Japanese government had run out of funds and, faced with major budget deficits, could not revive the economy by pump-priming. If anything, it became a drag. Korea, Taiwan, Hong Kong and Singapore, however, are still able to turn on the second growth engine when the first stalls even if they cannot get as far on it.

The other approach is much more promising since it is broad-based and long-lasting. That is to continue expanding the economy, deepening old sectors and opening up new ones. Here, alas, to varying degrees, the East Asians run up against their most serious problem which, in many ways, is actually a legacy of their past achievements.

While some of the economic slowdown is due to specific difficulties like rising raw material and labor costs or protectionism, the rest arises from the more general phenomenon of maturation. Economies, like human beings, grow and age. As they do, they use up many of the opportunities which once existed and find that ever fewer remain. This is particularly important for the Five, since their success was based largely on an ability at catching up. They could only benefit as fully from the manifest advantages of neo-development because they were latecomers and because there was so much to learn from others.

Back in the 1950s and 1960s, these were all relatively fresh economies with innumerable possibilities before them. The Five had just come out of the war with their productive facilities seriously damaged, if they had any. This meant that they could first revive agriculture. Then they could restore or create one branch of industry after the other. Next, they could tackle modern services. Production was at a very low level and could be increased massively both by introducing new products and expanding old lines. They could also enter one foreign market after another. This contributed to the startling rise of the region and spawned tales of economies that were "dragons" or "tigers."

Now, some decades later, there are no longer so many new sectors, new products, or new markets left. This means that there are fewer chances of increasing production. In fact, in many of the older fields, output has reached or is rapidly approaching its peak. And, for the first time, there are actually some declining industries. This is either because the markets are saturated or, due to high costs of raw materials or labor, the Five are no longer competitive. The "dragons" are not breathing fire the way they used to and the "tigers" have lost some of their teeth.

Yet, this is not really a sign of failure. Maturation is not peculiar to the "miracle" economies, it occurs everywhere. It has only happened more swiftly, and more suddenly, in East Asia because these economies grew and thereby matured so rapidly. The test, however, will be how the various countries rise to this unexpected challenge. Here, to see things more clearly, some distinction must be made between Japan and the rest, the "newly industrialized countries." This is quite understandable considering that Japan began its ascension so much earlier than the NICs and has obviously encountered these problems sooner.

Japan's economy is by far the most mature. There are really very few sectors that its industry has not yet developed and, in fact, where it has not reached a certain degree of maturity as well. Limits have appeared even for leading articles like steel and automobiles while electronics only prosper because new items replace the old ones. There are still some remaining frontier sectors, like biotechnology and aerospace, but they are not so numerous. And the competition will be stronger than ever. At this point, one can ask where Japan goes from here. For, strange as it may seem, the Japanese do not know despite their penchant for visions.

While the "old tiger" is uncertain which way to turn, the "young tigers" are in a distinctly better position. Fortunately for them as it were, they are not so highly developed. They only fit into the category of semi-industrialized nations which means that they still have a fair way to go. There are further industrial sectors they can introduce or fill out, there are vast numbers of new products they can launch. Taiwan and Korea, due to their larger size, have reasonable hopes of producing almost the same range as Japan aside from several of the high tech items. While the city-states are more limited, they can certainly add many finished products and many more components for sophisticated articles produced elsewhere.

But there is another whole line of items which is even more promising. This includes the thousands and tens of thousands of parts and components that are needed for the very articles they already produce. The levels of local content in many of their leading industries remain low. That is the case of electronics throughout the region or shipbuilding and automobile production in Korea and Taiwan. Not only is the need for localization great, the chances of filling it are particularly good since the parts are used by domestic assemblers which can readily be encouraged to acquire them. Alas, the NIC's gain will be Japan's loss, since it is presently the major supplier of these intermediate goods.

Beyond this there are even more possibilities that were woefully overlooked by all Five during the many years of intensive industrialization. The tertiary sector, services in

the broadest sense of the word, offer tremendous opportunities even now. One category consists of business-
related operations. Some few have been upgraded and
modernized, in some of the countries at least, such as
banking and securities. But they remain backward in
Taiwan and Korea. For the others, even Japan has a lot
to do. They include things like advertising, leasing, consulting (law, accounting, architecture, etc.), computer
software and programming, data banks, and so on.
There is also more than enough room to enhance the efficiency of the distribution system and some aspects of
transportation and communications.

There is another group of services which are directed
toward individuals and families. The spectrum here is
also extremely broad, from domestic servants like maids
and *amahs* to small enterprises that handle laundry and
dry cleaning, from nurseries and kindergartens to
cinemas and theaters, from restaurants and fast food
joints to amusements centers like bowling alleys and
pachinko parlors. Some few sectors are on a larger, more
organized scale like travel agencies and hotels. In all of
them, there is ample need for upgrading or modernization and very considerable expansion can be expected in
some as people have more free time and disposable income as well as more relaxed and sophisticated lifestyles.
In particular, the "leisure boom" which already swept
Japan has now arisen in the other Four.

Actually, throughout the region, the tertiary sector has
already become active and is taking up some of the slack
left by the slower growth, or decline, of agriculture and
manufacturing. Japan was the first to enter the post-in-
dustrial era and the others are following behind. This expansion is particularly welcome because, in addition to
boosting gross national product, it contributes even more
significantly to employment. Services are sectors which

naturally use larger quantities of labor, some of it highly trained and specialized, the rest consisting of quite ordinary people. The chances of rationalization are smaller. They therefore counteract an otherwise inevitable proclivity toward unemployment.[6]

So, judging by the trends, it is possible to remain relatively optimistic about the future of all five countries. They have repeatedly shown an exceptional ability to develop in an otherwise rather unexceptional world environment. No matter how great the problems and difficulties, there is good reason to believe that they will do a much better than average job of overcoming them and staying in the vanguard. There will be some slowing down of all the economies, Japan to what is regarded as low growth but should be a mite ahead of the other industrialized nations. As for the NICs, they should be

High time for the tertiary sector to catch up

Credit: Woronoff

able to achieve medium growth, somewhere between their earlier level and what is attained by Japan. With this, the NICs will continue treading on Japan's heels and all Five will keep catching up with the United States and Europe.

But there is another assortment of opportunities that has not been mentioned here and is even more neglected by the East Asians. That is perhaps because they do not offer as much growth, or are harder to deal with, or make unwanted demands on the government. Yet, they are no less promising in other ways. And, like it or not, they will have to be tackled. Three seem to be particularly important for the coming decades: housing, amenities and welfare.

In the midst of a strong push for development, private and public expenditures were strongly skewed to channel as much money as possible into economic infrastructure and production factilities. This meant that less was available for even such an essential item as housing. Of course, there were variations. Singapore, with its socialist creed and an awareness of the importance of home ownership in creating a responsible citizenry, devoted much more to public housing. Hong Kong was pushed in that direction by the crying needs. In Japan, Korea and Taiwan, the situation is far worse and sometimes outright derelict. Thus, throughout the region and especially in the larger countries, there is an unsatisfied demand for housing, both in quantity and quality, that should be met.

Amenities have fared even worse. The governments were often very stingy in allocating funds to such "unproductive" purposes as piped water, sewage, garbage disposal or parks and gardens. Schools were built, but often they were too small and poorly equipped. The public transport network, roads and highways, buses and

subways, were often inadequate or crowded. Again, only
Singapore was an exception by creating a "garden city"
while ordinary Japanese hardly lived as if they were part
of an affluent society. Here, too, are needs which should
be filled and can finally receive proper attention now that
most of the major projects relating to economic development have been completed and social overhead can get its
due.

The third sphere is harder to define since every country
has its own idea of what welfare means. Still, given the
rapid aging of the population, it should certainly include
two basic aspects. One is suitable health care and the
other, appropriate care for the aged. This requires the
construction of more hospitals, old age homes and other
facilities, all endowed with the essential equipment and
staffed by trained professionals. It also implies adequate
budgets to run them. The other side of this, as opposed
to actual care, is the people's knowledge that they will be
able to receive proper treatment when it is needed. This
means the introduction or expansion of health and old
age insurance, company pensions and state-run social
security. Nowhere in the region is any of this sufficient.

In fact, when considering the sectors of housing,
amenities and welfare, it becomes clearest that the East
Asian Five are still just developing countries and have a
long way to go. Whether they will get there is more open
to question than their past achievements in industrialization and future accomplishments in certain services. For,
this time, it is more a matter of spending or sharing
wealth than creating it. Housing, amenities and welfare
are all terribly expensive and individual or collective decisions must be made that are particularly painful in a time
of less rapid growth.

While individuals seem disposed to invest more in housing, improved amenities will be harder to come by.

Welfare and social security, however, will face the stiffest resistance. That is not only because they involve extraordinary costs but because the mentalities have not changed enough. It is argued that people can look after themselves or the Oriental family will rise to the needs. But that is improbable given the size of the coming case load and replacement of the extended family by the nuclear family. And there is reason to believe that these are only pretexts anyway. The real fear is that by making people's lives too easy and comfortable, by removing the pressure to work and perform, the essential will could be undermined while the state's finances are dilapidated.

Of course, rational answers can be found to rational worries. With the primary and secondary sectors stagnant, a shift to the teritary sector is all that remains and housing, amenities and welfare offer a lot of growth. They also contribute to employment and, more important, improved living conditions. As growth slackens, and it is harder to earn more, at least one can try to live better. Far from weakening the work ethic, these are goals which appeal to many segments of the population and can justify their efforts. Moreover, welfare is not an individual or family concern but one that can best be met by society as a whole. Still, it is not such rationalizations so much as the rise of younger generations that will turn the economy in these directions.

Thus, with more delay than it took to move into the high growth trajectory, the East Asians may get onto another path that is more in keeping with the present and future situation. Admittedly, the economy will not expand as rapidly. But at least it will fulfill the new goals that have emerged. Exports could slow down even more. And the primary thrust would be to meet domestic needs. The economy could become less productive, yet considerably more fruitful. If that happens—and it is too early to tell—the Five would finally come of age and might create a "miracle" that would rival anything that has been accomplished so far.

NOTES

1. For a description of how the oil crises affected Japan, see Yoichi Shinkai, "Oil Crises and Stagflation in Japan," in Kozo Yamamura, *Policy and Trade Issues of the Japanese Economy*, pp. 173–96. For Taiwan, see Shirley W. Y. Kuo, *The Taiwan Economy in Transition*, pp. 181–222. The situation was relatively similar in the other three countries.
2. The biggest problem has not actually been acquiring Western technology but getting Japan to transfer more of its technology to the NICs.
3. See Jon Woronoff, *Japan's Wasted Workers*.
4. See Woronoff, *Japan: The Coming Social Crisis*.
5. Books on protectionism abound, especially as regards Japan's difficulties. See, among others, I. M. Destler and Hideo Sato (eds.), *Coping with U.S.-Japanese Economic Conflicts*, and Woronoff, *World Trade War*.
6. How Japan could react positively to the challenges is sketched in Woronoff, *The Japan Syndrome*.

14

Allies or Rivals?

Ever since the East Asian Five emerged as enterprising manufacturers and traders, there has been a tendency to see the group more and more as a bloc. The similarities have been accentuated by various writers, some even referring to the region as "Eastasia" to enhance this image.[1] Such an approach is understandable since there is no doubt that these countries do have much in common. If not for that, it is hardly likely that they would have risen at roughly the same time and in roughly the same manner.[2]

If one takes a very broad view, and looks back far enough, it is possible to show the quite close racial and historical relations. While the Koreans, Japanese and Chinese are equally proud of their racial uniqueness and homogeneity, they are still members of a broader family. Over the ages, there were times of immigration and intermarriage amongst them and they have periodically been ruled over or strongly influenced by one another.[3]

The cultural similarities are fairly noticeable. The earliest religions were clearly indigenous, and owed less to borrowing, and yet there were parallels between Shintoism, Taoism and Shamanism. Buddhism, which was ultimately accepted as the state religion throughout the region, was an even more pervasive shaping force despite any differences in sects and practices. Finally, Confucianism as a philosophy and also a political system spread widely, although it was much stronger on the mainland than the offshore islands.

One particular aspect of this common background, Confucianism, has frequently been taken up as a key to the economic success of present days. The stress placed on hard work and frugality, education and loyalty, harmony and hierarchy, was regarded as crucial in pulling the economy up by the boot-straps. This is what made it possible for these different peoples to work effectively. And they only plugged at it so hard because of the pervasive influence of these putative Confucian virtues.

Viewing things in more practical and concrete terms, there is no doubt that the development model adopted by all five countries was very similar. Each one of them started with labor-intensive production and moved on to capital and then technology-intensive sectors. Each one, with the exception of Hong Kong, reserved a significant economic role for the state and only later shifted the balance toward private enterprise. Each one oriented its sales toward exports. Even smaller details of policy and implementation were so amazingly alike that, having understood the pattern in one economy, it was easier to grasp what happened in any other.

While this economic style doubtlessly arose from common approaches and attitudes among the leaders and people, it would be unwise to forget that similar endowments and starting positions were also determinant. All five suffered from a dearth of land and natural resources, which would have made it impossible to develop through mining or agriculture even if they wanted to. As time passed, and wages rose, there was little choice but to move toward more capital and technology-intensive sectors. With a modest domestic market, they would never have gotten very far without launching exports.

Beyond this, the similarities had a further cause which is probably most germain in this context. The five countries did feel some intangible bond with one another as master and apprentices of economic development. There is no doubt that Japan, the first to rise, proposed its own model as an example for the others. This was done by force during the colonial period and left an imprint which was easier to build on after its postwar economic "miracle." The others, following in its wake, located so nearby and influenced by investment and trade, could hardly ignore Japan even if it was only recently that any imitation was not only surreptitious but proudly proclaimed by some. Meanwhile, outsiders began to call the foursome "new Japans."

With the years, the ties between the countries have grown. But they are still extremely lopsided in certain ways. One is that the connection is overwhelmingly economic in nature. As they developed, all five tended to trade less with the United States or Great Britain, originally the main trading partners, and more with one another. Japan in particular enhanced its share of sales to the NICs by exporting large quantities of intermediate and capital goods. It also became a major source of financial assistance through loans and, more rarely, grants. Its companies gradually claimed the largest share of investment and were equally important as suppliers of technology.[4]

However, even the economic aspect is sharply skewed because most of the relations emanate from Japan. The NICs do not, in return, provide it with aid, investment or technology. They are not suppliers of raw materials. And they find little receptiveness for what they do produce since this overlaps with Japan's range, although their goods are more labor-intensive and often cheaper. This means that the relations are not always auspicious since they create a form of one-sided dependence which weighs heavily on those bearing it.[5]

While the ties with Japan have intensified, there has been considerably less movement among the NICs. There is relatively little trade with one another since the products are so similar. Korea and Taiwan have tried to remedy this by special commercial agreements, but to little avail. They are hardly in a position to aid one another financially or by providing technology. And there is very little reciprocal investment aside from the efforts of Overseas Chinese who operate in Hong Kong, Singapore and Taiwan. While there may ultimately be room for more exchanges than at present, the scope will remain rather limited.

Outside the economic sphere, there is even less to report. Since it took time to overcome the bitterness of the colonial and wartime experiences, it was not until relatively late that Japan could finally establish relations with Taiwan and Korea. It then tried to bring some substance into the relationship by offering aid or sending missions. Yet, it never dared go much further since it was more concerned about consolidating links with Peking, which soured relations with Taipei and Seoul. Not until a pragmatic leadership arose in China could Japan even develop the political side more fully. With Hong Kong, business was the only thing that ever counted. Only with Singapore was there some warmth as shown by periodic visits of the respective leaders and high sounding declarations of friendship. Thus, broader intercourse among the Five never progressed much beyond lip service to common aspirations.

There is no doubt that cultural similarities, common interests and increased economic transactions have brought the Five closer together and strengthened the affinity to one another. But this is certainly not enough to view them as a formative bloc, something that is done all too often by those speaking of East Asia. At most, they are a group of countries with certain commonalities where mutual interests, usually diffusely felt more than explicitly defined, have resulted in a tendency for policies and, on occasion, actions to run parallel. Rarely did the relationship go much beyond that!

In fact, a careful look at the situation would provide more than enough evidence to espouse a contrary view. One could make a very good case for the argument that the Five are characterized by a notable lack of cohesion and that there are more than enough causes for rivalry and competition. It would be pointless to push the argument to the extent of predicting glaring rifts or open conflicts. But the idea of East Asia as a united or distinct bloc would surely be discredited.

First of all, any view of the East Asian Five as even a potential bloc immediately runs up against the fact that, although they are often thought of as a geographical unit, they are actually separated by vast distances. Japan and Korea are close neighbors, and Taiwan is not much further off, but Hong Kong and Singapore are pretty far away from Japan. With modern means of transport, this is not an unsurmountable obstacle. But it inevitably means that the Five cannot have the same relationship to one another as the European countries amongst themselves or Canada and Mexico to the United States.

Also, lest one forget, there is not just water filling the spaces. Japan's closest neighbor happens to be the Soviet Union, with whom relations have frequently been strained, and it is also close to the People's Republic of China, with whom the relationship has seen many ups and downs. South Korea borders on North Korea, its implacable enemy. Taiwan faces Communist China, its foe of over four decades. And Hong Kong is perched on Chinese territory. Singapore, while part of the group in many ways, has opted for a more intimate affiliation with its partners in the Association of Southeast Asian Nations.

This means that the possibility of moving from a loose affinity to one another or a community of interests to any kind of formal relationship, let alone integration, would be out of the question without radical changes in the geopolitical situation of the globe. The Five will doubtlessly trade more and more with one another, more investment will flow, they will keep looking over their shoulder at what the others are doing, and they may occasionally offer a kind word or make a friendly gesture. But this will rarely go beyond a sentimental or philosophical attachment such as expressed by the excessively vague policy of "looking East" or Japan's "heart-to-heart" relationship with ASEAN.

Moreover, while the East Asian Five are located in the same general region, manifest many cultural similarities, and have maintained substantial contacts for centuries, none of this means that they must be on good terms. Every historian knows that those with the closest relations are not always the best friends. They could just as well be rivals or enemies. A look at East Asian history will readily bear this out when one thinks of the bloody round of invasions, wars and domination imposed on one another and which created very deep undercurrents of division and distrust.

The Chinese, Koreans and Japanese have long questioned one another's motives for persuasive reasons, some of whose origins are only faintly remembered. But the memories of the period of Japanese colonialism still remain vivid in the region. Although the old wounds have been healing, they left scars that are very sensitive and can be opened by any slight or offense. Even today, the mere proposal of tighter links arouses immediate suspicions of a return to the thoroughly discredited concept of a Greater East Asian Co-Prosperity Sphere. Thus, while relations appear relatively calm and superficially amicable, there is little love lost among the various peoples.

Japan has been trying to refurbish its image in several ways, although not always to the complete satisfaction of the other four. They regard its reparations as not overly generous given the damage it caused and add that this also did Japan a lot of good by letting its companies get a foothold in their markets. Japanese development aid has never been considered sufficient, especially since it consists much more of reimbursable loans than outright grants. While the amounts have grown somewhat, it was

Building bridges: Singapore's Lee and Japan's Nakasone

Credit: FPC/Kyodo

all too often under pressure. The most notable case arose in the early 1980s when Tokyo reacted to Seoul's call for more loans with incredulity and then whittled the request for $10 billion over five years down to $4 billion over seven.

While the Japanese have invested substantially, they are criticized for doing so only in their own self-interest. They sought very definite commercial gains and, if they were not forthcoming, did not hesitate to withdraw. Japanese investors also won a nasty reputation for being the least willing to transfer technology. Given the acute dependence on outside technology, this also became a bone of contention when, for example, Japanese firms shunned the science-based industrial park in Hsinchu and initially refused to transfer VTR knowhow to Korea or participate in constructing the second POSCO steel mill. Korea again had to take energetic steps to wrest a verbal commitment from the Japanese government to encourage more technology transfer.

The most disturbing aspect of the relationship, however, stems from trade. The NICs purchased so much more than they sold that it was almost embarrassing for Japan and quite distressing for them. True, they did not have as much to offer. But there was no reason that the garments, toys, watches and electronic goods which did so well in the West should not be absorbed by Japan given the cost differentials. This failure seemed to indicate a closed market. Whatever the cause, the Four accumulated deficits running into billions of dollars with little hope of reversing the trends. Even trying to shift purchases elsewhere or placing special tariffs on Japanese imports, as Taiwan sporadically did, could not stop the hemorrhage.[6]

While this exposition of grievances would lead one to assume that Japan was on the winning side, the situation is far more complex. Certainly, in the relations among the Five, Japan is getting more than it gives. Yet, and this has hardly been noticed by most, it is actually the four NICs which are gaining ground. In fact, they are advancing so rapidly and aggressively that they have become the biggest threat to Japan's continued progress and prosperity.

This arises almost inevitably from the circumstance that the five countries have roughly the same factor endowment, the same comparative advantage in the initial stage, and even the same development strategies. The "new Japans" with only a slight delay, are following in the "old" Japan's footsteps and doing exactly the same thing it had done somewhat earlier. They are establishing the same industries, they are making the same products, they are upgrading the quality of these articles, and they are then exporting them to the same markets. This sort of harassment hardly appeals to the Japanese and explains why they often speak disparagingly of the "Gang of Four."

The upshot is that the NICs are constantly treading on Japan's heels and forcing it to press ahead more rapidly than it otherwise would. This has several disadvantages. The most noticeable is that, no sooner does Japan launch a product or conquer a market than it finds the other Four busily competing with it, admittedly from a somewhat lower position. While it goes upmarket, and tries to compensate with new sales, it loses considerable numbers of earlier customers. Its actual sales growth, subtracting what is lost from what is gained, can be marginal and sometimes even negative. Yet, to keep ahead, it is forced to compete frontally with producers from the advanced countries, which is more disconcerting and can result in restrictions on its exports.

This means that, in a sense, Japan is running interference for the "Gang of Four". It introduces each new export product and creates a market for it by penetrating other countries. In so doing, it usually crushes some of their domestic industry. When the NICs later appear with the same product, the complaints are not as loud because many of the makers have since disappeared. As much of this effort is geared to taking sales away from the Japanese, the locals do not really mind. Indeed, if they get yet cheaper prices, they are quite happy. After all, the only ones who lose are the Japanese manufacturers.

There are two other aspects to the chasing-up process that make things even more vexatious. As its own wages increase, Japan is gradually forced to invest in countries with lower wage scales. The places of predilection, for rather obvious reasons, have been the nearby Asian NICs. While this permits it to produce more cheaply, by having more and more of the manufacturing done abroad it is losing its relatively backward industries at home. This creates what is known as the "doughnut" phenomenon. When the NICs then become proficient enough to export, they may tackle the Japanese market as well, which is likened to a "boomerang."[7]

Certainly, the appearance of a "boomerang" arising out of their own investment is very annoying for Japanese business circles. But that is not the real problem, since they have erected more than enough non-tariff and commercial barriers to keep the NICs out despite the fact that they usually possess a genuine competitive edge. Where the Japanese are really in trouble is abroad, in more open markets where the goods compete fairly and squarely for sales. No matter how much better the quality may be, the Japanese often lose on price. And price has been increasingly decisive during the recession or in generally poorer markets. Comparing the growth of exports by the NICs to that of Japan shows clearly that they have been catching up.

This similarity of approach does not prove, by any stretch of the imagination, that the NICs have a common policy or that they are particularly united amongst themselves. The "Gang of Four" is not even loosely organized. Once again, a careful and objective look at the situation would more likely show the opposite. These economies are even closer to one another in endowment, comparative advantage, and product range. This means that they are drawn into even more direct competition against one another than against Japan.

The fiercest confrontations arise for a series of manufactured products made by Hong Kong, Taiwan and Korea. As it happens, their basic lines could hardly be more alike with all three specializing in textiles and garments, toys, digital watches, and certain electrical and electronic articles. Having gotten off to a faster start, Hong Kong has usually provided goods of a somewhat better quality for a slightly higher price. But Taiwan and Korea make almost identical items and a slight edge on quality or a petty advantage in price is enough for one or the other to win. Meanwhile, both try to nibble at Hong Kong's share.

This race is so tight that the three contestants constantly keep an eye on one another and, as much as possible, take specific measures to counter any threat. Lower labor costs in Taiwan is regarded as a valid reason to keep Korea's wages down or to devaluate the won. This sort of thing would immediately unleash demands in Taiwan's business circles to devaluate the N. T. dollar. When Korean industry got into difficulty after Park's assassination, the Taiwanese obtained windfall sales. Both got worried when the Hong Kong dollar started slipping, not because they feared for its economy but because this made their own goods relatively more expensive.

The intensity of this contest is only accentuated by the action of the purchasers, most of them from the West and many representing major clients. For, during the seasons, the garment buyers regularly take a swing through all three countries to compare quality and price and they will not hesitate to shift large orders one way or the other if they feel some country is out of line. The same applies to purchases of toys, or watches, or sundries. It is not as easy for electronics firms to take advantage of such differentials, especially if they have set up their own subsidiaries. Still, since the larger ones often have branches in two or three countries, they can gradually increase production at one site and reduce it elsewhere once the gains seem to justify this.

For any naive observers who think that creating a strong economy and dynamic companies is enough to survive in a cruel world, it must be added that this emulation is not just an interesting sidelight on the excitement and passion aroused by free enterprise. There is not the least doubt that on many occasions the intense competition has seriously punished all of the parties, the winners and the losers. It has repeatedly happened, for products like garments, watches, electronic components and even ships, that everyone had to sell under cost and take a loss. This rarely lasted very long but, before the prices snapped back, some companies had gone under.

Singapore is only partially involved in this particular race since its industrial production is considerably smaller in general and it depends less on articles where the toughest competition arises. But it is keenly interested in what happens in the tertiary sector because it has been promoting certain services very strongly. This includes shipping, tourism, and banking. Hong Kong is a serious rival for all three. While each port has its own advantages and natural clientele, and ships may well visit both, the choice of where to lay up or have repairs made is significant. Tourists will probably want to see both Singapore and Hong Kong. But, staying an extra day in one and spending a day less in the other, if this becomes a general trend, would have redoubtable consequences. In the offshore banking field, where decisions are made by large international banks which control huge sums of money, the competition is even sharper.

There has recently been an additional form of rivalry, one that would normally be in bad taste. For, although the year 1997 is still far enough off, its three competitors have already begun courting companies which may wish to leave Hong Kong at that time. They are also soliciting for the funds and knowhow of Overseas Chinese businessmen. This has been done quite openly as some circles at least appear to be gloating over Hong Kong's untimely demise. Their attitude indicates, as everyone who has ever studied the East Asian economies must realize, that all is fair in love, war *and* business.

From this brief account of the frictions and wrangling it must be obvious that, whereas one "miracle" is wonderful, and two are acceptable, five in the same region can be almost unbearable. This is especially true when the "miracles" all follow the same pattern with companies and countries copying one another and then vying for the same products and markets.

This gives us a considerably more variegated and rounded view of what is happening among the Five than one usually obtains from their official spokesmen or the media. It shows that there is an intriguing mixture of common interest and mutual benefit, on the one hand, and serious bones of contention and causes of confrontation, on the other. It is these two very different elements which will continue shaping their behavior in the future as they have done in the past.

The extent to which cooperation or competition will prevail will also be influenced by the kinds of relations that exist between the East Asian Five and the rest of the world as well as between each one of them and its specific foreign partners. The directions these external relations are likely to take are even more important given this very divisive background.

If things go well, and the world economy improves, this will take some of the pressure off the Five. They will be able to expand production and exports. This will permit them to satisfy their perceived needs for any essential imports and growth. On the other hand, if things get worse and the economic climate becomes chillier, the pressure will build up. This would put more of a bite in their relations as they become hungrier for sales, sources of technology, machinery and raw materials. If things are tough enough, the internecine struggle could become terribly bitter.

The idea has been expressed that somehow the Five might draw together in the face of such adversity. They would trade more than ever with one another, get technologies and machinery from within the group, and so on. That solution may appeal to some. But it is highly idealistic and not very realistic. The main hitch is the existing imbalance. Most of the new benefits would therefore flow in the same old direction, from the other four toward Japan. Trade and technology gaps that are hardly tolerable now would be further inflated and Japan could only get by through squeezing as much as possible from the others while they would basically have nowhere to turn.

What is much more likely is that any incipient relations among the Five, and especially between the NICs and

Japan, would be loosened. What they need more than anything is markets, places to sell their goods. And that can still be found more readily in the affluent West. The West, for all its decay, can also provide plenty of capital, technologies, and even raw materials. This makes closer bilateral East-West relations considerably more attractive. Any residual or potential "Eastasian" solidarity would weigh little against the concrete gains of leaving the circle.

Thus, the East Asians would probably be tempted to accentuate a policy that has already been used by some in fostering better relations with the West. This consists, among other things, of sending special "purchasing missions" to buy as much as possible in an attempt to balance bilateral trade. It would also be shown more prominently by acquiring major capital goods there, such as nuclear power plants, communications satellites, or steel mill equipment, to say nothing of armaments.

This would attenuate some of the trade imbalances with the West. However, while it could be applied massively by the NICs, which still have many needs, it would not help Japan as much since it is so advanced. And Japan would lose most if the "Gang of Four" were to shift purchases from its own companies to Western ones. This would make Japan the "odd man out" again unless it were finally willing to bring down its barriers and seek a greater complementarity with other economies.

Which of these scenarios is more probable, the one of an improving economic environment which reduces pressures or the one of a worsening climate that only aggravates rivalries, is not hard to guess for the short and even medium term. Most of the trends point toward mounting trade conflicts, protectionism and even autarky. Countries are more worried about their own domestic problems than whether their solutions create difficulties for others. There will be more trouble in the future and East Asia cannot remain unaffected!

NOTES

1. Roy Hofheinz, Jr. and Kent E. Calder, *The Eastasia Edge.*
2. The parallels are shown with particular clarity in Edward K. Y. Chen, *Hyper-growth in Asian Economies.*
3. See Key-Kiuk Kim, *The Last Phase of the East Asian World Order.*
4. See Jon Woronoff, *Japan's Commercial Empire*, and Kunio Yoshihara, *Japanese Investment in Southeast Asia.*
5. For Japan's relationship with Korea, which is similar for the others, see Toshio Watanabe, "An Analysis of Structural Dependence between Korea and Japan," in Wontack Hong and Lawrence C. Krause (ed.), *Trade and Growth of Advanced Developing Countries in the Pacific Basin*, pp. 393-434.
6. For some of the impediments to accepting more imports, see Ippei Yamazawa, "Adjusting to the ADCs in Face of Structurally Depressed Industries: The Case of Japan," in Hong and Krause, *op. cit.*, pp. 435-75.
7. See Woronoff, *op. cit.*, pp. 370-8.

15

Asian Spillover

It was out of the question for the East Asian Five to emerge as strong economic forces without having a pervasive impact on the rest of the world. This was only enhanced by the fact that, as trading nations, they had contacts with a broad range of countries. However, while the relations were just marginal or secondary in more remote areas, they were increasingly deep and intense in those which were nearer. The repercussions in Asia soon proved to be particularly significant.

Part of the impact was good, part bad. But the positive or negative aspects could hardly be traced to the good or bad will of the rambunctious "tigers". They were much too absorbed in the arduous task of restoring and then promoting their own economies to pay much attention to what happened elsewhere. While this is hardly admirable, it did leave more leeway for others to benefit from their actions or not, as the case may be. It also makes it easier to see the relatively natural consequences growth in one part of a region will have on the rest.

Given the development model they adopted, one based on importing raw materials, processing them, and then exporting manufactured articles, it is obvious that all five countries were exceedingly dependent on reliable access to various natural resources. The supplies could, of course, be obtained from many different sources and were originally acquired from the market wherever they were available at the lowest price. This did not imply any preference for Asian raw materials, for raw materials bore no nationality. But it was certainly more convenient and cheaper to procure them from the region because transport costs were lower.

Gradually, however, the importers did realize the advantages of working out more stable and durable arrangements with certain suppliers and buying from them even when the price was not the lowest or the quality the highest. One reason was to spread sourcing more broadly, which helped Asia because it was not among the traditional suppliers of certain items. Another was to avoid places that were more remote or more unruly because the supplies might unexpectedly be cut off. This benefited Indonesia quite substantially as a producer of oil and gas as well as Australia as a supplier of a broader range including coal, iron ore and also gas.

Trade in the other direction was no less important for the Five since they were eager to sell their products to as many customers as possible. Admittedly, the rest of Asia was long considered a rather second-rate market since it could not absorb as large quantities nor take the more costly articles when compared to the United States or Europe. But the additional sales were always welcome. And it was nice, especially during the earlier stages, to have some markets which were more concerned with low price than high quality. Subsequently, some of the Asian countries became even more interesting as capital goods and machinery were bought to encourage their own development.

Numerous attempts have been made to show that trade was primarily in the interest of the industrial powers, Japan and the NICs. Without it, they would have been unable to procure raw materials or unload their merchandise and their economic machinery would have stalled or come to an abrupt halt. But it should be obvious that the sales of raw materials also helped the producers while the ability to purchase cheaper, and sometimes better, Japanese and then Korean or Taiwanese articles was to the good. In fact, the entry of a new group of buyers definitely enhanced the gains of selling commodities while the fierce competition among the East Asians to sell most assuredly lowered prices.

Although most self-respecting developing countries rally around the slogan of "trade not aid," there is always a more than residual interest in receiving aid as well. On this particular, their neighbors were rather disappointed at first. There was hardly the generosity or concern which was expressed more spontaneously by the West, and especially the United States. Indeed, having pulled themselves up by the bootstraps, neither the Japanese nor the others had much desire to help those who seemed to be inadequately helping themselves. Nor did their traditions place that much stress on helping others to begin with.

Still, they were gradually convinced that it is not only right and proper for those better off to aid those less well off, they learned that it was in their best interest to do so. It was not so easy to buy raw materials or to sell finished products, especially when there was a trade imbalance, if the visibly richer and more powerful country did not offer something in return. Since this was already being done by the other members of the Organisation for Economic Cooperation and Development, it was impressed on Japan that it should do the same when it joined. More recently, Korea has taken to granting aid for economic reasons while Taiwan has long been in the game on political grounds.

Since Japan has already become one of the most advanced—and most prosperous—countries in the world, it might be assumed that its contribution would be sizable. In global terms it is, as it is now the third or fourth largest donor in the OECD. But, on a per capita basis, it is quite selfish, ranking only thirteenth among the seventeen members. Korea and Taiwan would be much lower on any listing. However, since the bulk of their aid is directed toward other Asian countries, especially those they are cultivating, they leave a rather good impression where it is most desired.[1]

Much of this aid, alas, is only aid under the present loose definitions. It consists of some loans at concessional rates, and more at nearly commercial rates, all of which have to be repaid with interest. There are relatively few grants or outright gifts. Moreover, the loans are usually earmarked for works that do not have much direct impact on economic development but rather contribute to the transportation, educational or health infrastructure. One notable exception, imposed on Japan more than offered by it, was a $1 billion loan for various ASEAN national projects.

The actual development, where it has occurred, can be traced back to something that is hardly as generous as aid, namely investment. The Japanese, and now the Koreans, Taiwanese, and even Singaporeans after them, have found there are valid economic reasons for investing in the rest of the region. Many Hong Kong Chinese have political concerns which only make the urge greater. Ever since the 1960s for Japan, and more recently for the others, the amounts invested abroad have grown rapidly and certainly exceeded a level of some $55 billion by 1983.[2]

Part of the investment, originally the largest share, was directed toward natural resources. In order to get the quantity of raw materials they needed, when they needed it, Japan, Korea and Taiwan invested in a series of mining operations, usually as a partner of local companies. Later on, they were persuaded to invest in processing as well. This occasionally took the form of political pressure rather than economic motivation, since their primary goal was to do the processing back home. But they could be convinced by politics, and sometimes also by economics, to process oil and gas near the well or metal ores in the producing country. Indonesia was the biggest beneficiary here, with a burgeoning LNG sector and the Asahan aluminum project.

There was distinctly less eagerness to invest in manufacturing, although there were soon some exceptions. All of the Five, including even Japan, at the outset, depended heavily on exceptionally low labor costs to get into certain industries. With time, this advantage was eroded as their wage levels rose. In order to benefit from the much cheaper labor abroad, they were often willing to set up rudimentary facilities in poorer parts of Asia. This first meant Japanese factories in the NICs but ultimately included both Japanese and NIC factories in suitable places. Most of them were for labor-intensive light industries like garments, toys and simple electronics.

A lot of this investment had a second motive. As trade restrictions on their own exports mounted, Japan and the NICs found it advantageous to have some of the goods produced offshore and then shipped to the advanced countries. This was known as a triangular strategy in which the investor managed to export but had to entrust the labor and some inputs to the less developed country. Since export processing zones were ideal for such operations, they were quickly filled and spread rapidly throughout the region. In fact, much of Asia became a site of offshore production for someone or other.[3]

Unfortunately, the articles produced on the basis of cheap labor or for export purposes were usually not very

Part of Japan's investment in Asian industry

Credit: Toray

sophisticated and did not involve much value added. They were therefore regarded less favorably by the host countries which were intent on more imposing projects. But they rarely found investors who agreed with them or put much store in their visions of industrial progress. So, they often had to buy machinery or whole turnkey factories and try to run them. For some, this method was preferred. Other still felt the transfer of technology would be smoother if the factories were run by reputable multinationals.

To make the investors more amenable, the host countries were usually willing to offer a number of tempting incentives like tax exemptions or customs rebates. If this were not enough, they might simply close their borders to trade in certain products and inform potential sellers that they had to produce domestically in the future. While this certainly resulted in some investment, it was often a moot point as to whether it was for the better or worse since not all of the projects were carefully chosen or effectively implemented.

While not always successful, there is no doubt that, on the whole, the flows of trade, aid and investment did stimulate growth in the broader Asian region. At least, they made a contribution where it was permitted since some places like Burma, Indochina and the People's Republic remained largely outside the circuits. While rarely as high as the NICs, the growth rates of several other countries attained fairly impressive levels and there were encouraging signs of development, some of which would never have materialized without the rise of a new economic center in East Asia.

Those who could see beyond the momentary circumstances were already aware that the conjunction of a multitude of such actions was swelling into something broader and deeper. There was manifestly an economic spillover, a phenomenon often predicated in the textbooks but all too seldom witnessed in practice. Just as the flows of trade, aid and technology from the West had permitted Japan to grow, and its flows to the NICs had boosted their economies, now all Five were providing massive amounts of capital and knowhow that made it possible for other, once sluggish economies to get moving. Far from laying waste to the surrounding countries, the "dragons" sparked the productive motors of Thailand, Malaysia and Indonesia and, to a lesser extent, the Philippines and Sri Lanka.[4]

There were also increasing interrelations between the two groups which presaged the eventual emergence of an economic sub-system. That is because the complementarity that did not exist within the Five did arise between them and the rest of Asia. Some of the outlying countries were becoming the principal purveyors of raw materials

for the Five while almost all were among their more promising markets. This first step, however, was now being
followed by others. Some were able to ship processed
raw materials to the Five while others manufactured
labor-intensive articles that would increasingly be purchased there. As the Five went upmarket, graduating into
more capital and technology-intensive sectors, this left
some room down below for the Asian newcomers to find
a niche. While this progression was in certain ways worrisome, it enabled the industrialized countries to sell
more factories, machinery and technologies.[5]

There was one further way in which the Five had a
notable impact on the rest of the region. This was much
less concrete and almost impalpable, but it was no less
decisive. Through their example, the East Asians proved
that it was possible for non-Westerners (or, more crude-
ly, non-whites) to build strong and dynamic economies.
This had already been demonstrated by Japan before the
war. Now it was clear that Japan was not an exception, a
unique case as it were, but rather part of a broader movement. This aroused considerable admiration and a desire
for emulation.

Before that, however, it was necessary to overcome
some other emotions that were far less congenial and
almost made it impossible to cooperate with Japan, and
hard to cooperate with the others, at certain times. This
process was bound to be a long one and, no matter how
much progress might be made, there could always be a
relapse.

When Japan initially surfaced as a potential economic
superpower, it was far from a comforting appearance.
Past experiences with a forceful Japan were almost
universally negative and, although it was now a
peaceable state, it was still alarming to see how rapidly
and explosively it grew. This was more than just an emo-

tional fear. Japanese companies were soon trading throughout the region in ways which upset the host countries and sometimes resulted in the stunting or destruction of domestic industries. They were also far too keen to get hold of raw materials and little else. This made Japan look like a predatory economic power which had scant interest in more balanced relations with its neighbors.

On such a background, there was little desire for yet closer relations with the "old tiger" since that seemed to imply subordination and domination. This led to a nasty backlash which reached its peak during Prime Minister Tanaka's visit to Southeast Asia in 1974. Demonstrations and riots broke out, claiming numerous lives, and the Japanese glimpsed the depths of passion that remained. This provoked an awakening in Tokyo and a realization that it was necessary to win friends and supporters by showing that Japan was willing to give as well as to take. The new policy was launched by Prime Minister Takeo Fukuda during his tour of Southeast Asia in August 1977, when he pledged an era of "heart-to-heart" diplomacy and sweetened it with a $1 billion loan. It was followed by his successors with similar, if not quite as spectacular, gestures.

The "young tigers" never encountered the same hostility or resistance. They were smaller and less intimidating and had no past to live down. If anything, as fellow developing countries, they could expect a fair degree of acceptance. The only problem was that they were not in much of a position to influence events at first. Singapore, despite its modest size, was actually the most active due to the vigorous foreign policy of its leaders and a showcase economy. Taiwan was on the defensive, as mainland China reasserted its influence. But economic relations flourished even if there were occasional political reverses. Korea, whose potential was considerable, only really looked outward after President Chun Doo Hwan came to power. However, as of 1982, he began visiting country after country to strengthen economic ties and show that Seoul was a vastly superior partner to Pyongyang.

Yet, no one had really expected that the 1980s would witness an extensive reversal of attitudes with ever more countries in the region looking toward Tokyo as a potential leader. There was little interest on either side in a political or military role, but as an economic partner Japan was increasingly desirable. Whoever had natural resources to develop turned in that direction. Any government that wished to promote a new industry called for its help. Those who were uncertain of how to go about economic development sent missions to study the experiences of the trading companies, QC circles, high tech ventures, and so on. Korea also appeared as a new mecca for studying economic development, while the others were admired more distantly.

What had originally been sporadic and spontaneous gradually evolved into a conscious policy of "looking East." It was inaugurated by Lee Kuan Yew of Singapore and followed yet more fervently by Mahathir Mohamad of Malaysia. Even if never officially proclaimed, the views were shared by many others. The basic idea was that the time had come to change models, cease the slavish adoption of what the West had to offer and see what could be gained in the East. This was bluntly put by Malaysia's prime minister.

"In the past we looked to the West to get new knowledge, to learn about technology, about the methods of production, even systems. This was what we looked at because at that time the West was very successful . . . so successful they conquered the whole world. Naturally, one wants to copy the successful example. Now the situation has changed somewhat whether people like it or not, we see a competition between the Japanese method and the Western method. And, in the contest, we see the Japanese have made headway while the West has not only not made headway, but appears to be regressing. So, in order for Malaysia to progress, we have to learn from the better example, and the better example is the Japanese example. That is why we now want to look East where before we were looking West.''[6]

However, what to borrow from Japan, or Korea, or the others, remained a bit obscure and each country had its own preferences. Mahathir talked of "Malaysia, Inc." and personally targeted the automobile industry. Singapore's Lee placed emphasis on higher productivity and better labor-management relations including even in-house unions. Some wanted to create their own *sogo shosha* and the concepts of quality control spread very widely. Beneath the purely material manifestations, there was always an underlying belief that Asians were indeed different because they placed more stress on harmony, discipline and close human relations. Yet, while there was a great eagerness to learn and to improve, it is far from certain that the other Asians truly understood why the "miracle" economies succeeded or were ready to make the indispensable efforts.

Still, although nobody knows what will come of the "learn from East Asia" boom, there is no question but that it expressed very deep admiration and respect. There is no finer compliment than imitation, and there has never been more copying of the methods applied by the East Asian Five. While this is the least tangible of their achievements, it may have the most far-reaching effects.

Their economic accomplishments and also the new moral ascendency have increasingly made the Five the focus of several circles of friends, supporters or partners in Asia. They have admittedly not won over all. And they also have a few adamant adversaries. But the very fact that so many countries even bother relating to them positively or negatively is an unexpected turnaround for places which were regarded as negligible quantities only a few decades ago.

The first circle consists of the countries of Southeast Asia with which relations are warmest and most structured. This derives from the longer historical contacts, closer proximity, and greater similarity of economic systems and political perspectives. It is further facilitated by the existence of the Association of Southeast Asian Nations including the Philippines, Indonesia, Thailand, Malaysia, Brunei and Singapore. Whereas most of the relations have remained state-to-state, especially for trade and investment, some of the assistance is distributed within the framework of ASEAN alongside any individual offerings. By appearing as a group, its partners felt less exposed and more able to contend with an economic superpower. This arrangement has clearly borne fruit for, over recent years, ASEAN has provided some of Japan's most avid admirers and staunch supporters.

While Japanese aid and investment was far larger, the "Gang of Four" also played a significant role in this grouping. Singapore is a full member of ASEAN, and a respected one, although it tries to avoid giving the impression of foisting its views on the rest. Taiwan, which retains diplomatic ties here, has consolidated them with assorted aid projects. The presence of a large Overseas Chinese population throughout the region has more often been a plus, although it could also be a minus, in encouraging trade and investment. Korea tried to make up for its earlier absence once President Chun initiated a more outgoing diplomacy. Signs thereof are increased purchases of raw materials, sales of manufactured goods, and participation of Korean contractors in major public works. Given a relative complementarity between the East Asian and Southeast Asian economies, there is no reason cooperation should not grow.

The second circle includes several Asian countries a bit further off, such as Burma, Sri Lanka, India and Pakistan. Historically, contacts with this group were slight and some espoused rather nebulous socialist ideologies or clung to a prickly autarky, which did not help political or economic relations. But they were more than happy to sell their raw materials, when they had them, or to import priceworthy consumer or capital goods, when the money was available. This rather constricted relationship, however, took a definite turn for the better when Burma opened up cautiously and Sri Lanka adopted an aggressive capitalism based on massive foreign investment. India, and Pakistan more so, were also willing to increase trade and investment from East Asia even if the actual amounts stayed relatively modest.

While stretching the boundaries somewhat, one must add the thriving exchanges with countries in the Middle East. Despite any lack of traditional links, markedly different cultures and political systems, and economies which could hardly be less alike, the Five actually found their ideal partners there. Each side had what the other wanted. The Arabs had oil and other natural resources and therefore also a tremendous capacity to buy all sorts of things they did not produce. The East Asians produced most of those things and needed raw materials desperately. This time, it was Japan and the NICs which ran deficits. But they did a better job of covering them than most by boosting sales of consumer and capital goods. The Koreans actually did best by undertaking some of the biggest construction projects around and winning considerably more contracts than the Japanese.

There was another, more distant circle, reaching into Oceania and the smaller islands of the South Pacific. Most prominent were Australia and New Zealand, geographically Asian but with a Western heritage and cultural affinities. Gradually, however, they realized that their economic, and perhaps also political, fate was bound to the other liberal countries in the region including both ASEAN and the Five. East Asia's relations with Oceania were not unlike those with the Middle East. They basically exchanged consumer goods for raw materials with the slight difference that, alas, Australia and New Zealand disliked being hewers of wood and drawers of water and had bothersome pretensions to making their own manufactured goods.

Unfortunately, it was the tightest geographical circle in the region which included the largest number of scoffers, opponents and enemies. There was North Korea, a bitter foe of the southern regime, with its troops stationed near the gates of Seoul. There was the People's Republic of China, an implacable rival of the Republic of China, whether wishing to prevail by force or guile. The Soviet Union, with a vast Asian expanse, worried Japan and the others with its military might. Vietnam, dominating the rest of Indochina, was no less of an irritant for ASEAN. For decades, relations passed through various degrees of tension, peaking when Peking bombarded Taiwan's offshore islands or refused to trade with Japan, when Hanoi absorbed the south or invaded Cambodia, or Moscow decided to transfer its missiles eastward. With antagonistic political and economic regimes, there was no great cause for hope.

Yet, subtly and imperceptibly there were changes. The

most drastic arose in the People's Republic when the ideological hardliners were replaced by pragmatists who tried to rebuild the economy after the setbacks of the Great Leap Forward and the Cultural Revolution. No one knew how far the economy would be reshaped and liberalized, but there was no doubt that economic ties would be vastly improved, not only for Japan which offered massive trade and aid but perhaps even for Korea and Taiwan. Instrumental in this reversal was the Hong Kong model, the safest and most accessible.[7] The Indochinese would probably also welcome a bit more trade and aid from East Asia, without transforming their economies as much. The Soviet Union, while maintaining strained diplomatic relations with Japan, was eager for investment in Siberia. Only North Korea seemed immovable.

Thus, in Asia at least, the standing and popularity of the Five has never been higher. There was nothing self-evident about this and the countries had worked hard to win the esteem of their peers. However, the honor itself could be costly because it is impossible to remain a leader without meeting some of the expectations of any followers. And pupils who have already changed teachers would be less hesitant to do so again. This involves onerous obligations like more generous development aid and financial assistance, a more open market and a receptive attitude to any special requests. It also means that the "dragon" and "tiger" economies have to live up to their reputation. They must continue breathing fire and bounding ahead or they will cease inspiring much awe.

NOTES

1. See Alan Rix, *Japan's Economic Aid*.
2. See Jon Woronoff, *Japan's Commerical Empire*, and Kunio Yoshihara, *Japanese Investment in Southeast Asia*.
3. See Yoshikuni Ohnishi, "Free Trade Zones in Asia," and F. A. Rabbani (ed.), "Economic and Social Impacts of Export Processing Zones in Asia," both Tokyo, Asian Productivity Organization, 1983.
4. See Woronoff, *op. cit.*, pp. 295–331.
5. See Roger Benjamin and Robert T. Kuderle (eds.), *The Industrial Future of the Pacific Basin*.
6. *Far Eastern Economic Review*, June 11, 1982, p. 38.
7. As the years pass, the value of "learning from Hong Kong" will only grow for China.

16

East Confronts West

The emergence of an East Asian group also had a notable impact on the West. In many ways, the effect was even sharper in Europe and North America than in Asia, because the methods used were bound to provoke more direct confrontations. The Five appeared as unwelcome upstarts in just those areas where the West had hitherto enjoyed an undisputed superiority, industrial production, procurement of raw materials, application of technology and sales of manufactured goods. That the Five should even attempt such a thing was startling. That they should succeed was most unsettling. It is only because they beat the West at its own game that it deigned take the "miracle" economies seriously.

Not surprisingly, there has been a tendency to exaggerate. In many circles, the East Asians are already condemned as an insidious threat to the continuing prosperity and leadership of the West.[1] In reaction to this, others countered that their rise could also be a source of hope, offering tremendous promise if only handled properly.[2] This debate was amplified by politicians, academics and writers whose credentials are very impressive, but who apparently never bother listening to one another. It must be obvious that East Asia cannot be both a threat and a promise of such proportions and probably is neither if one takes a more balanced view. But these are not times for taking balanced views.

The threat scenario is particularly compelling at present since preoccupying manifestations of it are already at hand. In fact, they are very hard to miss if one reads the daily newspapers which make repeated references to them. The danger is primarily, for the moment at least, economic. The Five have been able to do an awesome job of developing their productive machinery to the point where they are frightfully competitive in a growing range of goods and have been able to outsell the supposedly "advanced" nations on third markets. Worse, in many cases, they also penetrated Western markets so aggressively that some of their erstwhile competitors collapsed.

Their increasing ability to export to the West was compounded by a marked decrease in any Western ability to sell manufactured goods or even technologies to East Asia. In Taiwan and Korea this could occasionally be traced to trade barriers while in Hong Kong and Singapore, with more open economies, Japanese articles often prevailed. Most attempts to get into the Japanese market, the crucial test, were frustrated by competition from better or cheaper products or, when that was manifestly not the case, business practices which blocked sales. The only things that could readily be sold to East Asia were raw materials and foodstuffs, placing Canada, Australia, and the United States in the equivalent of a "colonial" relationship. European countries, which could not even offer that, were worse off. This failure took the very conspicuous and galling form of huge trade deficits which tended to grow from year to year.

However, as Kent Calder and Roy Hofheinz, Jr., plainly show in *The Eastasia Edge*, this might just be the beginning and the "list of disastrous consequences may be long indeed." Declining competitiveness would affect not only the economy but society ("it aggravates the deepening social ills") and international relations ("controls on foreign acquisitions may increase resentment abroad, but their absence could well generate domestic zenephobia''). It could even threaten national security. "Failures of industrial and technical leadership may impair our ability to match Soviet weapons production. An unsound industrial base could make it impossible for us to build up our military strength without serious inflation, further weakening our industry."[3]

It is frequently assumed that these trends, which are already appallingly noticeable, will continue indefinitely and that Western countries will keep sinking into decadence while Eastern countries go from strength to strength. That is because, as opposed to being mere time-servers, they are forward-looking and plan ahead. In fact, they are even now targeting the sectors they intend to take over in the future. All one has to do is read the lists, which are rather exhaustive, to know that they are already zeroing in on the last remaining bastions of Western enterprise. Having undermined its light industries like textiles and garments, its basic industries like steel and chemicals, they are now working on high tech without eschewing computers, aerospace and biotechnology.

There is no doubt that the Five have pulled off a few "miracles" in their time and proven their economic prowess. They have made exceptional strides in production capability and scale and are better organized than ever. Whereas they were once competitive mainly for reasons of cheaper labor, they have since shifted their advantage to a better use of machinery and advanced technologies. Henceforth, they will be engaging in much more research and development. Having proceeded from imitation to innovation, they hope to make their mark in invention. This may explan the uncomfortable feeling in some circles that the Asian "tigers" are stealthily prowling about in the underbrush and preparing to pounce again.

Still, the incipient dangers should not be exaggerated. The Five possess both the will and the ability to make further economic progress. They have been highly successful in the past and should do comparatively well in the future. But it is absurd to assume a continuation of their previous performance. Many things have changed since the early days and the "tigers" are getting winded and hemmed in. If we look at some of the factors which got the East Asians where they are, this immediately becomes obvious.

Raw material and energy costs, as noted, are rising. Labor costs are rising. Machinery, used to replace labor, is also more costly. Due to the aging of the population, fewer workers will have to carry more idle young or elderly persons. Due to a maturation of the economy, there are no longer as many new technologies that can be acquired, new products that can be manufactured or new markets that can be tapped. Some markets are actually shrinking and barriers to others are increasingly forbidding. Competition will be stiff all around. These are just some of the daunting hurdles to rapid growth and, even if some are cleared, the Five will be forced to slow down.

That should be more than enough to dismiss the concept of a linear rise of the East that could precipitate a no less linear decline of the West. The Five are already decelerating somewhat and this will take a bit of the pressure off the rest of the world, including the West. And that assumes that no defensive measures are taken. Most of the scenarios are grossly misleading because they tend to intimate that nothing has been done to counter the threat and the Western nations are meekly awaiting their economic defeat.

While there is no explicit policy or program that could be formally proclaimed as the Western reaction to an

1936: Launching Japanese automotive exports

Credit: Toyota

Eastern economic offensive, there have been many individual actions as well as a considerable change in attitude. During the 1950s and 1960s, there is no doubt that America and Europe felt vastly superior to the impoverished and nearly desperate Asian countries which seemed unlikely to overcome their crises. Moved by a reasonably selfless charity, assistance was provided to help their economies recover. This was then continued on grounds of enlightened self-interest and to strengthen the "free world." And close cooperation has since grown out of mutual interest, since the West also gained from the relationship.

But Westerners are no longer as naive as they used to be. They have finally realized that economic progress was not an exclusive talent of their countries. If anything, they were astounded by the speed of the recovery and growth in East Asia. When the Five began competing against their products and penetrating their markets, the reaction was even more charged. The change in mood, however, was still only partial because some segments of the public clearly benefited from the flow of imports. Not until the recession and the alarming increase in unemployment has the threat become so patent and the need for a suitable response so pressing that no leadership can ignore it.

The best policy would doubtlessly include a strengthening of the Western economies through some of the same methods used in East Asia. There is a crying need to construct new factories, introduce more efficient machinery, develop better production techniques and instill greater concern for productivity and quality in both labor and management. Yet more investment and R & D will be required to perfect even more advanced technologies. Some of these measures have been taken all along by responsible companies. But more support is likely to come from the government. If such a reindustrialization of the West took place, the ability to meet and also parry the economic thrust from the East would be decidedly improved.

The East Asians may actually find that their favorite techniques and strategies are turned against them. There is already an admission of the importance of exporting and measures are being taken to enhance export capability. The United States and Canada have adopted legislation to create trading companies and the Europeans, from long habit already, subsidize the exports of major items and offer generous credit terms for others. Japanese-style management, the so-called "non-adversarial" type, is zealously promoted and much fuss is made about QC circles and the like.[4] Governments are urged to cease interfering and preferably help local business with a striking shift in favor of promoting "sunrise" industries while letting "sunset" ones disappear. There has even been talk of establishing a Department of International Trade and Industry (DITI vs MITI) in America. No one knows yet what "Eastern technology and Western spirit" will concoct, but it is clearly designed to counter East Asia.

Other steps are also possible. In fact, they have already been taken in numerous cases. The best place to face the Japanese competition, which is the most telling, is not at home but in Japan. Thus, more investment is being made to produce locally and penetrate the Japanese market from within or, at least, to know what one's opponents are up to. The alternative, which makes very good economic sense, is to cooperate with the other four countries in order to get at Japan. The West has advanced technologies, the NICs still have cheaper yet competent labor forces. This means that products which are about as good as Japanese ones, and certainly cheaper, can be manufactured there. Most will be shipped back to the home market, which helps the NICs, but at least the profit will go to Western companies and they can check the Japanese advance.

Another series of measures is considerably less constructive, but no less likely to blunt the East Asian offensive. As noted, much of the impetus of industrial growth came from the ability to induce modern technologies in order to leapfrog ahead. This was largely possible because the proprietors were not fully aware of the value of technology or vainly assumed that backward countries would be unable to use sophisticated techniques and, even if they could, the clever Westerners would soon come up with new ones. That was not so easy. And now more companies are holding on to their technologies as precious assets or selling them for very high fees.

East Asian governments and companies were also able

to benefit from relatively broad and cheap access to foreign capital. They received gifts, grants and concessional loans from American, British and other agencies or various international bodies. Now, as semi-industrialized countries, many sources are closed to them and even World Bank loans will cease once per capita income rises a bit further. The Five will depend essentially on straight commercial loans at conditions which are far less advantageous. As major producers of certain goods, they are also being "graduated out" of the General Scheme of Preferences, reserved more exclusively for less proficient developing countries. This will cut off a particularly useful entry point.

However, it is the worst response, mainly because it is so negative, that has been the most widespread. When faced with too large an influx of Asian products, especially when there are surges or suspicion of dumping, the industries concerned will call for protection. This has resulted in higher tariffs, smaller quotas, countervailing duties and fines. It has also brought about demands for greater restraint on the part of the exporters, something they find it hard not to concede when asked forcefully enough. As the individual acts multiply, there has actually been a notable regression in trade relations and a perceptible move toward a new era of protectionism.

It is often pointed out that this "solution" is not good for anyone, either the exporters or the importers. It means that efficient foreign producers are hurt and the consumers are forced to buy from less efficient domestic producers. But there is no doubt that protection brings immediate relief to the inefficient producers at home, as well as their employees, and thereby decreases the pressure on the politicians who can adopt such measures. That is why there is every reason to believe that protectionism will continue spreading as long as the economic attack from the East is too aggressive. And there is nothing much the Asians can do about it. Their bargaining position is weak, especially if their own markets are closed. Worse, the advanced countries are beginning to realize that a market is an asset just like anything else and one should get the most out of it.

Protectionism is clearly the easiest way of defending the Western economies, at least in the short run, no matter how disreputable it may be in the eyes of some or how unfortunate the consequences in the long run. What is no less important is that it is particularly effective against East Asian incursions. That is because the Five have put themselves in a position of abject dependence on Western and other markets even when this was not truly necessary. By pushing export-oriented policies so single-mindedly without thinking of the devastating effect of losing markets, they do not have a very good fall-back position. Thus, it makes them the weaker parties whenever there is a trade conflict and it makes them give in to pressure whenever it is applied.

This alone should be enough to dispel the notion that the East Asian threat is somehow invincible and overwhelming. It can be stopped very readily. And the advance has regularly been blocked in this manner. Protectionism, of course, will hurt those applying it if it becomes their only response. But, if it is coupled with a conscious effort to rebuild the economy, it could just as well form the basis of a Western resurgence not unlike the one in the East. If a revitalized Western economy were pitted against a somewhat less vigorous Eastern one, the outcome would be significantly different.[5]

Some of this, of course, is just wishful thinking. Too many Western businessmen are unwilling to make the effort and it is not certain the governments can impose the necessary discipline. If they do not, then protectionism will only cushion the decline and the rot will continue to spread. Rather than taking over markets in a spectacular manner, the East Asians will be more subtle and discreet. They will increase exports more gently. And they will have the wisdom to send as much as possible through OEM, with the products made for and bearing the labels of national companies that serve as a Trojan horse of sorts.

Yet, even a gradual and gracious decline cannot really be accepted by certain governments, not so much because they have a deep concern for the economy as because they know that it is impossible nowadays to create a strong military force on a weak economic base. Increasingly, arguments of this kind have been used to take measures that should already have been adopted for economic reasons. Companies are urged to make greater efforts at research and development and not to part with their valuable technologies. They are encouraged to instal more machinery and make better use of their work force. They are carefully fostered and sheltered and, if need be, R & D and other expenses are subsidized. Alas, it is the excessive emphasis on military production that often weakens the sectors manufacturing consumer goods and results in economic devolution.

Whatever its effect on the economy, the military and political power of the West can be decisive even in the context of the economic confrontation and despite every effort by the East Asians to separate the two spheres. Whether they like it or not, the "dragons" are highly dependent on American military strength to maintain their own system and perhaps guarantee their survival as independent entities. This is particularly true of Korea and Taiwan, menaced by powerful military opponents, and Japan, which depends more generally on the nuclear umbrella. The others also feel more comfortable with an

American military presence in the region. In a broader and more diffuse manner, they all rely somewhat on European political support in world forums.

While it may not be especially nice to use political, let alone military, pressure on one's friends and allies, this cannot be entirely excluded. Indeed, it can hardly be avoided, at least implicitly, when they are perpetually engaged in economic conflicts. For, undercutting the economic base of their main partners and protectors would be sheer folly and the Five may be asked to make certain sacrifices to avoid this. Here lies the second basic fallacy in the idea of an invincible and overwhelming force arising in the Orient.

Whereas the threat is usually portrayed as imminent, the promise deriving from the rise of an East Asian group

Today: The automobile invasion escalates

Credit: Toyota

is regarded as more distant. This does not keep its proponents from waxing poetic about the countless benefits this can bring. If anything, it leaves them more leeway than otherwise. And they have already begun a lively campaign of proselytism for the coming of a Pacific Age.[6]

Great expectations are aroused by citing statistics showing the tremendous amount of activity that already exists in the Pacific Basin. The countries bordering it account for well over half the world's entire population, they generate almost as much of its total gross national product and they include many of the leading political and military powers of the globe. The various indicators are, of course, then extended indefinitely to project a continuing ascent of the region while everything else on Earth sinks into nothingness. Striking milestones on this path are avidly seized upon, such as the fact that in 1983—for the first time in recorded history—there was more trade across the Pacific than the Atlantic.

More dramatically, vapid orators recall that the East is the land of the rising sun while the West witnesses a setting sun. The Pacific is young and vigorous while the Atlantic is old and jaded. On the basis of such characteristics, it seems that almost anything would be possible if one would only make efforts commensurate with the challenge. Thus, visionaries like American Ambassador Mike Mansfield rally the faithful with stirring appeals. "The next century will be the century of the Pacific. When you look at the whole picture you have to admit that's where it all is, that's what it's all about, and that's where our future lies."[7]

While it is undeniable that trade, investment and even political relations have been improving here and there in the region, the arguments are greatly overstated. The first weakness becomes amply clear when one asks the simplest of all questions—which countries are committed to participation in a Pacific Community?

It then becomes painfully evident that some are pointedly indifferent. To take account of geographical facts, and make the whole vision that much more grandiose, various Latin American countries have been included in the potential membership such as Mexico, Peru and Chile, although no one has said much about those in Central America. They, alas, have dreadfully few relations with the rest of the countries which border the Pacific, with the one exception of the United States. With their North American partner, and the rest of the countries in the continent, the Latin Americans have such intense relations that there is little room for anything else.

Even more questionable is the mention of some countries which would probably be against any such grouping. Indeed, one wonders whether it was not an oversight or whether the love of illusion led some to include the People's Republic of China, the Soviet Union (and why not Vietnam and North Korea?) in the list of conceivable candidates. There is little hope they would wish for any closer relations with the staunchly capitalist countries which form the core of the unit. Yet, once they are excluded, it is no longer correct to speak of the vast population, the huge gross national product and the immense political and military potential of the region.

It would therefore seem that any realistic grouping would have to be shorn of several elements and would end up with, at most, the East Asian Five, the ASEAN group, the United States and Canada, Australia and New Zealand. This is still an impressive line-up. But it would take a formidable effort to shape it into more than it now is, just a string of countries primarily concerned with their own interests but smart enough to recognize, and occasionally pay lip service to, any broader interests.

This does not mean that parts of the Pacific Basin will not be drawn closer together. Probably they will. There are vital constructive links that bind them and many of the influences shaping today's world are more likely to unite than to divide them. But it is improbable that any rapprochement will extend beyond the field in which the influences are strongest, namely economics. The slightest hint that the grouping could spread to political, or especially military cooperation, would be liable to hinder rather than to help its establishment.

Yet, if the bonds are to be only economic, then one would have to take a more realistic look at the situation and admit that there are both positive and negative factors at work. That, if nothing else, is why the backers of a Pacific Community should listen to some of the comments coming from those who decry the insidious threat to the West. Many of the relations between East Asia and other industrialized countries wherever they may lie have gone from bad to worse. Numerous trade conflicts already exist and many more are on the way. Certainly, this would not encourage some to tie their fate more closely to the Five. And the promise of a broader market would not appeal much to the "Western" segment if it simply means that they will increasingly become suppliers of raw materials, and clients for manufactured goods, of the "East".

Still, even within this considerably restricted framework, there is some room for action. For the moment, it cannot be undertaken by dominant countries like Japan or the United States because that would only frighten the others (who would immediately suspect ulterior motives). The role of initiator has thus descended on places like Korea and Australia, a bit outside of the existing circuits and eager to join a larger group, but which do not arouse as much suspicion. On the other hand, they cannot exert the pressure that might be necessary to bring about more active participation by the rest.

The long march to a Pacific Community, one with an appreciably reduced geographic and functional scope, has thus been slow and hesitant. Much of the initiative has come from private businessmen who have formed friendly associations to discuss the matter. They even began working toward a Pacific Economic Community, Pacific Free Trade Area or a Pacific Basin Common Market.[8] But these are often just big words covering rather modest deeds since nothing more actually exists than small study groups or committees looking into the situation. No matter how great they are bound to find the ultimate potential, when they get down to the practical possibilities, they will appear distinctly less imposing.

This analysis should certainly not be interpreted as a rejection of a noble cause, any more than the previous one intended to underplay the dangers that do exist. It is simply that the threat is not quite as nefarious as often pictured nor is the promise as glorious. They are both real. They both deserve careful attention. But the very fact that there are such momentous currents pulling in opposite directions, some encouraging closer relations, others impeding them, signifies that the outcome will lie somewhere in the middle. And, once again, it is likely that things will get worse before they get better.

NOTES

1. The list of such books is growing rapidly and includes Jack Baranson, *The Japanese Challenge to U.S. Industry*, Lawrence G. Franko, *The Threat of Japanese Multinationals*, Roy Hofheinz,

Jr. and Kent E. Calder, *The Eastasia Edge*, and Marvin J. Wolf, *The Japanese Conspiracy*.

2. These books are not quite as numerous, although increasing, and include William J. Barnds (ed.), *Japan and the United States, Challenges and Opportunities*, Kiyoshi Kojima, *Japan and a New Economic Order*, and Endymion Wilkinson, *Misunderstanding: Europe versus Japan*.

3. Hofheinz and Calder, *op. cit.*, pp. 12–3.

4. Worthy of mention, but hardly of reading, are William Ouchi, *Theory Z*, Richard Tanner Pascale and Anthony G. Athos, *The Art of Japanese Management*, and so many others.

5. For more constructive alternatives, see Jon Woronoff, *World Trade War*, pp. 256–94.

6. See Roger Benjamin and Robert T. Kudrle (eds.), *The Industrial Future of the Pacific Basin*, and F. Q. Quo (ed.), *Politics of the Pacific Nations*.

7. *Japan Economic Journal*, February 28, 1984, p. 13.

8. See, among others, Kojima, *op. cit.*, pp. 168–87.

Epilogue:

Learning from East Asia

Over recent years, the rest of the world has gradually realized that something exceptional is happening in East Asia. While most nations are plodding along quite slowly, and many economies have actually slipped back, in that particular region there has been an unusual spurt of growth which has raised some of the most backward countries to the pinnacle of economic performance. The first to emerge, already before the war, was Japan. But it did not remain alone and was followed later by Taiwan, Korea, Hong Kong and Singapore.

This aroused a growing curiosity about what might be going on there which culminated in the "look East" policy of some Asian countries. It did not take long, however, for the interest to spread more widely as the "dragons" displayed their economic prowess on foreign markets, impressing even the Americans and Europeans. What had once been regarded as hopeless amateurs were taken more seriously and became worrisome competitors. Even places which had long been isolated, like the Soviet bloc and People's Republic of China, eventually took notice.

The next step, not surprisingly in a world so void of noteworthy examples, was to wonder whether it were possible to learn something worthwhile from the East Asian Five. They were manifestly succeeding where so many others failed, maybe they possessed some secrets that could be of use. The "learn from Japan" boom which ensued was as sudden as it was swift, taking hold not only in Asia but almost as deeply in the United States and Europe, circles which once thought there was no one they could learn from. Meanwhile, the range of teachers spread from Japan to the four NICs, whose attraction for developing countries was sometimes even greater.

Certainly, there are many things that can be learned from East Asia. This book and others like it would never have been written otherwise. The exemplary rise of five once undistinguished economies is an intriguing story which can encourage others. The various policies and strategies used to accelerate growth are even more pregnant with meaning. Their failures, just like their successes, can shed precious light on the development process as such.

But it is worthwhile adding a few more lessons which have not been dealt with directly thus far. They can be derived more intuitively from the experiences of the Five than as a result of their formal pronouncements and policies. Yet, without these several lessons, it would be extremely hard to learn very much.

The need for these additional pointers immediately becomes apparent when one considers the present approach to learning from East Asia. After all, what is it that people seemingly want to learn? To judge by their words and actions it is . . . magic formulas . . . pat models . . . universal recipes . . . infallible strategies . . . something neat and tidy to work another economic miracle.

Well, if there is one thing that is clearly taught by the development history of these economies, it is that there is no such thing as magic formulas, pat models, universal recipes, infallible strategies and the like. That is doubtlessly *Lesson No. 1*.

Not only do such miraculous means not exist, it could not be claimed that there is any one "right" way to develop an economy. That was shown very palpably by the fact that the East Asian Five adopted quite varied approaches to just about any possible problem. Some were highly *dirigiste*, others extremely liberal; some gave the leading role to the state, in others the state held back; some strongly promoted industry and exports, others left that to economic circumstances. There was absolutely nothing done by one that was not ignored or even contradicted by another.

It would therefore be very unwise to adopt any of the supposed "models" outright. What they did was only effective to the extent that it met the needs of the country concerned, and it is extremely unlikely that any other place would have exactly the same endowment or possibilities or wish to follow exactly the same policies. Moreover, none of these countries, no matter how successful, ever really found the "ideal" policy mix. This became clear from the fact that they periodically altered or discarded measures which had once been deemed suitable.

It would be even more perilous to just pick one or two institutions or strategies which are particularly appealing and claim that they were the true secret of success. It does not matter how striking or significant they may seem, whether the *sogo shosha* or planning boards, export orientation or targeting. For, each of them was part of a much broader approach and could only function in that context. Trading companies are pointless if there are no attractive products and targeting them is futile if industries are not competitive. Without the proper backup, these apparent "assets" have no value and can turn out to be liabilities to those who acquire them.

While there is no one "right" way, there is a multitude of wrong ways. That is clear from the failure of so many countries to show much economic progress which sharply highlights the pitifully few sucesses that were noted. The same "development decades" that saw the rise of the Five also witnessed the stagnation and sometimes decline of well over a hundred developing countries and a weakening even of the more advanced nations.

What is most paradoxical, however, is that the difference between "right" and "wrong" was not always one of kind but of degree. Most of the wrong policies were just unfortunate distortions of the right policies. Most of the mistakes came from an exaggeration of what could have led to success. No matter how good a policy was, it became negative and harmful when pressed too hard or inflexibly and planners or businessmen lost their sense of moderation. This might be *Lesson No. 2*.

This is easier to comprehend with some examples, all of them referring to already familiar characteristics of the East Asian growth strategies. This is necessary to show that even in the hands of relative masters things did not always work. If used foolishly by apprentices, the results could be far worse.

It was stressed that there was little hope for economic advancement without showing the necessary commitment. This means that it would be impossible to progress unless people were willing to accept sacrifices, show discipline and unite in a common task. If they fell to fighting over who would get the biggest slice of the prospective pie, they were in trouble. On the other hand, if it were assumed that simply by regimenting people, giving them orders and then pushing them in the right direction one could succeed, the failure might be just as great.

There is no doubt that the state could play an extremely important role, actually the leading role if there was little initiative from private businessmen. In the early years, it could launch plans and nurture industries. But, if it became too invasive, the private sector might never develop and the state would be left to carry the whole economy. Once it was forced to do more than it could, and especially engage in activities that were not really amenable to state control, the economy could suffer as much as if it had done nothing.

On the other hand, assuming that the state should not intervene at all, that private entrepreneurs could be trusted to run the economy alone, was just as risky. There are some things no private company wishes to do. There are other things that can clearly be done better collectively. And it is necessary to see that the businessmen do not get out of hand and abuse their position. A state that ignores this is more likely to encourage anarchy or corruption than sound economic endeavor.

Much waste is entailed in letting entrepreneurs proceed entirely by trial and error and enter sectors they know little about. Surely, it is possible to make a better use of manpower and resources if there is some organization. Planning is the most comprehensive way of doing this. Yet, if the stress on planning becomes excessive, this will create an undesirable rigidity. It will also overlook many vital details which simply cannot be taken into account by plans. The outcome could also be considerable waste.

Japan's latest export hit: QC Circles

Credit: Toyota

Industry is unquestionably important. A country cannot develop if it is unable to manufacture some rather basic products on its own and each additional article adds to the economy's diversity. But, it makes little sense to push industrial growth so far that it becomes a fetish. Promoting and protecting it excessively would result in superfluous or inefficient facilities. It would also mean not enough could be done for other sectors which are perhaps not as popular, but are just as useful in generating employment and wealth.

A country which cannot export anything is in sorry shape. For then it cannot import either. Or, if it imports more than it can pay for, it will quickly run up debts. So there must be enough exports to procure essential imports and perhaps a bit more to accumulate a surplus that can be used for development. But exporting should not be overdone. If exports are pushed too hard they may not even yield a sufficient return to justify the effort. And imports are equally useful in their own right.[2]

This all goes to show that there is plainly no precise "formula," let alone a single "key" to development. Even policies and strategies that are basically wise are only useful when they stay somewhere in the middle of the possible range of actions. This range is broad enough, as it were, to accomodate even the rather notable variations of the East Asian Five. Thus, to qualify as valid behavior, something one might be tempted to copy, it is necessary to maintain a reasonable balance.

Obviously, it is easy to say that balance must be maintained. It is not so simple to explain exactly how that is done, at which point one attains or loses this balance. Nor will there be any attempt made here to spell it out. For, as should be amply clear by now, it is not a question of specific positions but circumstances which vary from country to country and from time to time. Seeking a straight and narrow path would be foolhardy as the most one can hope for in economics is a path that is broad and winding.

There are, however, very good indicators of where that path may be at any given moment. They arise from something that is much deeper than any of the specific policies and strategies about which so much fuss is made. They derive from what have often been referred to as economic "laws," although they are repeatedly ignored or flaunted by many of the economic actors, from statesmen to businessmen. Heeding these economic laws would be *Lesson No. 3*.[3]

In order to obey these invisible laws, it is first necessary to ascertain one's factor endowment so as to see what sort of possibilities exist. Even if they are not particularly brilliant, it is still wise to admit it. For, the factor endowment will indicate most clearly which activities should be taken up and which shunned. They will point an economy more accurately than any planner to the comparative advantage which determines success or failure. In case one is not very certain of the direction, there is no shortage of market signals, not terribly unlike traffic lights, to tell one when to proceed and when to fall back.

The most precious attribute of the economic "laws" is that, unlike human laws, they are extremely responsive and natural, growing out of the inherent economic situation. They can temper the more static and categoric policies and strategies which are as often a reflection of hopes and desires as realities. The market signals are also more sensitive, recording minor movements as soon as they begin and well before they become major tremors. The corollary, of course, is that those in the best position to notice any changes should be allowed to adapt to them without too much interference from those who are more remote. This implies giving necessary leeway to farmers, merchants or manufacturers as opposed to politicians, planners and bureaucrats.

If balance and ability to follow market signals are to play such a crucial role, then it is extremely useful at this point to refer to another basic lesson, one which can be observed in the actions of the Five and saved them from going wrong more often than can be imagined. That is to adopt a pragmatic approach to economic development.

Lesson No. 4, pragmatism, takes many forms. As noted, it involves checking on circumstances to see that one goes far enough in each aspect of economic policy without going too far. It means that if the market signals indicate that something has gone wrong, if there is a distortion in the use of resources, if there is waste, this will be recognized. It will not only be admitted, the mistaken policies should be discarded and efforts made to correct any failings.

Pragmatism also implies a careful screening of economic policies, strategies, institutions and other elements which can be borrowed from other countries to be certain that they really meet the needs. It is essential for them to fit in as smoothly as possible with the existing conditions and lend themselves to local application. Naturally, the fit will not be perfect, so anything that has been borrowed should be modified and adapted to the prevailing circumstances.

Lesson No. 5, for those who do not realize this yet, is that there is no hope of economic development unless one is willing to learn from others. It was not until Japan accepted to learn from the West, and the "Gang of Four" from Japan, that any of them made progress. In fact, the more willing they were to learn, to accept, to adopt and to assimilate, the more rapid their progress. This did not mean blind admiration or blanket approval, but it did at least imply an admission that for certain things they knew less than others.

The willingness to learn is more important now than it has ever been in the past. That is largely because there is so much to learn. There has never been a greater reservoir of knowledge related to economic development than today. This consists not only of broad policies and strategies but specific agricultural and manufacturing techniques, more exact organizational and managerial procedures, and detailed knowhow in a thousand-and-one sectors. Actually, it is absurd that with all this available, much of it already tested and proven, more countries have not picked up the tricks that make neo-development so much easier than original development ever was.

Alas, it would be hasty to conclude without adding one final lesson. No matter how much simpler it is now, no matter how much can be learned from the Five, it is never easy to reform, improve and expand an economy. It still requires a lot of hard work, a lot of sacrifice, and a lot of patience. That this effort has remained beyond the capability of most is sadly evident.

Thus, it must be stressed time and again that development arises not out of policies, strategies, plans and the like but rather out of implementation. The former are nothing more than a starting point. Until they are put into practice, they are just noble sentiments and wishful thinking. Far more attention must therefore be paid to creating the appropriate institutions to supervise or carry out the work as well as mobilizing the population to participate actively and intelligently. If this can be achieved, then even the worst endowed country could proceed smartly along the path to development. Deeds, not words, might perhaps best sum up this indispensable *Lesson No. 6.*

Some of these rather moralistic lessons may sound simple, perhaps even simplistic. But the sad fact is that they have proven incredibly difficult to realize in the vast majority of cases and failure here has probably been as great a cause of economic mishaps as anything else. This makes it far from superfluous to add them to the more concrete ones displayed by the policies and strategies pioneered by the East Asian Five. For, if they are not duly considered, the learning process would be very badly flawed. And those who do their most to ape the master magicians could make a worse mess of their economies than before.

However, with these lessons in mind, as well as any others one may care to derive from the actual experiences of the Five, it is just possible that some of the many aspiring apprentices will do the right things. It is just possible that more developing countries will finally start growing and a few of the advanced countries will pull themselves back from the brink. It might even be conceivable to create a world in which there is a bit less poverty and squalor and a bit more affluence and ease. This would not be the best of all possible worlds, but it would certainly be better than what we have now.

NOTES

1. The danger is far from theoretical given the temerity with which the United States, Canada and Malaysia decided to establish general trading companies, Malaysia targeted autombiles and France electronics, Singapore adopted a system of in-house unions and the United States mooted the creation of a Department of International Trade and Industry (DITI).

2. The triumph of export orientation in East Asia has already enhanced its rating to the point that the strategy is being generally recommended to developing countries by think tanks and aid agencies although the chances of success for many are exceedingly slim.
3. See Jon Woronoff, *Hong Kong: Capitalist Paradise*, pp. 24–30 and 252–8.

Bibliography

1. Japan

Allen, G. C., *The Japanese Economy*, London, Weidenfeld and Nicolson, 1981.

Beasley, W. G., *The Modern History of Japan*, London, Weidenfeld and Nicolson, 1981.

Bronte, Stephen, *Japanese Finance: Markets and Institutions*, London, Euromoney, 1982.

Fukutake, Tadashi, *Japanese Society Today*, Tokyo, University of Tokyo Press, 1981.

———, *The Japanese Social Structure*, Tokyo, University of Tokyo Press, 1982.

Goldsmith, Raymond W., *The Financial Development of Japan, 1868-1977*, New Haven, Yale University Press, 1983.

Hanami, Tadashi, *Labor Relations in Japan Today*, Tokyo, Kodansha, 1979.

Hane, Mikiso, *Peasants, Rebels and Outcastes: The Underside of Modern Japan*, New York, Pantheon Books, 1982.

Johnson, Chalmers, *MITI And The Japanese Miracle*, Stanford, Stanford University Press, 1982.

Kahn, Herman, *The Emerging Japanese Superstate*, Harmondsworth, Penguin Books, 1970.

Kelley, Allen C., and Williamson, Jeffrey G., *Lessons From Japanese Development, An Analytical Economic History*, Chicago, University of Chicago Press, 1974.

Levine, Solomon B., and Kawada, Hisashi, *Human Resources in Japanese Industrial Development*, Princeton, Princeton University Press, 1980.

Lockwood, William W., *The Economic Development of Japan, Growth and Structural Change 1868-1938*, Princeton, Princeton University Press, 1954.

Ministry of International Trade and Industry, *White Paper on International Trade*, Tokyo, various.

Moore, Joe, *Japanese Workers and the Struggle for Power*, Madison, University of Wisconsin Press, 1983.

Nakamura, Takafusa, *Economic Growth in Prewar Japan*, New Haven, Yale University Press, 1983.

———, *The Postwar Japanese Economy*, Tokyo, University of Tokyo Press, 1981.

Roberts, John G., *Mitsui: Three Centuries of Japanese Business*, Tokyo, Weatherhill, 1973.

Shinohara, Miyohei, *Industrial Growth, Trade, and Dynamic Patterns in the Japanese Economy*, Tokyo, University of Tokyo Press, 1982.

Shirai, Taishiro (ed.), *Contemporary Industrial Relations in Japan*, Madison, University of Wisconsin Press, 1983.

Small and Medium Enterprise Agency, *White Paper on Small and Medium Enterprises in Japan*, Tokyo, various.

Stone, P. B. *Japan Surges Ahead, The Story of an Economic Miracle*, London, Weidenfeld and Nicolson, 1969.

Tanaka, Kakuei, *Building a New Japan*, Tokyo, Simul Press, 1972.

Uchino, Tatsuro, *Japan's Postwar Economy*, Tokyo, Kodansha, 1983.

Woronoff, Jon, *Inside Japan, Inc.*, Tokyo, Lotus Press, 1982.

———, *Japan's Wasted Workers*, Tokyo, Lotus Press, and Totowa, Rowman & Allenheld, 1983.

———, *Japan: The Coming Economic Crisis*, Tokyo, Lotus Press, 1979.

———, *The Japan Syndrome*, Tokyo, Lotus Press, and New Brunswick, Transaction Publishers, 1985.

Wray, William D., *Mitsubishi and the N. Y. K.*, Cambridge, Harvard University Press, 1984.

Yamamura, Kozo, *Economic Policy in Postwar Japan*, Los Angeles, University of California Press, 1968.

———, (ed.), *Policy and Trade Issues of the Japanese Economy*, Seattle, University of Washington Press, 1982.

Yoshino, M. Y., *Japan's Managerial System: Tradition and Innovation*, Cambridge, MIT Press, 1968.

Yoshihara, Kunio, *Sogo Shosha*, Oxford, Oxford University Press, 1982.

Young, Alexander K., *The Sogo Shosha, Japan's Multinational Trading Companies*, Boulder, Westview, 1979.

2. Taiwan

Barclay, George W., *Colonial Development and Population in Taiwan*, Princeton, Princeton University Press, 1954.

Chang, Kowie (ed.), *Economic Development in Taiwan*, Taipei, Cheng Chung Book Co., 1968.

Chen, Cheng, *Land Reform in Taiwan*, Taipei, China Publishing Company, 1961.

Chou, Shun-hsin, *The Chinese Inflation: 1937-49*, New York, Columbia University Press, 1963.

Fei, John C. H., Ranis, Gustav, and Kuo, Shirley W. Y., *Growth with Equity: The Taiwan Case*, London, Oxford University Press, 1979.

Galenson, Walter (ed.), *Economic Growth and Structural Change in Taiwan*, Ithaca, Cornell University Press, 1979.

Gold, Thomas B., *State and Society in the Taiwan Miracle*, Armonk, M. E. Sharpe, 1986.

Government Information Office, *Republic of China, A Reference Book*, Taipei, 1984.

Harrell, Stevan, *Ploughshare.Village, Culture and Context in Taiwan*, Seattle, University of Washington Press, 1979.

Ho, Samuel P. S., *Economic Development of Taiwan, 1860-1970*, New Haven, Yale University Press, 1978.

Hsing, Mo-Huan, *Taiwan*, London, Oxford University Press, 1971.

Hsiung, James C. (ed.), *Contemporary Republic of China, The Taiwan Experience*, New York, American Association for Chinese Studies, 1981.

Jacoby, Neil H., *U. S. Aid To Taiwan*, New York, Praeger, 1966.

Kuo, Shirley W. Y., *The Taiwan Economy in Transition*, Boulder, Westview, 1983.

Lin, C. Y., *Industrialization in Taiwan, 1946-72*, New York, Praeger, 1973.

Sih, Paul K. T. (ed.), *Taiwan in Modern Times*, New York, St. John's University, 1973.

Silin, Robert H., *Leadership and Values, The Organization of Large-Scale Taiwanese Enterprises*, Cambridge, Harvard

University Press, 1976.

Simon, Denis Fred, *Taiwan, Technology Transfer, and Transnationalism*, Boulder, Westview, 1985.

Wu, Yuan-li, *ROC Industrialization: The Future Outlook*, New York, Praeger, 1985.

Yang, Martin M. C., *Socio-Economic Results of Land Reform in Taiwan*, Honolulu, East-West Center Press, 1970.

3. Korea

Ban, Sung Hwan, Moon, Pal Yong, and Perkins, Dwight H., *Rural Development*, Cambridge, Harvard University Press, 1980.

Cole, David C., and Lyman, Princeton N., *Korean Development, The Interplay of Politics and Economics*, Cambridge, Harvard University Press, 1971.

Cole, David C., and Park, Yung Chul, *Financial Development in Korea*, Cambridge, Harvard University Press, 1983.

Hasan, Parvez, and Rao, D. C., *Korea: Policy Issues for Long-Term Development*, Washington, John Hopkins Press, 1979.

Hong, Wontack, *Trade, Distortions and Employment Growth in Korea*, Seoul, Korea Development Institute, 1979.

Jones, Leroy, and Il Sakong, *Government, Business, and Entrepreneurship in Economic Development: The Korean Case*, Cambridge, Harvard University Press, 1980.

Keon, Michael, *Korean Phoenix, A Nation From the Ashes*, Englewood Cliffs, Prentice-Hall, 1977.

Kim, Bun Woong, and Rho, Wha Joon (eds.), *Korean Public Bureaucracy*, Seoul, Kyobo Publishing, 1982.

Kim, Chuk Kyo (ed.), *Industrial and Social Development Issues*, Seoul, Korea Development Institute, 1977.

————, *Planning Model and Macroeconomic Policy Issues*, Seoul, Korea Development Institute, 1977.

Kim, Joungwon A., *Divided Korea, The Politics of Development*, Cambridge, Harvard University Press, 1963.

Kim, Kwang Suk, and Roemer, Michael, *Growth and Structural Transformation*, Cambridge, Harvard University Press, 1981.

Kim, Kyong-Dong, *Man and Society in Korea's Economic Growth*, Seoul, Seoul National University Press, 1979.

Krueger, Anne E., *The Development Role of the Foreign Sec-*

tor and Aid, Cambridge, Harvard University Press, 1979.

Kuznets, Paul W., *Economic Growth and Structure in the Republic of Korea*, New Haven, Yale University Press, 1977.

Lim, Youngil, *Government Policy and Private Enterprise: Korean Experience in Industrialization*, Berkeley, Institute of East Asian Studies, 1981.

Mason, Edward S., Perkins, Dwight H., Kim, Kwang Suk, Cole, David C., Kim, Mahn Je, et al., *The Economic and Social Modernization of the Republic of Korea*, Cambridge, Harvard University Press, 1980.

McCune, Shannon *Korea's Heritage, A Regional and Social Geography*, Tokyo, Tuttle, 1956.

McGinn, Noel F., et al, *Education and Development in Korea*, Cambridge, Harvard University Press, 1980.

Mills, Edwin S., and Song, Byung Nak, *Urbanization and Urban Problems*, Cambridge, Harvard University Press, 1979.

Park, Chong Kee (ed.), *Human Resources and Social Development in Korea*, Seoul, Korea Development Institute, 1980.

————, *Macroeconomic and Industrial Development in Korea*, Seoul, Korea Development Institute, 1980.

Park, Chung Hee, *The Country, The Revolution And I*, Seoul, Hollym Corp., 1962.

Reeve, W. D., *The Republic of Korea, A Political and Economic Study*, London, Oxford University Press, 1963.

Rhee, Yung Whee, Ross-Larson, Bruce, and Pursell, Gary, *Korea's Competitive Edge, Managing the Entry into World Markets*, Washington, John Hopkins Press, 1984.

Suh, Sang-Chul, *Growth and Structural Changes in the Korean Economy, 1910–1940*, Cambridge, Harvard University Press, 1978.

Westphal, Larry, Rhee, Yung, and Pursell, Gary, *Korean Industrial Competence: Where It Came From*, Washington, World Bank, 1981.

Whang, In-Joung, *Management of Rural Change in Korea: The Saemaul Undong*, Seoul, Seoul National University Press, 1981.

Woronoff, Jon, *Korea's Economy, Man-Made Miracle*, Seoul, Si-sa-yong-o-sa Publishers, 1983.

4. Singapore

Chen, Peter S. J., *Singapore Development Policies and Trends*, Singapore, Oxford University Press, 1983.

Drysdale, John, *Singapore: Struggle for Success*, Singapore, Times Books, 1984.

George, T. J. S., *Lee Kuan Yew's Singapore*, London, Andre Deutsch, 1973.

Hassan, Riaz, *Singapore: Society in Transition*, London, Oxford University Press, 1976.

Josey, Alex, *Singapore: Its Past, Present and Future*, Singapore, Eastern Universities Press, 1979.

Lim, Chong-Yah, *Economic Development in Singapore*, Singapore, Federal Publications, 1980.

——, *Economic Restructuring in Singapore*, Singapore, Federal Publications, 1984.

Ministry of Culture, *Singapore*, Singapore, annual.

Ministry of Trade and Industry, *Economic Survey of Singapore*, Singapore, annual.

Nair, C. V. Devan, *Socialism That Works, The Singapore Way*, Singapore, Federal Publications, 1976.

Ooi, Jin-Bee, and Chiang, Hai Ding (eds.), *Modern Singapore*, Singapore, University of Singapore, 1982.

Swee, Goh Keng, *The Economics of Modernization*, Singapore, Asian Pacific Press, 1972.

Yoshihara, Kunio, *Foreign Investment and Domestic Response: A Study of Singapore's Industrialization*, Singapore, Eastern Universities Press, 1976.

You, Poh Seng, and Lim, Chong-Yah (eds.), *Economic Development of Singapore in the Last Quarter Century*, Singapore, Eastern Universities Press, 1984.

——, *The Singapore Economy*, Singapore, Eastern Universities Press, 1971.

5. Hong Kong

Beazer, W., *The Commercial Future of Hong Kong*, New York, Praeger, 1978.

Cheng, Tong-Yung, *The Economy of Hong Kong*, Hong Kong, Far East Publications, 1977.

England, Joe, and Rear, John, *Chinese Labour Under British Rule: A Critical Study of Labour Relations and Law in Hong*

Kong. London, Oxford University Press, 1975.

Government Information Services, *Hong Kong*, Hong Kong, annual.

Harris, Peter, *Hong Kong: A Study in Bureaucratic Politics*, Hong Kong, Heinemann Asia, 1978.

Hopkins, Keith (ed.), *Hong Kong: The Industrial Colony*, London, Oxford University Press, 1971.

Hsia, Ronald, and Chau, Lawrence, *Industrialization, Employment and Income Distribution: A Case Study in Hong Kong*, London, Croom Helm, 1978.

Hughes, Richard, *Borrowed Place, Borrowed Time*, London, Andre Deutsch, 1968.

Jarvie, Ian C. (ed.), *Hong Kong: A Society in Transition*, New York, Praeger, 1969.

Lethbridge, David (ed.), *The Business Environment in Hong Kong*, Hong Kong, Oxford University Press, 1980.

Lin, Tzong-Biau, Lee, Rance P. L., Simonis, Udo-Ernst (ed.), *Hong Kong, Economic, Social and Political Studies in Development*, Armonk, M. E. Sharpe, 1979.

Miners, N. J., *The Government and Politics of Hong Kong*, Hong Kong, Oxford University Press, 1975.

Rabushka, Alvin, *Hong Kong: A Study in Economic Freedom*, Chicago, University of Chicago Press, 1979.

Sit, Victor Fung-Shuen, Wong, Siu-lun, and Kiang, Tsin-sing, *Small Scale Industry in a Laissez-Faire Economy*, Hong Kong, Centre for Asian Studies, 1979.

Szczepanik, Edward, *The Economic Growth of Hong Kong*, London, Oxford University Press, 1958.

Woronoff, Jon, *Hong Kong: Capitalist Paradise*, Hong Kong, Heinemann Asia, 1980.

6. Comparative

Akrasanee, Narongchi, Naya, Seiji, and Vichit-Vadakan, Vinyu (ed.), *Trade and Employment in Asia and the Pacific*, Honolulu, University Press of Hawaii, 1977.

Balassa, Bela, *Development Strategies in Semi-Industrial Economies*, Washington, John Hopkins Press, 1982.

———, *The Newly Industrializing Countries in the World Economy*, New York, Pergamon, 1981.

Bergsman, Joel, *Growth and Equity in Semi-Industrialized*

Countries, Washington, World Bank, 1979.

Blumenthal, Tuvia, and Lee, Chung H., *Development Strategies of Japan and the Republic of Korea*, Honolulu, University of Hawaii, 1983.

Chen, Edward K. Y., *Hyper-growth in Asian Economies*, New York, Holmes & Meier, 1979.

Corbo, Vittorio, Krueger, Anne O., and Ossa, Fernando (eds.), *Export-Oriented Development Strategies, The Success of Five Newly Industrializing Countries*, Boulder, Westview, 1985.

Czinkota, Michael R., *Export Promotion, The Public and Private Sector Interaction*, New York, Praeger, 1983.

Fields, Gary S., *The Labor Market and Export-Led Growth in Korea, Taiwan, Hong Kong, and Singapore*, Seoul, Korea Development Institute, 1982.

Geiger, Theodore, *Tales of Two City-States: The Development Progress of Hong Kong and Singapore*, Washington, National Planning Association, 1973.

Hayami, Yujiro (ed.), *Agricultural Growth in Japan, Taiwan, Korea and the Philippines*, Honolulu, University Press of Hawaii, 1979.

Hewitt, Robert (ed.), *Political Change and the Economic Future of East Asia*, Honolulu, University Press of Hawaii, 1981.

Ho, Samuel P. S., *Small-Scale Enterprises in Korea and Taiwan*, Washington, World Bank, 1980.

Ichimura, Shinichi (ed.), *The Economic Development of East and Southeast Asia*, Honolulu, University Press of Hawaii, 1975.

Kahn, Herman, *World Economic Development: 1979 and Beyond*, London, Croom Helm, 1979.

Kim, Key-Hiuk, *The Last Phase of the East Asian World Order*, Berkeley, University of California Press, 1980.

Kirby, E. Stuart, *Economic Development of East Asia*, New York, Praeger, 1967.

Lee, Eddy (ed.), *Export-Led Industrialization and Development*, Geneva, International Labour Office, 1981.

McMullen, Neil, *The Newly Industrializing Countries: Adjusting to Success*, Washington, National Planning Association, 1984.

Oshima, Harry T., *The Transition to an Industrial Economy in Monsoon Asia*, Manila, Asian Development Bank, 1983.

Shinohara, Miyohei, Yanagihara, Toru, and Kim, Kwang Suk, *The Japanese and Korean Experiences in Managing Development*, Washington, World Bank, 1983.

Skully, Michael T., *Financial Institutions and Markets in the Far East*, New York, St. Martin's Press, 1982.

Turner, Louis, and McMullen, Neil (eds.), *The Newly Industrializing Countries: Trade and Adjustments*, Winchester, Allen & Unwin, 1982.

7. East Asia and the World

Baranson, Jack, *The Japanese Challenge to U.S. Industry*, Lexington, D. C. Heath, 1981.

Barnds, William J. (ed.), *Japan and the United States, Challenges & Opportunities*, New York, New York University Press, 1979.

Benjamin, Roger, and Kudrle, Robert T. (eds.), *The Industrial Future of the Pacific Basin*, Boulder, Westview Press, 1984.

Davidson, William H., *The Amazing Race: Winning the Technorivalry with Japan*, New York, John Wiley, 1984.

Destler, I. M., and Sato, Hideo (eds.), *Coping with U.S.-Japanese Economic Conflicts*, Lexington, D. C. Heath, 1982.

Franko, Lawrence G., *The Threat of Japanese Multinationals*, New York, John Wiley, 1983.

Hanabusa, Masamichi, *Trade Problems between Japan and Western Europe*, London, Saxon House, 1979.

Hofheinz, Roy, and Calder, Kent E., *The Eastasia Edge*, New York, Basic Books, 1982.

Hollerman, Leon (ed.), *Japan and the United States: Economic and Political Adversaries*, Boulder, Westview, 1980.

Hong, Wontack, and Krause, Lawrence B. (eds.), *Trade and Growth of the Advanced Developing Countries in the Pacific Basin*, Seoul, Korea Development Institute, 1981.

Kojima, Kiyoshi, *Japan and a New World Economic Order*, Tokyo, Tuttle, 1977.

Okimoto, Daniel I., Sugano, Takuo, and Weinstein, Franklin B. (eds.), *Competitive Edge, The Semiconductor Industry in the U.S. and Japan*, Stanford, Stanford University Press,

1984.

Quo, F. Q. (ed.), *Politics of the Pacific Nations*, Boulder, Westview, 1983.

Rix, Alan, *Japan's Economic Aid*, London, Croom Helm, 1980.

Wilkinson, Endymion, *Misunderstanding: Europe versus Japan*, Tokyo, Chuokoron, 1981.

Wolf, Marvin J., *The Japanese Conspiracy*, New York, Empire Books, 1983.

Woronoff, Jon, *Japan's Commercial Empire*, Tokyo, Lotus Press, Armonk, M. E. Sharpe, and London, Macmillan, 1984.

———, *World Trade War*, Tokyo, Lotus Press, and New York, Praeger, 1984.

Yoshihara, Kunio, *Japanese Investment in Southeast Asia*, Honolulu, University Press of Hawaii, 1978.

Index